D1392305

STUDIO VISTA GUIDE TO CRAFT SUPPLIERS

STUDIO VISTA
GUIDE TO CRAFT SUPPLIERS

JUDY ALLEN

This book is dedicated to all those who only send for free samples and catalogues if they have serious intentions of buying.

The author and publishers would like to point out that all the information contained in this book was, to the best of their knowledge and belief, correct at the time of going to press.

Studio Vista a division of
Cassell & Collier Macmillan Publishers Limited, London
35 Red Lion Square, London WC1R 4SG.
Sydney, Auckland, Toronto, Johannesburg.
An affiliate of the Macmillan Publishing Co. Inc. New York

Printed in Great Britain by
Northumberland Press Limited
Gateshead

ISBN 0 289 70456 1 (hardbound)
ISBN 0 289 70471 5 (paperback)

Contents

Introduction

Craftwork is undoubtedly growing in popularity—perhaps because people have a very deep need to make things, and very little opportunity to do so in a society where so much is mass-produced and convenient—or perhaps because there is a feeling that sometime it may once again be important to know how to weave your own blankets and throw your own pots.

Compiling a guide to craft suppliers brings you face to face with world shortages almost every day. Remember that it is no longer O.K. to waste materials. Nor can firms afford to send out free catalogues to people who just want to look at the pictures, or free samples to people who are hoping that the sample itself will be large enough for the job they have in mind.

But, shortages apart, it is hoped that this will be a useful address book for anyone pursuing any craft. There is no attempt to suggest what you should do with the various materials when you have them. The assumption is that you already know what you want to do (or have an instructor or one of the scores of instruction books) and are simply held up by an inability to locate gold leaf, a tjanting, bobbins, leading, a custom-made hat shape, or whatever. Neither does the book promise to be totally comprehensive. It isn't possible to list every button stockist or every pottery that will sell clay out of the back door. But because so many firms produce good catalogues and undertake mail order it should be possible for anyone anywhere in Britain to come by whatever supplies may be required.

The words 'Mail Order' mean that you can order and receive the goods from afar. Clearly no-one is going to put a potter's kiln in the post, but rather than waste space specifying method of travel—which isn't too important so long as the kiln arrives—'Mail Order' is used as a covering term. Equally, 'Catalogue' covers everything from a posh eighty page book with photographs to a one page price list. 'Catalogue' means 'they will tell you through the post exactly what they stock'.

J. A.

1 Craft Shops

This chapter is made up of an alphabetical, town by town, list of general craft shops throughout Britain. Most stock 'general craft materials', some rely heavily on kits, and a few specialise in materials for particular crafts (in which case they are cross-referenced to the relevant chapter).

Craft shops have three main advantages over mail order dealers and wholesalers: they will sell small quantities, they will probably be able to order materials that are not in stock, and they may well be staffed by people who are knowledgeable about crafts and able to give help and advice.

Established craftworkers tend to be a little snooty about craft shops on account of the shelvesful of kits—but most of them stock unkitted materials as well, and in any case there are kits and kits. Good kits have all the necessary materials and tools in one box to save you the hassle of buying them separately. Then there are the kits that give you such limited materials and such detailed instructions that you work your way inexorably towards an end result already pictured on the outside of the box. Not much room for creativity. But on the other hand you are more or less assured of a successful end result which means that a beginner won't get discouraged and may well be inspired to go on to greater things.

And one vital function of a really good craft shop is that it provides facilities for browsing—which is a good way of generating ideas.

ABERDEEN

The Craft Centre
97 Claremont Street, Aberdeen AB1 6QR, Scotland   Aberdeen 20798

Open: Monday to Friday 09.30 to 13.00 and 14.00 to 17.30; Saturday 09.00 to 17.30; mail order; catalogue

Well stocked with kits and also with back-up materials. Kits for cold enamelling, plastic embedding, copper etching, candlemaking, stonecraft, soft toy and glove puppet making. Also a good supply of fabrics—pure silk chiffon, crêpe backed satin and continental damask—and of other things for needleworkers like felt, hessian, kapok and acrylic stuffing materials, trimmings, tapestry canvases and wools, embroidery fabrics and threads, crochet and macramé yarns and soft toy accessories. Also rug canvases and wools, tie-dye and batik materials, leather offcuts, marquetry kits, raffia and cane, lampshade frames and the fabrics and trimmings to adorn them, copper blanks, enamels and kilns, chain and findings in stainless steel, nickel, gilt and silver-plate, semi-precious stones, jewellers' tools and tumble polishing machines, seashells and modelling clays. Wide range of nice materials.

ALLENTON

Allenton Homecrafts
859 Osmaston Road, Allenton, Near Derby, Derbyshire   Derby 47214

Open: Monday to Saturday (excluding Wednesday) 09.00 to 18.00; Wednesday 09.00 to 13.00

Art and craft suppliers who have a fairly small stock of craft materials at the moment but say they plan to expand it. They have canvas, hessian, painting by numbers, plastic embedding and candlemaking kits, and will either make picture frames for you or cut timber and boards to size, cut mitres etc., to set you on the road to making your own.

ALTRINCHAM

The Handicraft Shop
5 Oxford Road, Altrincham, Cheshire WA14 2DY   Altrincham 3834

Open: Monday to Saturday (excluding Wednesday) 09.00 to 17.30; Wednesday 09.00 to 13.00; mail order (very rarely)

Will make lampshades for customers and also have frames, covering materials and trimmings for sale. Not to mention moccasin, candlemaking and marquetry kits; semi-precious and imitation stones; leather and the necessary tools, felt, canvas, hessian, various soft toy fillings and accessories, tapestry canvases and wools, evenweave fabrics and embroidery silks, plus most of the useful bits and pieces you would expect to find on a haberdashery counter; knitting, crochet and macramé yarns; rug-making materials; clear embedding plastics; raffia, cane and basketry materials; seashells and modelling clays.

ANDOVER

Arts and Crafts Centre
74 High Street, Andover, Hampshire
  Andover 2137

Open: Monday to Saturday 09.00 to 17.30

Most materials are initially sold in kit form backed up by accessories. Findings, chain and imitation stone for jewellery-making, also copper blanks, tumble polishing machines and cold enamelling materials; leather-working and lino-cutting tools; felt, canvas, kapok and toys' eyes and noses; potters' clays and glazes; a limited amount of rug-making materials and tie-dye, batik and silk screen printing materials; brass rubbing kits; veneers for marquetry and woods and tools for pokerwork and small woodwork; many kinds of plastic embedding kits; some glass for mosaic work; candlemaking kits; seashells; and various modern modelling materials.

ASHFORD

Graphic Art Supplies
30 North Street, Ashford, Kent
  Ashford 21460

Open: Monday to Saturday (excluding Wednesday) 09.00 to 17.30; Wednesday 09.00 to 13.00

An art shop specialising in artists' materials and drawing office supplies but with a few craft materials as well—the wherewithall for lino-cutting, brass rubbing, screen printing, candlemaking and modelling.

AYR

Contour Artists' Materials Limited
38 Sandgate, Ayr, Scotland   Ayr 62190

Open: Monday to Saturday (excluding Wednesday) 09.00 to 17.30; Wednesday

09.00 to 13.00 in the quiet seasons (open all day in summer); mail order; catalogue 15p (refunded with first purchase)

Art, craft, technical (for draughtsmen) and stationery supplies. Their large stocks warrant a 55 page catalogue. On the craft side they have a very large range indeed—mostly, but not exclusively, kits. And the kits are good ones. Chain and findings in base metals and sterling silver, semi-precious and imitation stones, jewellers' tools and tumble polishing machines; leather and leather-working tools and accessories; lino-cutting, brass rubbing, tie-dye and batik materials and tools; clays for pottery (and wheels and kilns to order); felt, canvas, hessian, kapok, trimmings, eyes, noses, bells, squeakers; macramé yarns and embroidery threads; marquetry and picture framing tools, woods and veneers; Plasticraft and Enamelcraft kits; candlemaking supplies; raffia, cane and basketry materials; lampshade frames, covering materials and trimmings; modelling materials (Das, Sofenbak, Superwood, clay), Artstraws, pipecleaners, buckram, picture framing and moccasin kits, hobby horse and bead loom kits—and the full complement of artists' materials as well.

BATH

Bath Handicraft Supplies
6 Bladud Buildings, Bath, Somerset
  Bath 61456

Open: Monday to Saturday 09.15 to 13.00 and 14.15 to 17.00; mail order

The shop has recently changed hands and the new owners have all kinds of plans to expand the range of stock. At the moment they have a lot to offer to lampshade makers—frames, fabrics, trimmings and parchment; also beads, chain, base metal findings, semi-precious and imitation stones and jewellers' tools; leather and leather-working tools; felt, canvas, hessian, kapok, and soft toy accessories; fleece for handspinning and dyes; candlemaking materials; raffia, cane and basketry materials; modelling clays and Enamelcraft and marquetry kits. Soon they hope to offer tumble polishers, tapestry and embroidery fabrics and threads, handweaving looms and yarns, spinning wheels and kilns for enamelling—in fact, by the time you are using this book they may have all these, so check.

Tridias
8 Saville Row, Bath, Somerset
  Bath 61730

Open: Monday to Saturday 09.00 to 17.30; mail order; catalogue

Best known as the place where you go to buy wooden toys and dolls' houses, but they also have Enamelcraft and Plasticraft kits, lino-cutting and brass rubbing accessories and materials, most of the requisites for tie-dye, batik and screen printing, candlemaking materials and several different kinds of modelling clay.

BEESTON

The Handicraft Shop
122 Chilwell Road, Beeston, Nottinghamshire Nottingham 254939

Open: Monday to Saturday 09.30 to 17.30

Especially good on lampshade-making supplies—frames, fabrics and trimmings, Also a lot of other handicraft materials—chain, copper and aluminium findings, copper blanks, semi-precious and imitation stones, jewellers' tools and tumble-polishing machines; leather offcuts and leather-working tools; fur fabrics, felt, hessian, terylene and acrilan fillings, buttons, buckles and soft toy accessories; macramé yarns and rug-making materials; Plasticraft and Enamelcraft kits; tie-dye, batik, brass-rubbing and marquetry materials and tools; tools and mouldings for picture framing; candlemaking supplies; raffia, cane and basketry materials; cold and kiln enamelling materials; seashells, clay, Plastone, Artstraws and various small kits.

BELFAST

Ato-Crafts Limited
12/16 Queen Street, Belfast, Northern Ireland Belfast 40853

Open: Monday to Saturday (excluding Wednesday) 09.00 to 17.30; Wednesday closed; mail order

General craft materials, but especially strong on lampshade frames and covering materials. Also tumble polishers, chain, semi-precious and imitation stones; everything for cold and kiln enamelling; leather and leather-working tools; felt, canvas, hessian, fillings and accessories for soft toys; tapestry and embroidery materials; macramé yarns; modelling clays; rug-making kits; marquetry and Plasticraft kits and accessories; candlemaking supplies; raffia, cane and basket bases and quite a good range of kits. Will send by mail on a cash-with-order basis.

BEXHILL-ON-SEA

Sackville Handicrafts (see page 140)

BIRMINGHAM

Midland Educational Company Limited
104/106 Corporation Street, Birmingham 4 021 236 2741

Open: Monday to Saturday 09.00 to 17.30

Materials primarily intended for schools —but anyone can call in and buy. They stock kits for macramé, tapestry, candlemaking, rug-making, marquetry, Plasticraft and Enamelcraft—also modelling clays and light construction materials. They are well able to supply you with soft toy making and some needlework materials—felt, canvas, hessian, kapok, Nu-stuffing, foam stuffing, trimmings, buttons and buckles, glass eyes and plastic noses. They have lino-cutting, brass rubbing and tie-dye and batik materials, some of the requirements for picture framing, leather and leatherworking tools. Also raffia, cane and everything for basket and lampshade making (including fringes and tassels). Geared generally to the smaller, quieter, less messy-in-operation crafts. There are branches in Coventry, Northampton, Worcester, Wolverhampton, Solihull, Leicester, Stratford-upon-Avon, Bristol and Shrewsbury (in Shrewsbury they trade as Wildings). Largest stocks are in Birmingham, Wolverhampton and Leicester—the rest have rather more limited supplies.

Type and Palette
724 Bristol Road, Selly Oak, Birmingham, Warwickshire B29 6DH
021 472 3021

Open: Monday to Saturday (excluding Wednesday) 09.00 to 18.00; Wednesday 09.00 to 13.00

Plasticraft and Enamelaire kits, chain, findings, copper blanks, tumble polishers, the necessities for lino-cutting and brass rubbing, felt, screen printing accessories, inks and papers, candlemaking materials and modelling clays.

BISHOP AUCKLAND

Auckland Studio
164 Newgate Street, Bishop Auckland, County Durham
Bishop Auckland 4668

Open: Monday to Saturday (excluding Wednesday) 09.00 to 17.30; Wednesday closed; mail order

Most art materials and quite a few craft materials including semi-precious stones (rough and polished), tumble polishers, lino-cutting supplies, frames and fabrics for lampshades, tapestry and needlework materials both in kit form and loose, felt, kapok, soft toy accessories and Plasticraft kits.

BISHOPS STORTFORD

Galaxy
90 South Street, Bishops Stortford, Hertfordshire   Bishops Stortford 52375

Open: Monday to Saturday (excluding Wednesday) 09.00 to 17.30; Wednesday 09.00 to 12.30

Artists' materials, craft books, and lots and lots of kits—Plasticraft, Enamelcraft, lino-cutting, brass rubbing, marquetry, embroidery, candlemaking, macramé, Airfix and so on. Also modelling clays, Sculptorcraft, moulds, powders, etc.; findings in nickel, gilt and stainless steel, beads, chain, semi-precious and imitation stones and tumble-polishing machines; tie-dye and batik materials; raffia, cane and basketry supplies; seashells; and plenty of materials for soft toy making— felt, kapok, foam, Modacryl, eyes and noses.

BOLTON

Bolton Handicrafts
150 Stall, Market Hall, Bolton, Lancashire   Bolton 26122

Open: Monday to Saturday (excluding Wednesday) 09.00 to 17.30; Wednesday closed

Strongest on the armchair crafts, with needlepoint tapestry canvases and wools, evenweave fabrics and embroidery threads, macramé yarns, hessian, kapok, acrylic and terylene fillings, eyes and noses for soft toys, basketry and lampshade materials, seashells and modelling clays. Also candlemaking supplies and some leather.

BOURNEMOUTH

Moordown Leather and Craft (see page 114)

BRIGHTON

Handicrafts
6 Circus Parade, Preston Circus, Brighton, Sussex   Brighton 64528

Open: Monday to Saturday 09.00 to 17.30; mail order

Good, basic general stock of art, handicraft and occupational therapy materials, sold by people who are happy to instruct you on any craft if you are buying your first materials. They have findings and chain, semi-precious and imitation stones, pewter and sheet copper; moccasin kits; lino-cutting and brass rubbing kits; some bookbinding materials, tools and accessories; embroidery fabrics, felt, tapestry canvas, hessian, kapok and soft toy accessories, buttons, buckles, tapestry wools, embroidery silks, trimmings and notions; rug-making materials; tie-dye and batik dyes and waxes; marquetry kits; embedding resins; candlemaking supplies; raffia and cane, basketry supplies; seashells and modelling materials. Also a good stock of lampshade frames, covering materials, braids, fringes and trimmings. Will also make lampshades to order.

Southern Handicrafts Limited
25 Kensington Gardens, Brighton, Sussex BN1 4AL   Brighton 681901

Open: Monday to Friday (excluding Wednesday) 09.15 to 13.00 and 14.00 to 16.00; Wednesday closed; Saturday 09.15 to 13.00 and 14.00 to 17.00; mail order; catalogue 3p

Specialise in sheet pewter and copper and soft toy materials, including fur fabrics, synthetic fillings and plastic features. Also have findings in various metals and imitation stones, some leather-working tools, macramé yarns, marquetry kits, lampshade frames, raffia, cane and candlemaking materials. Are agents for Dryad, so are in a good position to order other materials for you if you require them. Catalogue covers pewter and copper only.

BRISTOL

Bristol Handicrafts
20 Park Row, Bristol 1, Somerset   Bristol 25729

Open: Monday to Friday 09.00 to 17.00; Saturday 09.00 to 12.45; mail order

General craft suppliers who specialise in felt work, embroidery and soft toy making. They have felt and fur fabrics, embroidery and rug canvas, hessian, stuffing materials, eyes for toys, macramé yarns, rug wools, tapestry and embroidery kits. Also modelling clays, linocutting and brass rubbing materials, lampshade frames, tie-dye, batik and screen printing materials and accessories and marquetry kits. Good stock of candlemaking supplies, raffia and cane. No catalogue as such, but a sample card for fabrics which costs 10p.

Craftwise (see page 38)

Hobbies and Crafts
48 Temple Street, Keynsham, Bristol   Keynsham 4365

Open: Monday to Saturday (excluding Wednesday) 09.45 to 13.00 and 14.15 to

17.30; Wednesday closed; mail order (cash with order, please)

Specialists in art materials, sheet copper and pewterwork and also candlemaking supplies, of which they have a particularly rich variety. Also offer an exhibition and selling room for local artists. Wide range of craft kits and also silver and gold-plated findings, polished and rough semi-precious stones; leather offcuts; lino-cutting and brass rubbing materials and tools; fur fabric, felt, evenweave fabrics, canvas, hessian, embroidery silks and tapestry wools, washable fillings and soft toy accessories; macramé yarns; tie-dye, batik and screen printing materials in kit form; veneers; raffia, cane and basketry supplies; cold enamelling materials; modelling clays; and craft tools of various different kinds.

The Midland Educational Company Limited
71/73 Fairfax Street, Bristol, Somerset
   Bristol 27624

Open: Monday to Saturday 09.00 to 17.30 (see page 11)

BURNLEY

Northern Handicrafts Limited
Belle Vue Mill, Westgate, Burnley, Lancashire BB11 1SD   Burnley 33713

Open: Monday to Friday 08.00 to 17.00; mail order; catalogue 5p

Retail shop which does a lot of business by mail order. As well as artists' materials they offer various kinds of cane, canework tools, basket frames and handles, stool frames, natural and coloured seagrass, raffia and Plastistraw; wooden beads and polystyrene balls; felt in lots of colours and sold in 10p or 12p bundles; fur fabric, soft toy accessories and patterns and kapok; a well equipped 'candle pack' for the novice; Axminster carpet thrums, canvas, linen thread, hooks and sheepskin for rug-making; embroidery and sewing accessories, including embroidery canvases and threads, Singer sewing machine accessories and tapestry kits; Perspex sheet and offcuts; upholstery needles, pins, tacks and fabrics (including leathercloth and hessian); calfskins, suède, bundles of leather offcuts, leatherworking tools (and leaflets) and leatherworking kits, thonging, rivets, eyelets, etc.; marquetry kits and selected veneers and tools; lampshade frames, trimmings and fabrics; papercraft materials; jewellery findings, semi-precious and imitation stones; macramé yarns, etc. Extremely comprehensive range of stock in each category—the kind of catalogue to persuade anyone to take up a new craft.

CAERNARVON

Black Kettle Crafts
20 Bangor Street, Caernarvon, Caernarvonshire LL55 1AT   Caernarvon 3839

Open: Monday to Saturday (excluding Thursday) 10.00 to 17.30; Thursday 10.00 to 12.30; mail order

Large selection of books and leaflets on crafts and hobbies, and a metal detector for treasure-hunting. Kits for candlemaking, macramé, soft toy making, plastic embedding, cold enamelling and copper etching; also stainless steel findings and chain, semi-precious stones and tumble polishing machines; lino-cutting and marquetry materials; lampshade frames, covering fabrics and trimmings; tie-dye and batik dyes and accessories; seashells; raffia, cane and basketry materials.

CAMBRIDGE

The Leigh Gallery
19 King's Parade, Cambridge, Cambridgeshire   Cambridge 50303

Open: Monday to Saturday 09.00 to 13.15 and 14.15 to 17.45

Supercast chess kits, Plasticraft and Enamelcraft kits and comprehensive kits for lino-cutting, tie-dying, batik, silk screen printing, brass rubbing (especially good range), picture framing and candlemaking. Also seashells, modelling clay and various modern modelling materials. They plan to stock enamelling supplies soon and may have them by the time this book is available.

CANTERBURY

Canterbury Pottery
38a Burgate, Canterbury, Kent CT1 2HW
   (no telephone)

Open: Monday to Saturday 09.00 to 17.45 (Open on Sundays from Easter to September); mail order

Produce hand-painted tiles and all types of pottery and tile work to order, made on the premises—will also fire customers' own ceramic work by arrangement. You can watch them at work and buy or browse among the results. You can also buy prepared clays and glazes, modelling clays, leather offcuts and candlemaking supplies.
   The proprietor says he can obtain all kinds of craft materials for customers in any quantity at 'competitive prices'—so if there's something you need and can't find locally, go in and have a chat.

Needlecraft and Hobbies
83 Northgate, Canterbury, Kent CT1 1BA
   Canterbury 69888

Open: Monday to Saturday (excluding Thursday) 09.00 to 17.30; Thursday closed; mail order; catalogue 15p

Wholesalers and mail order suppliers who also run a retail shop at this address and one in Hythe (see separate entry). Probably strongest on the needlecraft side of things with fur fabric, evenweave embroidery fabrics and embroidery silks, hessian, handicraft and display felts, tapestry canvas and wools and rug-making canvas and wools, fabrics for covering lampshades (and the frames and trimmings), washable stuffing materials, eyes, noses and growlers for soft toys, buttons, buckles, trimmings, notions, knitting, crochet and macramé yarns, and net and lace-making requisites. But they can also sell you chain and findings in gilt, nickel plate, aluminium and stainless steel, copper blanks, enamels, kilns, tumble polishing machines and imitation stones; leather and leather-working tools; marquetry materials; plastic foil, plastic resin, plastic cane, plastic gold and silver kid; raffia, cane and basketry supplies; candlemaking supplies; and modelling clays. Also oddments like the frames for evening bags, flower looms, windows for dolls' houses, musical boxes and the necessary materials for making Christmas crackers.

CARDIFF

Handicrafts and Dressmakers' Aids
18 Merthyr Road, Whitchurch, Cardiff, Glamorganshire, Wales
Cardiff 612889

Open: Monday to Saturday (excluding Wednesday) 09.00 to 17.30; Wednesday 09.00 to 13.00; mail order

Strongest on the dress and soft toy making side, but the handicrafts side is expanding. Rely fairly heavily on kits, but the variety steadily increases; Candlecraft, Knit 'n make, brass rubbing and tapestry kits; also modelling and light construction materials; raffia, cane, seagrass, basket and lampshade making supplies and, for needlewomen, Crimplene, nylon fur, Lurex, felt, canvas, hessian, terylene, stuffing materials, buckles, buttons, notions, trimmings and plastic features for toys. Will send goods if really necessary and if you pay postage.

South Wales Arts and Crafts Suppliers
(see page 55)

CHANDLERS' FORD

Creative Crafts
Winchester Road, Chandlers' Ford, Hampshire   Chandlers' Ford 2241

Open: Monday to Saturday 09.30 to 18.00; mail order; catalogue

Here is a shop which is trying hard to stock everything for the home craftsman or 'hobbyist'. They extend their range all the time and like to hear if there is something you need that they are not at present supplying. Although they are a 'general' craft shop, they do specialise—in candlemaking, enamelling and jewellery-making. They have an impressive range of materials for all three crafts—findings in the full range of metals, chain, silver, lots of beads, semi-precious and imitation stones, jewellers' tools, tumble polishing machines, copper blanks, enamelling materials and kilns, and waxes, dyes, perfumes, wicks and whatnots for candlemaking, as well as waxes and dyes for batik and materials for tie-dye and silk screen printing. They are also strong in the natural cane, raffia, seagrass, etc., department. Also lino-cutting and brass-rubbing materials, macramé yarns, and pretty well everything for the soft toy maker—felts, fur fabrics, plenty of stuffing materials, noses, eyes and squeakers. They have woods and tools, marquetry and pokerwork supplies, a few seashells, modelling and light construction materials (including paper), the bases and frames for baskets, and plastic moulding resins. Kits as well as, and not instead of, loose materials. Happy to discuss crafts with customers or to send, free, about a dozen foolscap sheets close-typed with their multiplicity of wares.

CHELTENHAM

The Christmas Tree
2 Regent Street, Cheltenham, Gloucestershire   Cheltenham 21825

Open: Monday to Saturday 10.00 to 17.30; mail order; catalogue 15p

Good stock of craft materials and also some ready-made things like Indian bedspreads and made-up Stringcraft pictures. They have Enamelaire, Enamelcraft and Plasticraft kits, and candlemaking, marquetry, batik, tie-dye, plastercasting and felt toy making kits. Also silver, copper and gilt findings, copper blanks, Thai cottons and silks, seashells and modelling clays. And some oddments like sequins, wooden and seed beads, glass stones, bead looms and weaving looms for children.

The Colourman
6/8 Grosvenor Street, Cheltenham, Gloucestershire   Cheltenham 54687

Open: Monday to Saturday (excluding Wednesday) 09.00 to 17.30; Wednesday 09.00 to 13.00; mail order

An art material and handicraft supplier with quite a wide range of kits—candlemaking, cold enamelling, plastic embedding, leather-working, macramé, silk screen printing, picture framing and tissue flowers. Also copper and stainless steel findings, semi-precious and imitation stones, tumble polishing machines, chain, copper blanks and enamelling materials and kilns; leather-working and lino-cutting tools; modelling clays; lampshade frames, fabrics and fringes; brass rubbing materials and papers; veneers for marquetry; raffia and cane; seashells; felt, kapok and soft toys' features.

CHESHAM

The Tiger's Eye (see page 39)

CLITHEROE

Tattersalls
2 York Street, Clitheroe, Lancashire,
BB7 2DL Clitheroe 22285

Open: Monday to Friday 09.30 to 18.00; Saturday 09.30 to 17.30; mail order; catalogue

Tattersalls deal mainly in artists' materials and ready-made leather goods, but they also have Plasticraft, picture framing and lampshade making kits, a certain amount of felt, modelling clays, liquid plastic for moulding, raffia and ribbon (intended chiefly for the lampshades) and various light construction materials, such as Artstraws and papercraft.

COLCHESTER

Briggs Art and Book Shop
15 Crouch Street, Colchester, Essex
Colchester 74530

Open: Monday to Saturday (excluding Thursday) 09.00 to 17.30; Thursday closed; mail order

Artists' materials, art books and some craft kits—candlemaking, brass rubbing, lino-cutting, plastic modelling and marquetry. Also lampshade frames, covering fabrics and trimmings; felt, kapok and soft toy accessories; modelling clays, Sofenbak, Barbola etc.; raffia, cane and basketry materials; tumble polishing machines, copper blanks and the materials and kilns for enamelling. Good stock of craft books.

Johae Art Centre
17 St John's Street, Colchester, Essex
CO2 7AN Colchester 71760

Open: Monday to Saturday (excluding Thursday) 09.00 to 12.30 and 13.30 to 17.00; Thursday 09.00 to 12.30; mail order

Their speciality is graphics and graphic design, and they will undertake picture framing, dry-mounting and heat-sealing. For craftsmen they supply picture fram-

ing materials, fine papers, brass rubbing sticks and papers, acetate plastics, modelling clays and modelling and turning tools. Mail order if you send cash with order. Catalogue in preparation.

COLNE

The Art Shop
31 Albert Road, Colne, Lancashire
BB8 0RY

Open: Monday to Saturday (excluding Tuesday) 09.00 to 17.00; Tuesday closed; mail order

Specialise in plain white china and pottery and all the necessary paints and materials for decorating it—no catalogue as such, just a pottery painting list at 10p. They also sell leather and leatherworking tools and accessories; bookbinding leathers and cloths and some tools; lino-cutting and picture framing materials and tools; Perspex, acetate and glass; modelling clays; raffia, cane and basketry materials; lampshade frames and trimmings and, for needleworkers, embroidery fabrics, felt, canvas, hessian, kapok and plastic foam, tapestry and needlework materials; macramé yarns, soft toy accessories and some haberdashery items. Will undertake the firing of home-glazed pots.

COVENTRY

Midland Educational Company Limited
1/5 City Arcade, Coventry, Worcestershire Coventry 28618

Open: Monday to Saturday (excluding Thursday) 09.00 to 17.30; Thursday 09.00 to 13.00 (see page 11)

CREWE

Arts and Crafts
30 West Street, Crewe, Cheshire
Crewe 4776

Open: Monday to Saturday (excluding Wednesday) 09.15 to 17.30; Wednesday closed

Art and craft materials, mostly in kit form and quite a lot intended for children. They have lino-cutting and brass rubbing materials and tools, candlemaking kits, modelling clays, raffia, cane, basketry and lampshade making materials, embedding plastics and resins and acetate sheeting, marquetry kits and separate veneers, picture framing kits and mouldings, Scandinavian rug making kits and quite a lot of needlework materials—tapestry canvases and evenweave fabrics, tapestry wools, embroidery threads, felt and hessian—also knitting yarns, crochet and macramé yarns and soft toy accessories and fillings.

CROYDON

Barretts (see page 40)

CULLOMPTON

Crafts 'n Creations (see page 73)

DARTFORD

Jaybee Handicrafts
43 Hythe Street, Dartford, Kent
  Dartford 20150

Open: Monday to Saturday (excluding Wednesday) 09.00 to 13.00 and 14.00 to 17.30; Wednesday closed

Kits for marquetry, tapestry and painting by numbers; also a little leather and some tools; rug-making materials; candle-making kits; picture framing materials and tools; lampshade frames and plastic coverings; raffia and cane; felt, fillings and accessories for soft toys; and some model aircraft kits.

DEWSBURY

Marc Time
19 Broadway House, Crackenedge Lane,
  Dewsbury, Yorkshire
  Dewsbury 463109

Open: Monday to Saturday (excluding Tuesday) 09.00 to 17.30; Tuesday 09.00 to 13.00

Artists' materials, original paintings, hand-thrown pottery, costume jewellery, etc.— but with a crafts section which promises to expand if demand warrants it. Right now it can supply base metal findings, copper blanks, tumble polishing machines, lino-cutting tools and materials, felt, canvas, hessian, acrylic stuffing materials, soft toy accessories, tapestry canvases and wools, marquetry kits, plastic embedding kits (and shells), candlemaking supplies, raffia, cane, basketry supplies, lampshade frames and modelling clays.

DONCASTER

Busy Bee (see page 73)

DUBLIN

Gemcraft of Ireland (see page 41)

DUNOON

Dae-It-Yersel
45/47 Pretoria Crescent, Tom-a-Mhoid
  Road, Dunoon, Argyllshire, Scotland
  Dunoon 2514

Open: Monday to Saturday (excluding Wednesday) 09.00 to 13.00 and 14.30 to 17.30; Wednesday 09.00 to 13.00; mail order

General do-it-yourself suppliers who can also sell you felt, foam and mohair fillings and soft toy accessories, hessian, woods, veneers, picture framing materials and tools, plastic mouldings, Perspex, acrylic sheet, raffia and lampshade frames.

EASTBOURNE

The Sussex Handicraft Shop
5b Watts Lane, Eastbourne, Sussex
  Eastbourne 35802

Open: Monday to Saturday (excluding Wednesday) 09.30 to 17.30; Wednesday 09.30 to 12.30

Kits and raw materials for several crafts. Candlemaking and plastic embedding kits; beads, chain, gilt and nickel findings, copper blanks, materials for cold and kiln enamelling and semi-precious stones; lino-cutting, tie-dye and marquetry kits and materials; felt, kapok and plastic eyes; basket-making materials and sea-shells. Also lots of oddments—Artstraws, papercraft, etc.

EAST KESWICK

Westby Products
School Lane, East Keswick, Near Leeds,
  Yorkshire LS17 9EH
  Collingham Bridge 2527

Open: Monday to Friday 09.00 to 17.00; Saturday 09.00 to 12.30; mail order; catalogue

One of the leading mail order suppliers of craft kits (mostly their own make) who also have a retail outlet at the above address. They supply schools, institutions and craft shops, but are also very willing to deal with individuals and stipulate no minimum order. They also offer free advice on crafts—write to The Craft Adviser at the above address. Their products include clear plastic embedding kits, candlemaking kits, stone polishing kits (including the stones, tumble polisher, findings, etc.), cold enamelling kits, moulds for garden gnomes, leaping dolphins or chess sets; moulding and modelling materials (casting resin, moulding powder, paraffin wax and clear casting plastic). Also tropical seashells and quite a few craft books. Catalogue free, but send A4 s.a.e.

EPSOM

O W Annetts and Sons Limited
145 High Street, Epsom, Surrey
  Epsom 20323

Open: Monday to Saturday (excluding Wednesday) 09.00 to 17.30; Wednesday 09.00 to 13.00

Like the Sutton shop, primarily concerned

with art materials, pictures and a picture-framing service—but also with a stock of craft materials; Plasticraft and Enamelcraft kits, some findings and copper blanks, tumble polishing machines, linocutting tools, modelling clays, brass rubbing materials and papers, fabric dyes, marquetry kits, candlemaking supplies and raffias, canes, and basket bases.

EXETER

The Handicraft Shop
Central Station Buildings, Queen Street, Exeter, Devon Exeter 59718

Open: Monday to Saturday (excluding Wednesday) 09.00 to 17.30; Wednesday 09.00 to 13.00; mail order

Mostly craft kits (as and when available) and particularly strong on the needlework and embroidery side with linens and Glenshee fabrics, canvas and wools, embroidery threads and silks, buttons, buckles, trimmings, felt, kapok and soft toy accessories; also macramé yarns; lampshade frames; parchment; raffia cane and basketry materials; rug-making canvases and wools, hooks, etc.; leather and tools; marquetry materials and some picture framing materials and tools; candlemaking and cold enamelling kits and Plastone for modelling.

FALKIRK

Modelcrafts
112 High Street, Falkirk, Stirlingshire, Scotland Falkirk 21754

Open: Monday to Saturday (excluding Wednesday) 09.00 to 18.00; Wednesday closed

Rely heavily on kits, of which they have many. Can supply you with leathercloth and leather-working tools, lino-cutting tools and materials, felt, canvas, hessian, lampshade frames and trimmings, fillings and accessories for soft toy making, marquetry kits, pokerwork and picture framing materials and tools, embedding plastics, coloured acetate sheets, glass and leading for mosaic work, candlemaking supplies, raffia, cane and basketry materials, a few seashells and several kinds of modelling clay.

FORDINGBRIDGE

Caxton Decor
45 Salisbury Street, Fordingbridge, Hampshire Fordingbridge 53489

Open: Monday to Saturday (excluding Thursday) 08.00 to 13.00 and 14.00 to 17.30; Thursday 08.00 to 13.00

Primarily a specialist paint and wallpaper shop but keep a few craft materials for the convenience of customers who would otherwise have to travel miles. Chiefly for soft toy making and woodwork. They have felt, fur fabric remnants, eyes, noses, face masks, bells, squeakers, growlers, soft toy patterns, polyester stuffing and foam chippings—also a few marquetry sets and picture framing materials and tools.

FRINTON-ON-SEA

Frinton Handicraft and Art Centre
61 Connaught Avenue, Frinton-on-Sea, Essex Frinton-on-Sea 3707

Open: Monday to Saturday (excluding Wednesday) 09.00 to 13.00 and 14.00 to 17.30; Wednesday 09.00 to 13.00; mail order

Complete range of artists' materials and also a lot of handicraft materials—and not only in kit form, although kits are there as well. Copper, pewter and tools; chain, findings, copper blanks, semi-precious and imitation stones, jewellers' tools, tumble polishing machines, materials for cold and kiln enamelling; leather; lino-cutting, brass rubbing and candlemaking tools and supplies; felt, canvas, hessian, kapok and acrylic stuffing materials, tapestry canvases and wools, soft toy accessories; macramé yarns; prepared clays; rug-making equipment and some weaving yarns; tie-dye, batik and screen printing supplies; woods, pokerwork and marquetry tools and materials and woods and mouldings for picture framing; raffia, cane, basketwork materials and lamp shade frames; seashells; Plasticraft kits; modelling materials and Artstraws. They will get potters' wheels and kilns, looms for handweaving, and spinning wheels to order. They will also mount and frame pictures and tapestries, clean and restore paintings (and paint portraits), and offer lessons in art and craft subjects. Enquire for details. Very large stock.

GLASGOW

Miller's Art and Crafts Limited
54 Queen Street, Glasgow G1 3DH, Scotland 041 221 7985

Open: Monday to Saturday 09.00 to 17.30; mail order

Artists' materials and also craft kits and materials—Plasticraft and Enamelcraft, candlemaking and Polycraft kits and also chain, semi-precious stones, tumble polishing machines; leather and the tools for working it; lino-cutting and brass rubbing tools and materials; felt, tapestry canvas and wools, hessian, buttons and buckles, trimmings, knitting yarns, crochet yarns, macramé yarns and soft toy accessories; rug-making kits; tie-dye, batik and screen printing materials and accessories; marquetry kits; picture framing tools and materials; raffia, cane and basket making supplies; lampshade frames, fabrics and trimmings; and modelling clays and tools.

GLOSSOP

Homecrafts
18 High Street East, Glossop, Derbyshire
  Glossop 4134

Open: Monday to Saturday (excluding Tuesday) 09.30 to 17.00; Tuesday closed

Will frame pictures and cover or re-cover buttons and lampshades—or can sell you artists' materials, candle and rug kits, base metal findings, semi-precious stones, cold enamelling materials and accessories, leather and tools, lampshade frames, fabrics and trimmings, felt and soft toy fillings and accessories, tapestry canvases and wools and embroidery fabrics and threads, brass rubbing and marquetry materials, embedding plastics, picture framing materials and tools, modelling clays and craft books.

GODSHILL

The Island Craft Shop
The Bat's Wing, Godshill, Isle of Wight,
  Hampshire PO38 3HH   Godshill 634

Open: 10.30 to 13.00 and 14.15 to 17.30 seven days a week; mail order; catalogue

Particularly strong on jewellery-making, but with other craft materials as well. They have a 'Beginners' Tumbling Kit' (which slightly ambiguous term actually refers to stone polishing); a wide range of findings, both old-fashioned and modern; chain, tumbled stones, cut and polished stones, stone chips, rough rock (lots of agate, abalone, jade, wonderstone and others with equally appealing names), also glues, jewellers' tools and even small boxes in which to present the finished product. (Comprehensive kits as well as raw materials.) Also lots of lampshade frames, covering materials and trimmings; sticks and paper for brass rubbing; pokerwork machines and points; leather thonging; craft knives; natural and synthetic canes, basket bases and instruction leaflets; macramé yarns (also suitable for crochet and knitting); Enamelcraft and Plasticraft kits; starfish, shells, coral pieces etc. for embedding (coming soon: baby crabs—rather a sad thought). Also modelling materials, stool frames, sisal cord and seagrass for seating, and plenty of instruction books.

GORSEINON

Y Gegin Fawr (see page 74)

GRAVESEND

Tumble Kraft (see page 42)

GUISBOROUGH

Beecrafts
77 Church Street, Guisborough, Yorkshire

Open: Monday to Friday 10.00 to 15.00; Saturday 10.00 to 12.00; mail order; catalogue

Good range of general craft materials, although the speciality is really embroidery and soft toy making and they have embroidery linens and threads, tapestry canvases and wools, tapestry and needlework kits, kapok, foam, and a lot of soft toy accessories. But they also offer art materials (for children and adults); lots of craft books; chain and findings in silver, copper and gilt, semi-precious polished stones, cold enamelling materials; leather and leather-working tools; lino-cutting and brass rubbing accessories and materials; candlemaking supplies; a good stock of tie-dye, batik and screen printing materials; marquetry kits; eighty-four kinds of picture frame mouldings to order; raffia, cane, basketry materials; lampshade frames and seashells. Will also mount and frame paintings.

HARROGATE

Arts and Handicrafts
18 Station Parade, Harrogate, Yorkshire
  HG1 1UE   Harrogate 4772

Open: Monday to Saturday (excluding Wednesday) 09.00 to 17.30; Wednesday 09.00 to 13.00

Specialists in the materials for lampshade making, artists' materials and Black Forest clock kits (they will send you a special leaflet about the clocks). They also have things for jewellers—beads and chain, findings in silver-plate, nickel-plate and copper, copper blanks and enamelling materials, imitation stones and tumble polishing machines. Quite a lot of raffia and cane; trimmings and tassels (chiefly intended for the lampshades, but use them as you will); felt, canvas, hessian, kapok and fibre stuffing materials, noses and eyes for soft toys, and macramé yarns. The wherewithall for lino-cutting, brass rubbing and candlemaking; modelling clays and other modelling materials as available; clays and glazes for potters; art and craft paper; seashells; veneers, pokerwork tools, woods, and picture-framing materials and tools.

HATCH END

John Maxfield Limited
385 Uxbridge Road, Hatch End, Middlesex   01 428 6605

Open: Monday to Saturday (excluding Thursday) 08.30 to 17.30; Thursday 08.30 to 13.00; mail order

Publishers, and suppliers of artists' materials, mounting boards, air brushes, etc., who also sell craft kits—Plasticraft, Enamelcraft, Elamelaire, Supercast chess kits, candle kits and crystal craft kits; modelling clays and materials; copper and steel findings and copper blanks for enamelling; tumble polishers and imitation stones; brass rubbing and linocutting tools and materials and picture frame mouldings cut to size on the premises. They have another branch in Mill Hill, London.

HEMEL HEMPSTEAD

Arts and Crafts
81 High Street, Hemel Hempstead, Hertfordshire   Hemel Hempstead 55215

Open: Monday to Saturday (excluding Wednesday) 09.00 to 17.30; Wednesday 09.00 to 13.00; mail order; catalogue

A two-roomed shop—one room for art materials and one for crafts. They have Enamelaire and Allcraft kits, kits for candlemaking, batik, dye printing, linocutting, jewellery and soft toy making; also chain and findings in copper, gilt and stainless steel, silver wire, semi-precious stones, copper blanks and the materials for cold and kiln enamelling, screen printing and brass rubbing materials and accessories, embedding resins, seashells and modelling clays. They are prepared to advise on craftwork, and they arrange lectures and demonstrations.

HEREFORD

Winivere Crafts (see page 74)

HITCHIN

Homecrafts
8 St Mary's Churchyard, Hitchin, Hertfordshire   Hitchin 3945

Open: Monday to Saturday (excluding Wednesday) 09.00 to 17.30; Wednesday closed

Strongest on needlecraft with Penelope tapestry and embroidery kits, evenweave fabrics, felt, canvas, hessian, tapestry wools, embroidery silks, buttons, trimmings and soft toy accessories and fillings; also knitting, crochet and macramé yarns; the materials to make tufted rugs; some linen thread for lacemakers; marquetry and Plasticraft kits;

candlemaking materials both in kit form and loose; and raffia, cane and lampshade making accessories and materials.

HORSHAM

Annetts
7b Carfax, Horsham, Sussex
   Horsham 5878

Open: Monday to Saturday (excluding Thursday) 09.00 to 17.30; Thursday 09.00 to 13.00

Mainly for artists' materials but with a reasonable stock of Plasticraft kits, candlemaking supplies (in kit form and loose) and modern modelling clays.

HOVE

Handicrafts
58 George Street, Hove, Sussex
   Brighton 71688

Open: Monday to Saturday (excluding Wednesday) 09.00 to 17.30; Wednesday 09.00 to 13.00; mail order

Same stock as sister shop in Brighton—(see page 12)

HUDDERSFIELD

Arts and Crafts
PO Box 87, 10 Byram Street, Huddersfield, Yorkshire HD1 1DA
   Huddersfield 23402

Open: Monday to Saturday 09.00 to 17.30; mail order; catalogue 10p against goods

Such a wide range of stock it's difficult to know where to begin. Perhaps you should send for the catalogue (it costs 10p but they send you a 10p voucher with it to spend on goods). A very comprehensive range of kits, including all Atlas products. Beads, chain, findings and stones; copper blanks for enamelling; materials for cold and hot enamelling (including kilns); leather and leather-working tools; small weaving looms; tie-dye, batik and screen printing materials. For the needleworker there are hessian and felt and fur fabric, trimmings, tapestry kits and a lot of useful things for soft toy making—kapok and other stuffing materials, eyes, noses and masks. Very wide range of macramé threads and kits. Also clays and glazes and potters' kilns; candlemaking supplies; raffias and canes and everything you need for basket-making; origami paper; shells; modelling clays, Artstraws and light construction materials. They have lampshade frames in all shapes and sizes and plastic ribbon, raffia, parchment, silk, woven straw and Strylon to cover them with. They have everything you need for marquetry, including selected veneer packs, knives, cements and a full range of Multicraft Precision Tools. They have two lino-cutting sets and one set of tools and a complete brass rubbing kit with separate accessories. They continually add to their range and are happy to try and locate any materials for you if they are not already stocked.

HULL

Handicrafts of Hull
20/22 Hepworth's Arcade, Silver Street, Hull, Yorkshire   Hull 223489

Open: Monday to Saturday 09.00 to 17.00; mail order; catalogue

Lots of craft materials, including the full range of Supercast candle and chess-making kits, cold enamelling and macramé kits. Also a wide range of lampshade frames, braids and fringes. They have leather and tools; some beads, chains, findings and stones for jewellery-making; felts, buckles, trimmings and needlework materials; yarns for knitting and crochet; small weaving looms; tie-dye fabric dyes; modelling clays; veneers for marquetry and also raffias, canes and the bases and handles for basket-making. Plenty of bits and pieces to browse among and, in fact, their slogan is 'Exciting ideas begin at ...'

HYTHE

Needlecraft and Hobbies
3 Bank Street, Hythe, Kent   Hythe 67086

Open: Monday to Saturday (excluding Wednesday) 09.00 to 17.30; Wednesday closed; mail order (from Canterbury branch); catalogue 15p

Similar stock to that in the main shop in Canterbury (to whom you should apply if you want goods by mail order —see separate entry). Gilt, nickel and aluminium findings, copper blanks, en-amels and kilns, imitation stones, jewel-lers' tools and tumble polishing machines; leather and the tools for working it; fab-rics for embroidery and for covering lamp shades; felt, tapestry canvases and wools, hessian, washable stuffing materials, soft toy accessories, buttons, buckles, trim-mings, notions and yarns for knitting, crochet and macramé; rug-making can-vases and wools; net and lace making supplies; brass rubbing and marquetry kits; craft plastics; candlemaking sup-plies; raffia, cane and basketry materials; seashells; modelling clays and various toy-making accessories (dolls' house windows, fort walls, etc.).

ILMINSTER

Opie Gems (see page 43)

KEGWORTH

Kits 'n' Krafts (see page 75)

KEIGHLEY

Conways Arts and Crafts
53 Cavendish Street, Keighley, York-shire BD21 3RB   Keighley 4045

Open: Monday to Saturday (excluding Tuesday) 09.00 to 17.00; Tuesday closed; mail order

An artists' materials and model shop, specialising in plastic and balsa models, with a wide range of small craft kits—Plasticraft, Enamelcraft, brass rubbing, screen printing, tie and dye, batik, Mod-roc, weaving, marquetry, etc. Also leather and leather-working tools; lino-cutting tools; felt, tapestry canvases and wools, hessian, macramé threads, soft toy accessories and stuffing materials; pot-ters' clays and cold glazes; rug-making canvases and wools; picture framing mat-erials and tools; candlemaking supplies; frames and trimmings for lampshades; seashells; and a good range of modelling clays and modelling materials.

KENDAL

Kendal Handicrafts
7/9 Stramongate, Kendal, Westmorland Kendal 21174

Open: Monday to Saturday (excluding Thursday) 09.00 to 17.30; Thursday 09.00 to 12.30; mail order

A few beads and findings—also leather and tools, felts, trimmings and soft toy and tapestry kits, knitting and crochet yarns, small weaving looms and rug-making packs. Candlemaking and Plasti-craft kits, canes, raffia and basket-making supplies and a good stock of enamelling materials and kilns. They have the raw materials for pottery—clays, glazes and so on—and although they don't stock wheels and kilns they can, and are willing to, get them to order. They will mail materials to you, but there is no catalogue so you must know what you want.

KIDDERMINSTER

Arts and Crafts
102 Coventry Street, Kidderminster, Worcestershire   0562 4724

Open: Monday to Saturday (excluding Wednesday) 09.00 to 17.00; Wednesday 09.00 to 12.30; mail order

They carry a very large stock of artists' materials and will make picture frames to order. But they also sell mouldings for those who want to make their own frames and quite a lot of craft materials —beads, chain, pewterfoil, copperfoil and findings; leather and the relevant tools; felts, trimmings and tapestry kits; cold enamelling kits; a good range of tie-dye, batik and silk screening materials, including the right paper; modelling clays; woods and veneers; polyester casting resin and plastic construction kits; candlemaking supplies; canes, raffia and the wherewithall to create your own baskets. But no catalogue.

LANCASTER

Leisure Crafts
14 Lower Church Street, Lancaster, Lancashire Lancaster 66775

Open: Monday to Saturday (excluding Wednesday) 09.15 to 17.45; Wednesday 09.15 to 12.30

Plasticraft and Supercast kits, chain, findings, a limited supply of stones, cold enamelling materials, pewter and copperfoil; leather offcuts, thonging and tools; felt and tapestry canvases and wools; rug-making kits; lampshade frames and trimmings; basket-making materials including canes and raffia; modelling clays; candlemaking and batik materials; veneers for marquetry and various light construction materials—Artstraws, craft paper and so on.

LEAMINGTON SPA

A S Blackie Arts and Crafts
120 Regent Street, Leamington Spa, Warwickshire Leamington Spa 21719

Open: Monday to Saturday (excluding Thursday) 09.00 to 13.00 and 14.00 to 17.30; Thursday 09.00 to 13.00; mail order

Art and craft kits and back-up materials from Winsor and Newton, Reeves, Rowney, Atlas, etc.—also books. Jewellery findings and imitation stones, leather and leather-working tools; lino cutting and brass rubbing tools and materials; felt kits; soft toy accessories; silk screen printing materials and accessories; marquetry, pokerwork and picture framing supplies; candle, basket and lampshade-making supplies; modelling clays, raffia and cane.

LEATHERHEAD

Handicrafts (Leatherhead) Limited
Brick Bat Alley, High Street, Leatherhead, Surrey Leatherhead 73697

Open: Monday to Saturday (excluding Wednesday) 09.30 to 17.15; Wednesday 09.30 to 13.00

Here you can buy small soft toy kits and small leather kits; base metal chain and findings and imitation stones; fur fabric, felt, Courtelle fillings and soft toy accessories; sheet copper and pewter; moulds and powder for plaster casting; raffia, cane and basketry supplies; and the frames, covering materials and trimmings for lampshade making.

LEEDS

E J Arnold and Son Limited
Butterley Street, Leeds, Yorkshire LS10 1AX Leeds 442944

Mail order only; catalogue against goods ordered

The largest educational suppliers of materials in Britain who will deal by mail (minimum order £5.00) but are accustomed to supplying in bulk to schools—for instance, all their craft kits contain large quantities of materials and sufficient tools for up to twenty-four children to be working at the same time. They are therefore perhaps not of much practical interest to the individual craftworker but are included here because they are important, because you may be buying for a school or a group in any case, and because you might want to buy not a kit but £5 worth of modelling materials ... They offer kits for: texture rubbing, chromatography, marbling, lino-cutting, screen printing, enamelling (kits include a kiln), plastic embedding, plastic mosaic work, stone barrelling, raffia, basketry, weaving, tie and dye, batik, origami, modelling with plaster of Paris, polystyrene and balsa, candlemaking and paper flower making. They also have a good range of modelling tools and materials; clays and glazes for pottery and all pottery room accessories from plastic buckets to potters' wheels and kilns. They have yarns for knitting, crochet and macramé, embroidery fabrics and threads, sewing and dressmaking fabrics, threads, needles, scissors, thimbles, etc., a tremendous range of fancy papers and all kinds of woodworking tools and junior woodworking benches and toolboxes. Their kits contain everything except rigid ideas of how they should be used and leave plenty of room for creativity.

Headrow Gallery
52 The Headrow, Leeds 1, Yorkshire Leeds 22337

Open: Tuesday to Saturday 09.00 to 17.30; mail order

Quite a wide variety of craft kits in the following categories—lino-cutting, tie-dye, batik, screen printing, brass rubbing, marquetry and candle and toy making. Also back-up materials and accessories and lampshade frames, fabrics and trimmings, felt, canvas, hessian, soft toy accessories and fillings, raffia, cane and basketry supplies, seashells, modelling clays and picture framing tools and materials.

LEICESTER

Dryad

Northgates, Leicester, Leicestershire LE1 4QR   Leicester 50405

Mail order only; catalogue

Dryad, publishers of the books and leaflets you find in almost every craft shop, are possibly the best known craft suppliers in the country. They are, strictly speaking, educational suppliers, used by schools, colleges and organisations, and say that it is uneconomical to supply individuals. Nevertheless, they will sometimes supply, so if you are really stuck for some material you know them to have, try your luck.

They have all the necessary for bookbinding (paper, boards, cloth, leather, cords and laces, hand tools, brushes, adhesives, brass hand letters and figures, apparatus and instruction books); for canework (natural and synthetic cane and tools); for basketwork and stool seating; all kinds of art and craft papers; tools, blocks, inks, etc. for lino-cutting; everything for fabric printing (including the fabric); natural calf and hide, morocco, goat and sheep skins, thongs, threads, tools and accessories for leatherwork; lampshade frames, vellums and trimmings; powdered clay and powder glaze, kick wheels, electric kilns and kiln furniture and a good range of modelling clays (including plaster of Paris) and modelling tools; an excellent range of woodworking and woodcarving tools; the wherewithall for the making of musical pipes; various plastics (including coloured perspex offcuts) and the tools for working them; knitting and crochet yarns; embroidery linens, hessian, fabrics for needlework, upholstery and dressmaking, embroidery threads and tapestry wools, trimmings and notions, various kinds of raffia, felt and soft toy fabrics and stuffing materials and accessories; macramé twine; weaving yarns and looms and accessories; natural and synthetic dyes; spinning wheels, accessories and natural fleece; rug wool, rug canvas and the Dryad rug loom. And, of course, useful publications on all the above.

The Midland Educational Company Limited

17/21 Market Street, Leicester, Leicestershire   Leicester 29071

Open: Monday to Saturday 09.00 to 17.30 (see page 11)

LETCHWORTH

The Picture Shop

6 Station Road, Letchworth, Hertfordshire   Letchworth 4454

Open: Monday to Saturday (excluding Wednesday) 09.00 to 17.00; Wednesday closed

Artists' materials and a picture framing service, but for craftwork they offer the following kits—marquetry, casting plastics, mosaic, lino-cutting, Enamelcraft and tapestry. Also copper blanks and findings, enamelling materials and tumble polishing machines; hessian, felt, foam fillings and plastic eyes for toys; brass rubbing materials and papers; marquetry and pokerwork materials and picture frame mouldings; clear sheet plastic; candlemaking materials; raffia, cane and basket and lampshade making materials; seashells and a variety of modelling materials.

LONDON EC1

Crafts Unlimited

54 Fleet Street, London EC1   01 353 1688

Open: Monday to Friday 09.00 to 17.00; mail order; catalogue 35p

Similar stock to the Kensington High Street branch—see page 24. If they don't have some material that Kensington High Street does have, it can be made available on request within a day.

N1

Fine Art Supplies

294 Upper Street, Islington, London N1   01 226 7479

Open: Monday to Saturday 09.30 to 18.00; mail order

Specialise in artists' materials and stationery but, like many art shops, stock various boxed craft kits—for brass rubbing, candlemaking, modelling and lino-cutting. Also modelling clay by itself and fabric dyes suitable for tie-dye and batiking.

N1

The Pot Shop

8 Shillingford Street, off Cross Street, Islington, London N1   01 226 9607

Open: Monday to Saturday (excluding Thursday) 10.00 to 18.00; Thursday 10.00 to 13.00; mail order; catalogue (please specify which craft)

The Pot Shop is run by a potter, which means not only that they supply all necessary tools and materials for the craft but also that they can offer advice on materials and equipment. Well able to supply bulk orders (to schools and institutions) but equally happy to deal with individuals. They also have other craft materials and tools (some in kit form, but they say their kits are for craftsmen, or potential craftsmen, and come without fancy packaging) including some unusual ones. For instance, they make their own doll kits with ceramic head, shoulders and arms, kapok, calico, body and dress patterns, needles, thread, wig and glue and Victorian patterns for knickers, petticoat and boots. They manufacture pottery tool kits and kits for making stained glass windows. They have a very wide range of enamelling materials, kilns, tools and copper shapes; lots of bits and bobs for doll and toy making; leather thonging and leather-working tools; brass rubbing and lino-cutting tools and materials; glass and leading; candle-making supplies (natural beeswax is on order); raffia and cane and the essentials for basket-making; woodcarving tools and modelling materials. Good quality materials and a very 'alive' set-up. They actually invite criticism and comment and will try to provide any materials for which there is a demand if they are not already available.

N9
The Art and Craft Centre
333 Fore Street, Edmonton, London N9 0PA 01 807 0329

Open: Monday to Saturday 09.30 to 18.00

Specialises in artists' materials, but also has a very great many craft materials—canes and bases for basketry; rubbing sticks and paper for brass rubbing; candle-making materials and kits; clock making kits; embroidery silks and patterns; tapestry canvas, wools, needles and kits; materials for cold and kiln enamelling, including findings and copper blanks; mosaic kits; frames, covers and trimmings for lampshades; veneers, craft knives, polish and kits for marquetry; casting plaster, moist clay, Das and a battery operated potters' wheel; plastic embedding kits; a large selection of shells; felt, fur fabric, stuffing, eyes, noses growlers, squeakers and patterns for soft toy making; fabric dyes; macramé yarns and a wide choice of books on art and craft subjects.

NW3
Crafts Unlimited
311 Finchley Road, London NW3 01 435 6934

Open: Monday to Friday 09.00 to 17.30; Saturday 09.00 to 13.00; mail order; catalogue 35p

Similar stock to the Kensington High Street branch—see page 24. If they do not have some material that Kensington High Street does have, it can be made available on request within a day.

NW7
John Maxfield Limited
9 Broadway, Mill Hill, London NW7 3LN 01 959 3127

Open: Monday to Saturday (excluding Thursday) 08.30 to 17.30; Thursday 08.30 to 13.00; mail order

Another branch of the Hatch End shop. Wide range of artists' materials; Plasti-craft, Enamelcraft, Enamelaire and candlemaking kits; brass rubbing and lino-cutting tools and materials; modelling clays and materials; copper and steel jewellery findings, imitation stones and tumble polishers.

SW3
Harrods (see page 75)

SW10
Hobby Horse
15/17 Langton Street, Chelsea, London SW10 01 351 1913

Open: Monday to Saturday 10.00 to 17.30; mail order; catalogue 15p

Will send you a nice chunky catalogue with clear line drawings setting out everything they have in stock and also giving stray pieces of useful information (such as how a basic macramé knot should look). But try to go in person because they sell so many lovely things that you will probably decide to take up three or four new crafts before you leave the shop. They have weaving looms and yarns; felts; a staggering array of wooden, glass and ceramic beads; an inspired range of jewellery findings (including wire in silver, silver-plate, rolled-gold and copper) and jewellers' tools; macramé kits, cords and accessories; leather-working tools; modelling materials and tools; everything for candle-making (and not just kits, either); everything for batik and silk screen printing and lino-cutting; drilled wooden balls in various sizes; the Enamelaire kit, cold enamelling kits, and also kilns, tools and materials including a really good choice of copper blanks; the full Plasticraft range; natural cane in bundles; plywood basket bases; rolls of natural sea grass and various light construction materials, like sisal cord with wire, pipe cleaners and so on. A very good place to browse and ask advice. (There's a map in the catalogue and they even tell you which bus to catch.)

SW11
Leisure Crafts
123 Falcon Road, London SW11 2PE 01 228 0140

Open: Monday to Saturday (excluding Wednesday) 09.00 to 18.00; Wednesday 09.00 to 12.30

Tapestry and candlemaking kits, macramé, soft toy and marquetry kits; also leather and leather-working tools; linocutting and brass rubbing tools and materials; raffia, cane and basketry supplies; lampshade frames and trimmings; felt, canvas and Nu-stuffing; and some modelling materials.

SW17
Homecraft Supplies Limited
27 Trinity Road, London SW17 7SF
  01 672 7070

Open: Monday to Friday 09.00 to 13.00; mail order; catalogue

Although opening times for the public are somewhat limited, they are well equipped to send orders all over the country, which they do on a cash against a pro forma invoice system. For leather-working they have whole skins in various grains and colours, linings, thonging, leather offcuts and accessories and cut-outs for bags and purses; lampshade frames, kits and trimmings; mosaic pebbles and glues; Rotacane and natural cane and basket and tray frames and handles; picture framing kits (and pictures to frame); fur fabric, felt in all colours, fillings, eyes, noses and patterns for soft toys—also special packs for making a teddy bear, a rabbit or a panda; chair and stool frames and seating cords; knitting yarns in wool and nylon sold by the pound pack (or in pound packs of assorted colours for knitting blanket squares); thrums of wool, canvas and binding for rug-making; lots of embroidery threads and traced cushion covers, aprons, tablecloths etc. to work with them. Also wood and leatherworking tools, needles, scissors and other craft tools. (And all kinds of aids for the disabled—bed hoists, lazy tongs, bath safety rails and so on.)

W1
Hamleys of Regent Street Limited
200/202 Regent Street, London W1R 5OF
  01 734 3161

Open: Monday to Saturday (excluding Thursday) 09.00 to 17.30; Thursday 09.00 to 19.00; mail order; catalogue

Hamleys the toy shop has a craft department. There you will find a lot of different craft kits, mostly chosen because they are suitable for children. Kits for cold enamelling, candlemaking, Plasticraft, marquetry, tie and dye, batik, screen printing, brass rubbing and basket making. Also modelling clays, raffia, cane, seashells, expanded polystyrene and a craft compendium.

W1
George Rowney and Company Limited
12 Percy Street, London W1A 2BP
  01 636 8241

Open: Monday to Friday (excluding Tuesday) 09.00 to 17.30; Tuesday 09.30 to 17.30; Saturday 09.00 to 12.30; mail order; catalogue

Chiefly artists' materials, but they do a nice line in brushes useful for bookbinders—also lino-cutting and fabric printing kits, modelling clays, brass rubbing sticks and papers and mouldings for picture frames. No order is too small for them to send by post, and the catalogue is free.

W1
Selfridges Limited
Oxford Street, London W1A 1AB
  01 629 1234

Open: Monday to Saturday (excluding Thursday) 09.00 to 17.30; Thursday 09.00 to 20.00; mail order; catalogue at Christmas only

Selfridges have craft materials but, as with most large stores, they are not all collected in one department. Go to the Jewellery Department for precious, semi-precious and imitation stones; to the Do-It-Yourself Department in the basement for leather offcuts, lino-cutting materials and tools, woods, veneers and picture framing materials and tools; to Haberdashery for kapok, buttons, buckles, trimmings, notions and tie-dyeing materials and to Needlework for tapestry and rug-making materials and knitting wools.

W8
Crafts Unlimited
178 Kensington High Street, London
  W8 01 937 5370

Open: Monday to Saturday 09.00 to 17.30; mail order; catalogue 35p

There are several branches of Crafts Unlimited in London and the provinces, all owned by Reeves and all priding themselves on stocking a very wide range of craft materials. Like so many large craft shops they are adding to their range all the time and so it's probably worth spending 35p on the latest catalogue.

For jewellers they have beads, chain, findings in gold, silver and nickel, semi-precious and imitation stones, jewellers' tools and tumble polishing machines—also copper blanks, enamelling materials and kilns. They have the tools and materials for leather-working and lino-cutting. For needleworkers they can supply cambric, felt, canvas, hessian, kapok and the eyes and noses to give expression to your soft toys. They have modelling clays and also prepared clays for potters—also glazes, wheels and kilns. They have a good stock of macramé yarns and rug-making equipment. For weavers they have small looms and for spinners they have wheels. They have all the requirements for tie-dye, batik and silk-screening (including their own dyes), and for candlemaking and brass-rubbing. They have some woods, woodworking tools, veneers and other marquetry and pokerwork supplies. And for miscellaneous crafts they have seashells, raffia and cane.

WC2
Crafts Unlimited (see pp. 24, 53)

WC2
Tridias
44 Monmouth Street, London WC2
01 240 2369

Open: Monday to Friday 09.30 to 17.30; Saturday 09.30 to 13.00

Similar stocks to the Bath branch (see separate entry on page 10) but rather less on account of being a smaller shop.

LOUGHBOROUGH

Artcraft and Do-it-Yourself
36 Pinfold Gate, Loughborough, Leicestershire 050 93 63439

Open: Monday to Saturday (excluding Wednesday) 08.00 to 13.30 and 14.30 to 18.00; Wednesday 08.00 to 13.30 and 16.00 to 18.00

Well-stocked with candlemaking, tie-dyeing and moulding kits as well as a number of other materials such as beads, chains, findings, metals and stones for jewellery-making; leather offcuts; bits and pieces for needleworkers, like buttons, trimmings, notions, felts, etc.; yarns for knitting and crochet; rug-making kits; potters' clays and glazes; woods and veneers for marquetry; and raffias, canes and general basket-making materials. When asked if they specialised the proprietors replied that they specialise in advising on artcrafts, which is comforting.

LYTHAM

Lytham Woodcrafts Limited
52 Clifton Street, Lytham, Lancashire FY8 5EW Lytham 5796

Open: Monday to Saturday (excluding Wednesday) 08.30 to 17.30; Wednesday 08.30 to 12.30

At Lytham Woodcrafts you can buy woods and veneers for marquetry, but also general craft materials—leather, art and craft papers, felt, canvas, hessian,

Nu-foam, kapok, foam chippings, tapestry wools, soft toy accessories, macramé and candlemaking kits, raffia and cane, basket bases and lampshade frames, and covering materials (of the raffia rather than the fabric type).

MALVERN

Fearnside and Company
40 Belle Vue Terrace, Malvern, Worcestershire WR14 4PZ Malvern 3221

Open: Monday to Saturday (excluding Wednesday) 09.00 to 13.00 and 14.00 to 17.30; Wednesday 09.00 to 13.00; mail order; catalogue of art materials only

A shop for artists' materials, posters, cards, incense, mobiles and so on which began to stock craft materials because of local demand and is continually adding to its stock. At the moment it can offer Plasticraft and Enamelcraft kits and kits for batik, screen printing, stone tumbling, candlemaking and lino-cutting—also nickel and silver plate findings, copper blanks, felt, canvas, macramé yarns, picture framing kits (and a picture framing service), coloured and clear acetate sheet, raffia and seagrass, seashells—and plasticine, Plastone, Barbola, Das and plaster of Paris for modelling work. They have a good selection of art and craft books and it's worth noting that they are prepared to take good craftsman-made items on a sale or return basis and, if quantity and quality are sufficient, to stage window displays of them. Happy to give professional advice on art and craft problems.

MANCHESTER

Fred Aldous Limited
37 Lever Street, Manchester, Lancashire M60 1UX 061 236 2477

Open: Monday to Friday 09.00 to 17.00; Saturday 09.00 to 16.00; mail order; catalogue

Wholesalers and retailers of an enormous range of handicraft materials. They supply various retail outlets throughout the country, but you can call in and choose from their vast stocks or order by mail against the catalogue (minimum order £1.00). They stock embroidery and tapestry kits; raffia (natural and synthetic), basketwork supplies and tools, Centre cane and Rotacane, tray and basket bases, stools and seating cord; lampshade frames, covering fabrics, trimmings and raffias; marquetry kits; candlemaking supplies; modelling compounds, clays and tools; pewter and copper sheet, metal working tools, ceramic stones, gilt and silver plate, chain and findings, semi-precious stones, copper shapes for enamelling, enamels and kilns; all kinds of beads; macramé threads; soft toy kits, felts, squeakers, masks (including 'doll, flesh, glad eyes'), safety eyes and noses; leather-working tools and accessories (rivets, eyelets, thonging, bag fasteners, etc.), leather and leathercloth; Plasticraft and Enamelcraft kits; rug canvases, wools and fur pieces; an electric poker machine and whitewood mats and boxes; moccasin kits; batik kits and fabric dyes. Very wide range, chiefly but not all in kit form—and a lot of books and instruction leaflets.

Arts and Crafts (see page 77)

B Wilson and Sons
11 Precinct Centre, Oxford Road, Manchester 13, Lancashire   061 273 2000

Open: Monday to Saturday 09.00 to 17.30; mail order; catalogue

This is an art shop, with little in the way of craft materials, but the proprietors plan to open a shop next door (number 12) and to devote it exclusively to crafts. Opening date will just about coincide with publication date of this book, so it isn't possible to go into any details—except to say that opening times should be as above and the range of stock available should be extensive so, if this is your local shop, check up on it.

MIDDLESBROUGH

J Goldstein and Son
145 Linthorpe Road, Middlesbrough, Yorkshire   0642 46748

Open: Monday to Saturday 09.00 to 17.30

Here you can buy kits for the following crafts—marquetry, tapestry, Plasticraft, Enamelcraft, batik, candlemaking, macramé, soft toy making, gem polishing and jewellery work. Also separate dyes for tie-dye and batik, silk screening dyes and paper (paper for origami, too) beads, chain, findings, imitation and semi-precious stones, leather and leather-working tools, felts and trimmings, modelling clays, packs of wood veneers, synthetic and natural raffias and canes and, as well as the cold enamelling kits, materials and kilns for hot enamelling. They don't undertake mail order as such, or print a catalogue, but they will send your materials by post if you know what you want and can't get in to the shop yourself.

MILTON KEYNES

Milton Keynes Day Centre
3 Victoria Road, Bletchley, Milton Keynes, Buckinghamshire
Milton Keynes 73730

Open: Monday to Saturday (excluding Wednesday) 09.00 to 18.00; Wednesday 09.00 to 13.00

Most of the things you need to make soft toys—felt, stuffing materials and eyes, noses and growlers; woodworking supplies—the wood itself, veneers, carpentry tools, marquetry kits, pokerwork tools and picture framing materials and tools; also candlemaking and cold and kiln enamelling supplies, raffia, cane, basketry accessories and lampshade frames.

MORPETH

Tallantyre Wallpapers
43 Newgate Street, Morpeth, Northumberland NE61 1AT   Morpeth 2261

Open: Monday, Tuesday, Wednesday and Saturday 9.00 to 17.30; Thursday 09.30 to 13.00 and Friday 09.00 to 18.00

Plasticraft, Enamelcraft and Stringcraft kits, light construction materials and modelling clays—also marquetry and picture framing materials and tools (and they will undertake framing for you, if you wish). Small weaving looms—some hessian, felts and canvas and several kinds of stuffing materials; also paper for papercrafts; lino-cutting tools and materials; beads, tumble polishing machines, copper blanks and the materials for cold enamelling. And plenty of artists' materials.

NANNERCH

Craft O'Hans (see page 53)

NEW ASH GREEN

The Hobby House
10 Upper Street North, New Ash Green, Near Dartford, Kent
Ash Green 872136

Open: Tuesday to Saturday 09.00 to 17.30; mail order

Artists' supplies, drawing office supplies and equipment, kits and engines for model cars and planes, a picture framing and photocopying service—but somehow there is still the space for them to stock macramé and Plasticraft and Cosmetic kits; tapestry, embroidery and Enamelaire kits; lost wax casting, pin and wire and soft toy kits—and seagrass, feathers, modelling clays, stainless steel and copper findings, gemstones and polished pebbles, jewellers' tools and tumble polishers, leather offcuts and leather-working tools, lino-cutting and brass rubbing materials and accessories, candle and lampshade making supplies and raffia and cane, felt, canvas, hessian, toy fillings and accessories and most of the necessities for rug-making, tie-dye, batik and screen printing.

NEWBURY

Newbury Fine Art Limited
87 Bartholomew Street, Newbury, Berkshire Newbury 43171

Open: Monday to Saturday (excluding Wednesday) 09.00 to 13.00 and 14.00 to 17.30; Wednesday 09.00 to 13.00

Stockists of artists' materials who offer a picture-framing service which they do on the premises. Can also supply you with various Reeves Craft Sets, as available. Always in stock are materials for lino-cutting, brass rubbing, candlemaking and also modelling clays, plasticine, Das and so on.

NEWCASTLE UPON TYNE

Ashbourton Gifts and Crafts
Shop 4, Kenton Park Shopping Centre, 123a Kenton Road, Gosforth, Newcastle upon Tyne, Northumberland Newcastle upon Tyne 855717

Open: Monday to Saturday 09.00 to 18.00

This is where you go for stationery, haberdashery, gifts, craft books and craft kits. It is a fairly new venture which wants to expand with demand. Already there are macramé, marquetry, candlemaking, Plasticraft and Enamelcraft kits, craft papers, felt, hessian, washable cotton stuffing materials, trimmings, needlework and tapestry kits, soft toy accessories, notions, tools and materials for pewter and copperwork, raffia and Raffene, lampshade frames and trimmings, Das and plaster of Paris.

The Do It Yourself Foam Centre
70 Shields Road West, Byker, Newcastle upon Tyne 6, Northumberland Newcastle upon Tyne 653544

Open: Monday to Saturday (excluding Wednesday) 09.30 to 17.30; Wednesday 09.30 to 13.00

This is a new business, and although the craft materials available at the moment are slightly limited the intention is to build up the supply. Even now they promise to do their very best to get hold of any materials within a few days—so if what you want is not listed here it's still worth while asking for it. At present

they have tumble polishing machines, fur fabric, felt, kapok, foam and terylene stuffing materials and soft toy accessories (eyes, noses and masks). Also the materials and tools for picture framing, and basketry; Plasticraft, Enamelcraft and candlemaking kits; raffia, cane and modelling clays.

NEWTON STEWART

Country Crafts
2 Albert Street, Newton Stewart, Wigtownshire, Scotland

Open: Monday to Saturday (excluding Wednesday) 09.00 to 17.30; Wednesday 09.00 to 17.30 March to November— 09.00 to 12.30 November to March

Chiefly concerned with selling the finished work of craftsmen, but for those who want to do it themselves they offer a few bits and pieces—buttons and buckles, semi-precious stones (polished) and seashells.

NEW WALTHAM

Joseph Ogle and Sons Limited
259 Station Road, New Waltham, Grimsby, Lincolnshire Grimsby 822772

Open: Monday to Thursday 08.30 to 17.30; Friday 08.30 to 19.00; Saturday 08.30 to 17.00

In a way a general craft shop—but most of the stock seems to relate to jewellery making and woodwork. They offer chain and findings in base metals, copper blanks, semi-precious stones, jewellers' tools, tumble polishing machines and materials for cold and kiln enamelling; woods and veneers, marquetry and pokerwork tools and accessories, and picture framing tools and materials. Also modelling clays, light construction materials and candlemaking kits.

NORTHAMPTON

Abington Handicrafts
140 Abington Avenue, Northampton, Northamptonshire NN1 4PD Northampton 33305

Open: Monday to Friday (excluding Thursday) 09.00 to 12.45 and 14.00 to 17.45; Thursday 09.00 to 13.45; Saturday 09.00 to 12.45 and 14.00 to 17.00

A general craft shop, leaning towards the needlework side. They have embroidery linens and cotton, fur fabric, felt, tapestry canvas, hessian, Penelope needlework packs, beads and sequins, soft toy kits, eyes, noses, bells, masks, chimes, hair and, for stuffing the toys, polyester and acrilan stuffing materials, cotton flock and foam chips. Also Plasticraft and marquetry kits; chain, nickel findings and tumble polishing machines; candle and basket-making materials; raffia and cane; cold enamelling kits and some modelling materials. Will supply by mail but prefer not to.

Arts and Crafts Shop
21 Abington Square, Northampton, Northamptonshire Northampton 36521

Open: Monday to Saturday (excluding Thursday) 09.00 to 17.30; Thursday 09.00 to 13.00; mail order

General craft materials and some kits, including home-packaged Christmas cracker kits, needlework and tapestry kits. Also base metal and sterling silver findings, pewter and copper sheets and tools, polished cabochons, imitation stones, tumble polishers, copper blanks, enamels and the Enamelaire kiln; leather skins and offcuts; lino-cutting and brass rubbing materials and tools; felt, hessian, polyester, Nu-stuffing and crumbled foam; soft toy accessories; tapestry canvases and the full range of wools; evenweave fabrics and Anchor stranded cottons; macramé yarns; Ryagarn rug kits and cut wools for tufted rugs; batik kits and screen printing inks; marquetry materials; picture frame mouldings and tools; rigid PVC sheet and embedding plastics; glass for mosaic mural work; candlemaking supplies in kit form and loose (including natural beeswax); raffia, cane and basketry supplies; lampshade frames and modelling clays.

The Midland Educational Company Limited
27 The Drapery, Northampton, Northamptonshire Northampton 39400

Open: Monday to Saturday 09.00 to 17.30 (see page 11)

NORTHWICH

Country Crafts
5 Leicester Street, Northwich, Cheshire

Open: Monday to Saturday (excluding Wednesday) 09.30 to 13.00 and 13.30 to 17.30; Wednesday 09.30 to 13.00 (Don't close for lunch on Friday or Saturday)

Kits for candlemaking and marquetry, tapestry sets and Plasticraft and Enamelcraft kits. Also, useful things for needlework and soft toy making—felt, canvas, hessian, kapok and polyester fillings, buckles, buttons, beads, notions, trimings and soft toy accessories; knitting, crochet and macramé yarns; lampshade frames and covering fabrics; raffia, cane and basketry materials.

NOTTINGHAM

Home Pastimes
69 Mansfield Road, Nottingham, Nottinghamshire Nottingham 44974

Open: Monday to Saturday (excluding Thursday) 09.00 to 17.30; Thursday closed; mail order

Specialise in basketry and soft toy making and have plenty of materials for both crafts. Also Plasticraft and cold enamelling kits, tumble polishers, leather and tools, marquetry materials and lampshade frames.

OLDHAM

The Art and Craft Shop
194 Union Street, Oldham, Lancashire OL1 1EN   Oldham 2163

Open: Monday to Saturday (excluding Tuesday) 09.30 to 17.00; Tuesday closed; mail order; catalogue

Large range of craft kits—and a picture framing and tapestry stretching service. You can buy the necessary tools and materials for leather-working, lino-cutting, jewellery-making (beads, chain, semi-precious and imitation stones, copper blanks and enamelling materials), rug-making, tie-dye and batik, marquetry, picture framing, candlemaking, lampshade and basket making. Also self-drying clays, raffia, cane, felt, acrylic stuffing materials, soft toy accessories and canvas and wools for tapestry.

OXFORD

Brush and Compass
20 Broad Street, Oxford, Oxfordshire Oxford 46481

Open: Monday to Saturday 09.00 to 17.30; mail order

Stationers and artists' materials suppliers who have candlemaking, wire and nail and Stringcraft kits; enamelling materials, kilns and copper blanks; lino-cutting and brass rubbing tools and materials; tie-dye and batik dyes and accessories; modelling clays and tumble polishing machines.

Colegroves
4 Lincoln House, Turl Street, Oxford, Oxfordshire OX1 3EH   Oxford 43437

Open: Monday to Saturday 09.00 to 17.30

Full range of artists' materials and also a good stock of tools and materials and accessories for enamelling, candlemaking and crystal casting. They have kits and loose materials for all three, also batik kits and all the necessary for lino-cutting, brass rubbing and screen printing. Also silver plate chain and findings, tumble polishers, modelling materials, light construction materials and fancy and art papers.

PERTH

Dunn's Art Stores
35 Scott Street, Perth, Perthshire PH1 5EH Perth 24540

Open: Monday to Saturday (excluding Wednesday) 09.00 to 17.30; Wednesday 09.00 to 13.00; mail order

As well as artists' materials and a picture framing service they offer marquetry, macramé and plastic embedding kits; beads, chain and a few gilt and nickel findings; some leather offcuts; lino-cutting and brass rubbing tools and materials; buckram, Raffene, felt, hessian, canvas, kapok and cotton fillings, trimmings and soft toy accessories; macramé yarns; screen printing materials and accessories; candlemaking materials; raffia, cane and basketry supplies; lampshade frames; cold enamelling materials; modelling clays and glass mosaic materials.

PETERBOROUGH

Art and Educational Crafts
22a Lincoln Road, Peterborough, Huntingdonshire

Open: Tuesday to Saturday 09.00 to 17.30

Artists' materials and a picture framing service; also Enamelcraft and Plasticraft and batik kits, and rubber moulds for garden ornaments; beads, chain, findings, semi-precious and imitation stones and tumbling machines; materials for cold and kiln enamelling; leather; lino-cutting and brass rubbing tools and materials; felt, fabric dyes and screen printing materials; picture framing kits; candlemaking materials; lampshade frames and raffia; seashells; and clays, glazes, wheels and kilns for pottery.

PORT TALBOT

Cliffords (see page 78)

PRESCOT

The Art Shop
12 Church Street, Prescot, Lancashire Prescot 3722

Open: Monday to Saturday (excluding Thursday) 09.30 to 17.30; Thursday closed

The Art Shop has kits and craft materials as well as art materials. Kits for pin and wire and Stringcraft, marquetry, enamelling (cold only), plastic embedding and the making of artificial flowers. Materials for lino-cutting and brass rubbing, tie-dye, batik and screen printing, candlemaking, basket-making and needlepoint tapestry—also semi-precious stones, tumble polishers, leather, felt, hessian, stuffing materials, buttons, buckles, trimmings, lampshade frames, notions, crochet and macramé yarns, soft toy accessories, raffia, cane, various modelling clays and seashells. There are plans to open another branch in the High Street.

PRESTON

The Arts and Crafts Shop
17 Station Road, Kirkham, Preston, Lancashire Kirkham 3128

Open: Monday to Saturday (excluding Wednesday) 09.30 to 18.00; Wednesday 09.30 to 12.30; close 17.30 Saturday

Sells artists' materials and will frame your pictures for you. Also offers the necessary for lino-cutting, marquetry and pokerwork and stocks fur fabric, felt, kapok and soft toy accessories; canvas and wools for tapestry; buttons and buckles; Barbola and Plastone; and lampshade frames and Raffene.

READING

Inspirations (see page 48)

Reading Fine Art Gallery Limited
81 London Street, Reading, Berkshire Reading 50413

Open: Monday to Saturday (excluding Wednesday) 09.00 to 17.30; Wednesday 09.00 to 13.00; mail order; catalogue

Tremendous stock of artists' materials, pictures, prints, stationery, art and craft books and so on—with an on-the-premises picture framing and picture restoring service. Also very extensive stocks of tools and materials for jewellery-making, enamelling, tie-dye, batik and silk-screen printing, lino-cutting, brass-rubbing, modelling, candlemaking and working with plastic resins. Not just kits (though kits are there, too) but loose materials and tools—truly anything you could want for those ten crafts. Also picture framing materials and tools if you want to do it yourself. Will mail any quantity and the catalogue is free.

REDBOURN

Atelier
51 High Street, Redbourn, Hertfordshire Redbourn 3275

Open: Monday to Saturday (excluding

Wednesday) 09.30 to 13.00 and 14.00 to 17.30; Wednesday closed

General art and craft materials and a picture framing service. For jewellers there are silver and gold plate findings and chains, beads, semi-precious stones (polished and rough), and tumble polishing machines. There are also kits for candlemaking, tie and dye, crystal casting and plastic casting; lino-cutting and brass rubbing materials and tools; felt, canvas, kapok, soft toy accessories, macramé yarns, marquetry tools and materials, seashells and modern modelling materials.

RICHMOND

Richmond Art and Craft
9 King Street, Richmond, Surrey
  01 748 3036

Open: Monday to Saturday 10.00 to 18.00

All Reeves craft kits, and Plasticraft and Enamelcraft kits; also chain, copper and gilt findings, copper blanks, jewellers' tools; leather offcuts and skins; lino-cutting and brass rubbing materials and tools; felt, canvas by the yard, hessian, kapok, tapestry wools, embroidery fabrics and silks and soft toy accessories (eyes, noses, voices, whiskers even); potters' tools, wheels and kilns to order; tie-dye materials, screen printing materials and accessories to order; marquetry kits; coloured acetate sheeting; craft knives; candlemaking materials in kit form and loose (beeswax to order); raffia, lampshade frames and parchment; modelling clays of various kinds. Prepared to consider ordering any material they don't at present stock, but the shop is small so they can't stock kilns, potters' wheels and so on.

ROCHDALE

The Art Shop
75 Drake Street, Rochdale, Lancashire
  Rochdale 46563

Open: Monday to Saturday (excluding Tuesday) 08.00 to 17.30; Tuesday 08.00 to 12.30

Artists' materials and some craft materials; tumble polishers, lino-cutting and brass rubbing materials and accessories; marquetry kits; and picture framing, candlemaking and cold enamelling materials. Also felt, soft toy accessories and modelling clays.

ST ANNES ON SEA

The Handmaiden
50 Wood Street, St Annes on Sea, Lancashire St Annes 29564

Open: Monday to Saturday (excluding Wednesday) 09.00 to 18.00; Wednesday 09.00 to 13.00; mail order

Stockists of all Reeves art and craft kits and materials, where you can buy the basic necessities for embroidery, beading, raffia work, straw plaiting, basketry, lampshade making, leather-work, marquetry, candlemaking, modelling, jewellery (copper blanks, kilns, enamels, base metal findings, semi-precious stones and tumble polishers); and soft toy making (including felts, fur fabrics, kapok, eyes, squeakers, growlers, etc.).

SALISBURY

The Compleat Artist (see page 125)

SHEFFIELD

H R Whitehead
21 Chapel Walk, Sheffield 1, Yorkshire
  Sheffield 24858

Open: Monday to Thursday 09.00 to 17.30; Friday and Saturday 09.00 to 18.00; mail order; catalogue

General craft materials, chiefly in kit form—candlemaking, marquetry, Plasticraft, Enamelcraft and tapestry kits are all there—as well as a few semi-precious and imitation stones; leather-working kits complete with tools; felt and toys' eyes and noses; fabric dyes for tie-dye and batik; plastic cane, when available; seashells; modelling clay and various light construction materials like Art-straws, flower-making kits and so on.

SHREWSBURY

W M Freeman
18 Wyle Cop, Shrewsbury, Shropshire
  Shrewsbury 3657

Open: Monday to Saturday (excluding Thursday) 09.00 to 13.00 and 14.00 to 17.45; Thursday closed

Wide range of artists' materials and also lino-cutting and brass rubbing materials and tools, felt, hessian, soft toy accessories, Frame-maker picture framing kits, Isopon clear casting resin kits, candlemaking and modelling materials, raffia, cane, basketry materials and lampshade frames.

Wildings
The Midland Educational Company Limited, 33 Castle Street, Shrewsbury, Shropshire SY1 2BL
  Shrewsbury 51274

Open: Monday to Saturday 09.00 to 17.30 Limited stock of craft materials. (see page 11)

SITTINGBOURNE

Homecrafts
23 East Street, Sittingbourne, Kent
Sittingbourne 3655

Open: Monday to Saturday (excluding
Wednesday) 09.00 to 17.30; Wednesday
09.00 to 13.00

Soft toy making specialists (offering man-
made fibre stuffing materials and plastic
eyes and noses) who also have plaster of
Paris, Artstraws, marquetry and picture
framing kits, raffia, cane, and the frames
and coverings for lampshade-making.

SOLIHULL

*The Midland Educational Company
Limited*
24/26 Station Road, Solihull, Warwickshire 021 705 2112

Open: Monday to Saturday 09.00 to
17.30. Limited stock of craft materials
(see page 11)

SOUTHAMPTON

Hampshire Hobbies and Handicrafts
46b Nichols Road, Six Dials, Southampton, Hampshire
Southampton 27985

Open: Monday to Saturday (excluding
Thursday) 10.00 to 17.30; Thursday
closed; mail order

Corn dolly kits, plastic resin casting kits,
macramé kits, enamelcraft, supercast and
candlemaking kits—also modelling materials, chain, findings in gilt, nickel,
stainless steel and silver, semi-precious
and imitation stones, tumble polishing
machines and materials and kilns for
cold and kiln enamelling; leather and
leather-working tools and accessories;
lino-cutting and brass rubbing materials;
felt, hessian and soft toy accessories and
fillings; macramé yarns and the threads
and bobbins for lace-workers; tie-dye,
batik and screen printing dyes, inks and
accessories; marquetry and pokerwork
kits; basket making materials and lampshade frames, raffias and trimmings; seashells and small weaving kits. Thinking
about producing a catalogue.

SOUTHSEA

Solent Lapidary (see page 50)

SKIPTON

Craven Art Centre Limited
21 Coach Street, Skipton, Yorkshire
Skipton 4015

Open: Monday to Saturday (excluding
Tuesday) 09.00 to 17.30; Tuesday closed

Full range of artists' materials—(and
they will frame pictures and clean and
restore engravings and oil paintings)—
and also Plasticraft and Enamelcraft
kits, basic candlemaking packs, macramé kits, screen printing and brass
rubbing materials, marquetry kits, modelling clays, seashells, raffia, cane
and basket and lampshade making supplies. They have wax for batik, many
kinds of art paper, felt and hessian,
acrylic fillings and eyes, noses and
squeakers for toy-making.

STRATFORD-UPON-AVON

*The Midland Educational Company
Limited*
10/11 High Street, Stratford-upon-Avon,
Warwickshire Stratford 2787

Open: Monday to Saturday 09.00 to
17.30 (Limited stock of craft materials)
(see page 11)

STROUD

The Christmas Tree
21 Gloucester Street, Stroud, Gloucestershire Stroud 5425

Open: Monday to Saturday (excluding
Thursday) 09.15 to 17.30; Thursday
09.15 to 13.00; mail order; catalogue
15p

Same stock as the parent shop in Cheltenham—see page 14.

STURMINSTER NEWTON

Clarkes Handicraft Supplies
Bridge Street, Sturminster Newton, Dorset Sturminster Newton 72732

Open: Monday to Friday 09.00 to 17.00;
Saturday 09.00 to 13.00

Artists' materials and craft materials,
the latter chiefly in kit form. Can offer
tools and materials for lino-cutting, tie-
dye, batik, screen printing, brass rubbing,
woodwork, marquetry, pokerwork, picture framing (120 moulding designs
always in stock), candlemaking, basket
and lampshade making. Also raffia, cane,
seashells, modelling clay, felt, hessian,
kapok, foam crumbs, soft toy accessories,
tapestry wools and canvases and macramé yarns. They have a good range of
instruction leaflets and books, and craft
tools which are useful on all kinds of
materials. No mail order, but will post
materials to regular customers.

SUDBURY

Art and Craft Shop
21 Friars Street, Sudbury, Suffolk
Sudbury 72030

Open: Monday to Saturday (excluding Wednesday) 09.00 to 17.30; Wednesday 09.00 to 13.00

Artists' materials and a good range of craft materials (with kits kept to a minimum). Beads, chain, base metal findings; leather and the tools for working it; lino-cutting and brass rubbing tools, materials and accessories; some leather and tools relevant to bookbinding; art and craft papers; felt, tapestry canvas, wools, hessian, stuffing materials and soft toy accessories, macramé yarns, dyes for batik, screen printing and tie and dye; balsa wood, veneers and marquetry supplies; candlemaking materials; raffia, cane, basketry and lampshade supplies; and a wide range of modern modelling compounds.

SUTTON

O W Annetts and Sons Limited
159 High Street, Sutton, Surrey
  01 642 0990

Open: Monday to Saturday 09.00 to 17.30

Primarily concerned with art materials, Letraset, pictures and a picture-framing service—but they also stock craft materials; Plasticraft and Enamelcraft kits, some findings and copper blanks, tumble-polishing machines, lino-cutting tools, modelling clays, brass rubbing materials and papers, fabric dyes, marquetry kits, candlemaking supplies, raffias, canes and basket bases.

SWANSEA

Arts and Crafts
3 Shoppers Walk, Oxford Street, Swansea, Glamorganshire, Wales
  Swansea 55438

Open: Monday to Saturday (excluding Thursday) 09.15 to 17.30; Thursday 09.15 to 13.00; mail order

Retail craft shop with a very wide range of craft kits (all the famous makes) and also base metal findings, tumble polishers, copper blanks for enamelling, cold enamelling materials; leather-working tools; lino-cutting and brass rubbing materials and tools; felt, tapestry canvas and wools, embroidery fabrics and threads, British Standard washable stuffing materials, buttons, buckles, trimmings, macramé yarns and soft toy accessories; prepared clays and glazes for pottery; rug-making canvases and wools; tie-dye, batik and screen printing materials, both in kit form and loose; marquetry kits; embedding plastics; candlemaking supplies (including true beeswax); raffia, cane and basketry

supplies and lampshade frames and trimmings; seashells and modelling clays. All the materials come from the cash-and-carry warehouse in Singleton Street, from which is offered a delivery service for the whole of South West Wales.

Dragon Crafts
12 Singleton Street, Swansea, Glamorganshire, Wales Swansea 55438

Open: Monday to Saturday (excluding Thursday) 09.15 to 17.30; Thursday 09.15 to 13.00; mail order

A cash-and-carry warehouse. You are welcome to buy from here, or from the retail outlet in Shoppers Walk. See previous entry for range of stock. As wholesalers, Dragon Crafts supply many Welsh craft shops as well as individual customers. Offer a delivery service for the whole of South West Wales and a mail order service for the whole of Britain.

THORNBURY

Arts and Crafts
8 The Plain, Thornbury, Near Bristol, Somerset Thornbury 2484

Open: Monday to Saturday (excluding Thursday) 09.30 to 13.00 and 14.15 to 17.15; Thursday 09.00 to 13.00; mail order.

Good selection of artists' materials and instruction books—also gilt, nickel and sterling silver findings and chain, silver wire, semi-precious and imitation stones, tumble polishing machines, copper blanks and cold enamelling materials; leather offcuts; lino-cutting, brass rubbing and marquetry supplies; felt, hessian, kapok and soft toy accessories; cane, raffia and basketry materials; Das, Artstraws, seashells, candlemaking and plastic embedding kits. Will make up jewellery and frame pictures on the premises.

TORQUAY

Forestreet Model Centre
68 Fore Street, St Marychurch, Torquay, South Devon Torquay 36980

Open: Monday to Saturday (excluding Wednesday) 09.30 to 13.00 and 14.15 to 17.30; Wednesday closed

Specialise in radio controlled model aeroplanes and boats, plus all accessories, but also sell marquetry kits, lampshade frames, fur fabrics, soft toy accessories like eyes and noses, Nu-stuffing, nylon and kapok, and also raffia and cane. (Has anybody ever made a radio controlled fur fabric aeroplane and called it a moth? And if not, why not?)

TRURO

The Hobby House (Cornwall) Limited
2 Little Castle Street, Truro, Cornwall
TR1 3DL Truro 6980

Open: Monday to Saturday (excluding Thursday) 09.00 to 17.30; Thursday 09.00 to 13.00; mail order; catalogue

Very good stock of handicraft materials (as well as things like playing cards, jig-saws and home-brewing kits). Felt, canvas, hessian, beads, sequins, suède pieces, kapok, foam chips; tapestry canvas and wools; crochet and macramé yarns; soft toy accessories; cane, basket bases, Raffene, seagrass; rug-making kits; candlemaking supplies (in kits as well as loose); lampshade frames, materials, fringes, etc.; a complete range of Plasticraft, Enamelcraft and Supercast kits—and plaster, resin and moulds for modelling. Also a lot of craft books. Very good place to look for a present. Send s.a.e. for stocklist.

TUNBRIDGE WELLS

G B Butler (see page 51)

TWICKENHAM

Bits and Bobs (see page 54)

WATFORD

Allcraft
11 Market Street, Watford, Hertford-shire Watford 38131

Open: Monday to Saturday 09.00 to 17.30; mail order (from Greenhill Crescent); catalogue

The retail showroom of Allcraft and Enamelaire whose kits and materials are available in craft shops all over the country. The mail order division is at Greenhill Crescent, Holywell Industrial Estate, Watford, Hertfordshire, WD1 8SE and you should write there for supplies or for the catalogue. They have kits and back-up materials for candle-making (including beeswax) and for crystal casting. A good stock of lapidary tools, machines and accessories, the Enamelaire kit complete with kiln, a useful range of general craft tools (including drills), several soft toy kits (and separate safety glass eyes), a good range of modelling materials and tools; all the necessary for tie-dye, batik and screen printing (tjantings, beeswax, cold water dyes, frames, squeegees, screen printing colours, and kits for all three crafts); lino-cutting tools and kits, brass rubbing and lampshade making materials, marquetry and cosmetic kits, lost wax casting kits and materials; and things like paper flower kits, armies of rubber moulds (chess sets, soldiers, Dickensian characters etc.) and Dip-it-kits. Also a good range of useful books.

WELLING

Crafts Unlimited
88 Bellegrove Road, Welling, Kent
Welling 3038800

Open: Monday to Saturday (excluding Wednesday) 09.00 to 17.30; Wednesday 09.00 to 13.00; mail order, catalogue 35p

Similar stock to the Kensington High Street branch, see page 24. If they do not have some material that Kensington High Street does have, it can be made available on request very quickly.

WELLINGBOROUGH

Happicraft
7 Cannon Street, Wellingborough, North-amptonshire Wellingborough 79542

Open: Monday to Saturday (excluding Thursday) 09.15 to 17.30; Thursday closed

Specialise in plastic embedding materials and novelties like felt pictures and mobiles. Will frame pictures to order or make party hats. Also offer craft kits —candle and corn dolly making, cold enamelling and crystal casting, Penelope collage and tapestry kits, brass rubbing and marquetry kits. And stainless steel and nickel findings, tumble polishing machines, felt, canvas, hessian, kapok, soft toy accessories, raffia, cane, basket and lampshade making materials, sea-shells and modelling clays. Hope to extend their range in future, so if there is something you think they should have, go in and mention it.

WELLINGTON

New Age Handicraft Centre
8 Mantle Street, Wellington, Somerset
Wellington 2254

Open: Tuesday to Saturday 09.15 to 13.00 and 14.00 to 17.30

Can offer a wide range of craft kits and plenty of reject yarns for macramé, crochet and knitting. Also cheap findings and imitation stones, beads, tumble polishing machines, seashells, copper blanks and enamelling kits; lampshade frames and suitable fabrics and trimmings; felt, canvas, hessian; noses and eyes for soft toys, kapok, foam and Nu-stuffing; raffia, cane and basketmaking supplies; candlemaking kits; veneers for marquetry; and rug kits.

WELWYN GARDEN CITY

Boon Gallery
45 Wigmores North, Welwyn Garden
City, Hertfordshire AL8 6PG
Welwyn Garden City 25875

Open: Monday to Saturday (excluding
Wednesday) 09.00 to 17.30; Wednesday
closed

The Gallery say their speciality is Letraset, but they also sell plenty of craft
kits and materials—copper findings and
shapes for enamelling, enamels, kilns,
cold enamelling kits, tumble polishers;
lino-cutting and brass rubbing materials
and tools; hessian, felt, canvas, lampshade frames and trimmings, accessories
and fillings for soft toy making, macramé yarns, tie-dye, batik and screen
printing materials; marquetry kits and
picture frame mouldings; Plasticraft
and Crystalcraft kits; candlemaking kits;
raffia, cane and modelling clays.

WEST DRAYTON

Colberre Limited
48 Station Road, West Drayton, Middlesex UB7 7DB   West Drayton 43373

Open: Monday to Saturday (excluding
Wednesday) 09.30 to 17.30; Wednesday
09.30 to 13.00; mail order; catalogue

A hobby and handicraft shop which is
trying to expand its range. At the time
of going to press they had a large range
of plastic kits and also tie and dye
materials, tapestry sets, candlemaking
kits, marquetry kits and modelling clays.
Also copper shapes for enamelling and
enamelling powders and kilns. If you
want the free catalogue, please send an
A4 s.a.e.

WEYMOUTH

The Art Shop (see page 92)

WIRRAL

Arts and Crafts
241 Greasby Road, Wirral, Cheshire
051 677 0350

Open: Monday to Saturday (excluding
Wednesday) 09.15 to 17.30; Wednesday
09.15 to 13.00

Art and craft materials and a picture
framing service. Most of the craft materials are in kit form and they will order
a kit if they don't have one you want.
Can supply, in this form, tools and
materials for lino-cutting, brass rubbing,
tie-dye and batik, marquetry, picture
framing, candlemaking and basket and
lampshade making. Also felt, hessian,
foam and kapok fillings, tapestry wools

and canvases, soft toy accessories, macramé yarns, Plasticraft kits, modelling
clay, cane and raffia, findings in non-
precious metals and imitation stones.

WOKING

Arts and Crafts Shop
Arthur's Bridge Wharf, Woking, Surrey
Woking 5371

Open: Monday to Thursday 09.00 to
17.00; Friday and Saturday 09.00 to
18.00

General craft materials, including beads,
chain, copper and gilt findings, copper
blanks, enamelling materials, semi-
precious stones, jewellers' tools, tumble
polishing machines; brass rubbing materials; plastic-embedding kits; marquetry
and picture framing supplies; felt, kapok
and plastic eyes and noses for toys;
macramé yarns; candlemaking materials;
raffia and cane and basketwork supplies;
lampshade frames only (no coverings);
seashells and modelling clays.

WOLVERHAMPTON

*The Midland Educational Company
Limited*
24/25 Wulfrun Way, Wolverhampton,
Staffordshire   Wolverhampton 8787

Open: Monday to Saturday 09.00 to
17.30 (see page 11)

WOOLER

Glendale Crafts (see page 80)

WORCESTER

Feamside and Company
56 The Tything, Worcester (see Malvern
branch for details, page 25)

*The Midland Educational Company
Limited*
A O Jones, 14/15 Broad Street, Wor-
cester, Worcestershire
Worcester 25115

Open: Monday to Saturday (excluding
Thursday) 09.00 to 17.30; Thursday
09.00 to 13.00 (see page 11)

YEOVIL

Draytons Decorations Limited
103a Middle Street, Yeovil, Somerset
Yeovil 3120

Open: Monday to Saturday (excluding
Thursday) 09.00 to 17.30; Thursday
09.00 to 13.00

Quite a wide range of general craft materials—Plasticraft kits (with all kinds of accessories), candlemaking, marquetry, tapestry, needlework and Enamelcraft kits; chain, findings, copper blanks, semi-precious stones, tumble polishers; leather thonging; PVC for upholstery; felt, canvas, hessian, foam, kapok, buckles, trimmings, fur fabric, soft toy accessories, macramé yarns; brass rubbing and lino-cutting materials and tools; pokerwork and picture framing mouldings and tools; raffia, cane, lampshade frames and modelling tools.

YORK

Derwent Crafts
6 The Shambles, York, Yorkshire
   0904 27701
and 50 Stonegate, York, Yorkshire

Open: Monday to Saturday (excluding Wednesday) 10.00 to 17.00; Wednesday closed

Two shops under the same management and carrying much the same stock. They are general craft shops but with the emphasis quite firmly on jewellery-making—jewellers' tools and tumble polishing machines, stones, precious metals, copperfoil, beads, chain and findings. They also have macramé, marquetry and embedding resin kits. They have leather, and the tools for working it, a good range of hessian and felt in various colours, a few weaving looms, tie-dye and batiking materials, kilns for pottery and enamelling, potters' clays and glazes (though no wheels), candlemaking supplies, raffias and canes. Will advise on jewellery-making.

2 Jewellery

Possibly the most popular craft in Britain today, and surely the best catered for with precious stones and metals and specialised tools readily available in any quantity—so long as you can afford them.

Some people prefer to collect their own stones—not necessarily even semi-precious ones, just attractive ones—and tumble polishing machines are now on sale in most craft shops and many toy shops. (If you particularly want to collect semi-precious stones, Lythe Minerals of Leicester have a useful map.) Or stones can be bought in their rough state or ready cut and polished—and there are plenty of places to buy findings and fittings in precious or base metals, and silver in sheet or wire form, and copper in all forms (and indeed copper can often be bought from electricians, plumbers and hardware stores).

Most shops listed sell a full range of materials. The following are worth a special look—for silver, Johnson Matthey of Birmingham, London and Sheffield—for gold and silver, Blundell's of London—for tools, Rockcraft of Chichester, Barretts of Croydon, Pond and Sutton of Birmingham and Hirsh Jacobson, Gould, Charles Cooper and E Gray of London—for diamond abrasives, Kristalap of Hitchin—for jade, Jacinth Gems of Southampton—for opal, H and T Gems of Hartlepool and John Harrison of Kings Langley—for amber, Holt of London—for mother-of-pearl and abalone shell, Ruskins of Bristol—for ebony and ivory offcuts, Tumble Kraft of Gravesend—for precious metal findings, Caverswall Minerals—for a very wide range of stones, Baines Orr of Redhill, Scotrocks Craftshops in Edinburgh, Glasgow and Paisley, Peacocks of Bristol and Gemset of Broadstairs—and for the almost lost craft of lost wax casting, Allcraft of Watford, Barretts of Croydon and Tumble Kraft of Gravesend and The Rock Shop in Cowbridge.

ABERDEEN

The Craft Centre (see page 9)

ALDEBURGH

The Beachcomber
160 High Street, Aldeburgh, Suffolk
  Aldeburgh 3298

Open: Monday to Saturday (excluding Wednesday) 09.00 to 13.00 and 14.15 to 17.30; Wednesday 09.00 to 13.00; mail order; catalogue

A comber of the world's beaches. Rough rock mineral, shells and polished stones from all over the world; silver and gold findings and chains; tumble polishing machines, grits and polishing agents; stone cutting and drilling tools. Also Plasticraft and Enamelcraft kits. Ask for Peter Mill if you want advice or information.

ALTRINCHAM

The Handicraft Shop (see page 9)
Stones only

Lapidary Abrasives
14 Market Street, Altrincham, Cheshire
  Altrincham 4220

Mail order only; catalogue 10p

Manufacturers and mail order suppliers of specialised labidary products—abrasives, lapping wheels and grindstones, diamond saws, grinding and polishing machines; kilns for lost wax casting, enamelling and the firing of small pots; a wide range of grits and polishes; gold and silver findings; precious stones; and silver in sheet, wire and tube form. Supply to schools and to amateur and professional jewellers all over the country. Happy to give written assistance and advice on receipt of a stamped addressed envelope.

ANDOVER

Arts and Crafts Centre (see page 10)

AYLESBURY

Natural Gems Limited
Kingsbury Square, Aylesbury, Buckinghamshire Aylesbury 83604

Open: Monday to Friday 09.00 to 17.00; Saturday 09.30 to 16.00; mail order; catalogue 10p

All lapidary supplies and equipment with the emphasis on jewellery fittings and polished stones. They have findings and fittings in all metals, jewellers' tools, tumble polishing machines and a great range of precious, semi-precious and imitation stones. Also lapidary kits. Good people to ask for advice.

AYR

Contour Artists' Materials (see page 10)

BALLOCH

Agate and Pebblecraft
'Swingle Tree', Balloch, Inverness, Scotland Culloden Moor 674

Open: May and June—Monday to Saturday 10.00 to 18.30; July to September—seven days a week 10.00 to 18.30; November to April—Monday, Wednesday and Saturday 10.00 to 17.00; mail order

Agate and Pebblecraft is, as the leaflet (no catalogue) says, 'a highland cottage craft industry'. They offer a selection of ready-made agate and pebble jewellery (and will point out which are the genuine Scottish stones). But they also have rock, mineral and crystal specimens, tumble polishers, slab and trim saws, chain and findings in silver and plated metals and books on minerals and gemstones. Off the A96 Inverness to Nairn road, in the direction of Culloden battlefield.

BARNSLEY

Mineralcraft (North)
192 Barnsley Road, Cudworth, Barnsley, Yorkshire S72 8UJ Barnsley 710468

Open: by appointment; mail order; catalogue

Mr Hirst sells lapidary supplies from home, and you can call in the evenings or at weekends to see the stock—but please telephone for an appointment first. He can supply plated, stainless steel and silver chain and findings, semi-precious and imitation stones and tumble polishing machines—also advice and information.

BATH

Bath Handicraft Supplies (see page 10)

BECKENHAM

H S Walsh and Sons Limited
243 Beckenham Road, Beckenham, Kent Beckenham 7061

Open: Monday to Friday 09.00 to 17.00; A branch of Gray of Clerkenwell—(see page 37)

BEESTON

The Handicraft Shop (see page 11)

BELFAST

Ato-Crafts (see page 11)

BIRMINGHAM

Johnson Matthey Metals Limited
Vittoria Street, Birmingham, Warwickshire B1 3NZ 021 236 9811

Open: Monday to Friday 09.00 to 16.15 (see London branch for details— page 44)

Bernard C Lowe and Company Limited
73/75 Spencer Street, Birmingham, Warwickshire B18 6DG 021 236 7760

Open: Monday to Friday 09.00 to 17.00; Saturday 09.00 to 13.00; mail order

Wholesalers of jewellery and of precious and semi-precious stones who will nevertheless entertain groups, or even individuals, who are interested in jewellery-making, and will supply single items. Good stock, including faceted and cabochon stones, pearls, cameos, agate slabs, free form stones and also gold and silver chains. Will undertake all kinds of jewellery repairs—pearl re-threading, replacing of lost stones, making rings small enough to fit, and so on.

W Pond (see page 130)

Suttons
37 Frederick Street, Birmingham, Warwickshire B1 3HN 021 236 7139

Open: Monday to Friday 09.00 to 17.00; mail order; catalogue

Specialist supplier of every kind of jewellers' and silversmiths' tool—and also tumble polishing machines. A retail shop which will also fulfil any order by mail.

Type and Palette (see page 11)

BISHOP AUCKLAND

Auckland Studio (see page 11)

BISHOPS STORTFORD

Galaxy (see page 12)

BOURNEMOUTH

Moordown Leather and Craft (see page 114)

BRIGHTON

M L Beach (Brighton) Limited
7 Kings Parade, Ditchling Road, Brighton, Sussex   Brighton 500813

Open: Tuesday to Saturday 10.00 to 17.30; mail order; catalogue

Another branch of the Twickenham shop with the same stock of stone polishing machines and accessories, stones, precious metal findings and fittings and chains, relevant books and useful advice at the ready. One rather dramatic addition—a metal detector. These machines offer lots of exciting possibilities but are rather frowned on by professional archaeologists on the grounds that they encourage amateurs to despoil possibly important sites. So be careful.

Geobright and The Glass Animal Man
28 Queens Road, Brighton, Sussex   Brighton 28965

Open: Monday to Saturday 09.00 to 17.00

Geobright and The Glass Animal Man are mostly concerned with rocks, minerals and enamelling materials—and there is available a 24″ diamond saw if you have any large rocks you want to dismember. They also supply chain, copper blanks, precious and semi-precious stones, enamelling kilns, candlemakers' supplies, modelling clay and seashells. No mail order, but rock shops should in any case be visited—every piece of rock is wholly unique and naming it tells you only a little about it.

Handicrafts (see page 12)

Southern Handicrafts (see page 12)

BRISTOL

Craftwise
7 Christmas Steps, Bristol 1   Bristol 291411

Open: Monday to Saturday 09.30 to 18.00; mail order

A wide range of craft materials here, some in kit form, and a particularly good lapidary section where you will find beads, chain, findings in base and precious metals, rough and polished semi-precious stones, jewellers' tools, tumble polishing machines, silver wire and silver sheet, copper blanks and all the necessary materials for cold and kiln enamelling, including the kilns. The kits cater for corn dolly making, beadloom work, batik, candlemaking, marquetry, moulding and plastic embedding. There are also leather-working tools, felt, foam and kapok, macramé and crochet yarns, tie-dyes, woods and veneers, basketry kits, seashells, modelling materials and broken coloured glass for mosaic work. If you buy by mail, the minimum order is £3.00.

Hobbies and Crafts (see page 12)

Peacocks
7 Brookside Road, Brislington, Bristol BS4 4JS

Mail order only; catalogue

Mail order suppliers (minimum £1.00) of precious and semi-precious stones, crystals and minerals. Order form has no pictures, but the range is good and service (they promise) prompt. Willingly give advice (by post) if it is asked.

Ruskin's
515 Main Wells Road, Bristol, Somerset BS14 9AL   Bristol 76456

Open: Monday to Saturday 10.00 to 18.00; mail order; catalogue

Lapidary specialists who claim they are the main UK agents for polished mother-of-pearl and abalone shell shapes for jewellery and craftwork. They are also the largest lapidary dealers in Bristol who can sell you chain and findings in most metals; precious metals for working; precious, semi-precious and imitation stones and rough rock; tumble polishing machines and accessories and a good range of jewellers' tools. Well worth a visit if you can manage it.

BROADSTAIRS

Gemset of Broadstairs Limited
31 Albion Street, Broadstairs, Kent CT10 1LU   Thanet 65360

Open: Monday to Saturday (excluding Wednesday) 09.00 to 17.30; Wednesday 09.00 to 13.00; mail order; catalogue 10p

Lapidary specialists who can sell you everything you need from the beginning to the end of the grinding and polishing process. You can also make an appointment to be instructed in the cutting, faceting and setting of stones. They have rough gem rock, chain and findings in base and precious metals and traditional designs, precious and semi-precious stones, jewellers' tools, tumble polishing and stone cutting and faceting machines and equipment. Also a large range of related books and Plasticraft and Enamelcraft kits and spares. (No order ever refused—however small.)

BURNLEY

Northern Handicrafts Limited (see page 13)

CAERNARVON

Black Kettle Crafts (see page 13)

CAMBRIDGE

Timgems
164/167 East Road, Cambridge, Cambridgeshire

Open: Tuesday to Saturday 09.00 to 17.30

Similar stock of lapidary supplies and cabochons as that in the Ludham shop (see separate entry on page 46) but no mail order. Personal callers only.

CANTERBURY

Needlecraft and Hobbies (see page 13)

CARDIFF

Little Rocks
36 Oakwood Avenue, Cardiff, Glamorganshire, Wales Cardiff 36341

Open: by arrangement; mail order; catalogue 5p

Mail order suppliers of all the necessary for lapidary work—send 5p postage for the catalogue. They have tools, tumble polishing machines, grits, polishes and accessories, chain and findings in nickel plate, silver plate, stainless steel, gilt, silver and rolled gold and semi-precious stones. If you particularly need some material that is not offered in the catalogue they will try to acquire it for you.

South Wales Arts and Crafts Suppliers (see page 55)

CARK-IN-CARTMEL

Banbury Craft Supplies Limited
Shrine Yards, Halker Hall, Cark-in-Cartmel, Lancashire Flookburgh 450

Open: Monday to Friday 10.00 to 18.30; mail order

Wholesalers, not retailers, but you can telephone for an appointment during their working hours. They are specialists in jewellery findings for craftsmen and have a very wide range—also chain, pewter and copperfoil, semi-precious stones, copper blanks for enamelling and enamelling materials and kilns.

CARLISLE

Merricrafts (see page 141) Beads, imitation stones and findings only

CAVERSWALL

Caverswall Minerals
The Dams, Caverswall, Near Stoke on Trent, Staffordshire
Blythe Bridge 3838

Open: Monday to Friday 09.00 to 13.00 and 14.00 to 17.00; mail order; catalogue 5½p (postage)

Paul and June Bunn operate from home, so please telephone first if you want to call and view their lapidary materials. They say they have the largest range of precious metal findings available anywhere, and can also sell you findings in gilt, nickel plate and stainless steel, tumble polishing machines and precious and semi-precious stones (including rough rock for tumbling).

CHANDLERS FORD

Creative Crafts (see page 14)

CHELTENHAM

The Christmas Tree (see page 14)
Findings and beads only

The Colourman (see page 14)

Cotswold Craft Centre (see page 72)
Beads only

CHESHAM

The Tiger's Eye
7 High Street, Chesham, Buckinghamshire Chesham 3108

Open: Tuesday to Saturday (excluding Thursday) 09.30 to 17.30; Thursday 09.30 to 13.00; mail order

As you might infer from the name—lapidary supplies, semi-precious stones and minerals (also hand made silver jewellery). They have chain and findings in base metals and silver and can occasionally order precious stones. Also quite a wide range of craft kits—candlemaking, collage, plastic embedding, cold and kiln enamelling, lino-cutting, marquetry, batik, tie and dye, soft toy making and stone polishing. And for modelling—Newclay, plasticine and plaster of Paris.

CHESTER

Gemcraft
9 Main Road, Broughton, Chester, Cheshire CH4 0NW Chester 533146

Mail order only; catalogue

Offer rough and polished gemstones, slabbed gemstones, custom cut cabochons—and house names hand cut in Welsh slate. Mail order only—(minimum order 50p, which isn't asking a lot).

CHICHESTER

Rockcraft
6a Northgate, Chichester, Sussex PO19 1BA   Chichester 82766

Open: Tuesday to Friday 09.15 to 16.30; Saturday 09.00 to 17.30; mail order; catalogue

Lapidary and silversmith suppliers who also make and repair gold and silver jewellery. They have lapidary tools and machines and silversmithing tools and sundries. Also silver sheet, rod, wire and tube, rough rock, mineral specimens, cut stones (semi-precious and imitation), findings in silver, stainless steel and base metals, enamelling kilns and powders and copper blanks, cold enamelling kits and also Plasticraft kits. And presentation boxes and relevant recommended books. Terms are cash with order.

COLBY

Manninart
Dildawn, Glen Road, Colby, Isle of Man Port Erin 3481

Open: Monday to Saturday 09.00 to 17.00; mail order

Manninart is run by June Niven from her home, so telephone to make an appointment first. She makes jewellery to order from customers' own stones if they are suitable and also sells chain, plated and solid silver findings, semi-precious stones, tumble polishing machines, saws and lapidary supplies, copper blanks and enamelling materials, candlemaking and tie-dye materials, modelling plaster, plastic resins and kits for enamelling, plastic embedding, crystal growing and stone hand polishing.

COWBRIDGE

The Rock Shop
Llandow Industrial Estate, Cowbridge, Glamorganshire, Wales Cowbridge 2029

Open: Monday to Friday 09.00 to 17.00; Saturday and Sunday 14.30 to 18.00; mail order; catalogue 15p

The Rock Shop is run by Ammonite Limited, and they do indeed have ammonites and other fossils for sale (as well as plastic replicas for teaching), books on geology, and books on all aspects of stone collecting and stone jewellery making. They sell rough

material for cutting and tumble polishing (quite as beautiful in the rough as it is when it has been smoothed); also supplies and equipment for lost wax casting; tools for silversmiths and jewellers; tumble polishing machines and cutting, grinding and boring tools; adhesives; little jewel boxes; findings in real gold and silver or in gold or silver finish or stainless steel; tumble polished or cut stones—precious, semi-precious and imitation. They offer a professional casting and design service in precious metals and their catalogue contains instructions and information on all aspects of jewellery making and stone identification.

CREETOWN

Creetown Gem Rock Museum
Old School, Creetown, By Newton Stewart, Wigtownshire, Scotland Creetown 357

Open: Monday to Saturday 09.30 to 18.00; Sunday 14.00 to 18.00; mail order; catalogue

In the museum the exhibits are arranged to show the various lapidary processes, together with rock samples and corresponding cut gems, local and exotic stones. In the 'walk around workshop' you can watch slabbing, tumble polishing, cabochon cutting and stones being set in base and precious metals. And in the shop you can buy natural gemstone jewellery in base and precious metals, rough rock and all the necessary equipment for amateur lapidary enthusiasts; chain, findings, precious and semi-precious stones, tumble polishing machines, hand-polishing kits and jewellery kits (of findings and stones). They will undertake the slabbing of customers' own rock in the workshop and they offer residential weekend courses in stone cutting—details from address above. Very much geared to making visitors feel welcome. (They offer parking facilities, a café, and the vital information that Creetown is on the A75 Dumfries to Stranraer Road.)

CROYDON

Barretts
1 Mayo Road, Croydon, Surrey CR0 2QP 01 684 9917

Open: Monday to Saturday 09.30 to 17.30; mail order

Suppliers of new and used scientific equipment and, in particular, jewellers' tools. You can call in at the showroom in Mayo Road (off Pawsons Road), which is attached to the factory and warehouse.

Because of demand from craftsmen Barretts are, at the time of going to press, opening a craft shop in Lower Addiscombe Road where they hope to stock a wide range of jewellery making equipment (especially for the making of jewellery by the lost wax casting process) and also candlemaking supplies and general craft kits. Their intention is to supply demand and be as helpful as possible to local craftsmen, so they are worth a visit if you are in the area.

Barretts
290 Lower Addiscombe Road, Addiscombe, Croydon, Surrey   01 654 5395

Open: Monday to Saturday (excluding Wednesday) 09.30 to 17.30; Wednesday 09.30 to 13.00 (see above)

CULLOMPTON

Crafts 'n Creations (see page 73)

DEWSBURY

Marc Time (see page 16)

DUBLIN

Gemcraft of Ireland
Grafton Court, 44 Grafton Street, Dublin 2, Ireland   Dublin 782844

Open: Monday to Saturday 10.00 to 18.00; mail order; catalogue

Lapidary suppliers who have tumble polishers, rough rock, base metal findings and diamond saws and drills always in stock. And they also have cold enamelling kits, copper blanks, kilns and the materials for kiln enamelling; tie-dye, batik and screen printing tools and materials; candlemaking kits; macramé kits; modelling clays and seashells. Would probably think about stocking other craft materials if they were persuaded.

EASTBOURNE

Gemstones Limited
70 Seaside Road, Eastbourne, Sussex BN21 3PE

Open: Monday to Saturday 09.00 to 17.30; mail order; catalogue

Same stock of lapidary supplies as the main shop up in Hull—see separate entry on page 43.

The Sussex Handicraft Shop (see page 16)

EAST KESWICK

Westby Products (see page 16)

ECKINGTON

Avon Gems
Strathavon, Boon Street, Eckington, Near Pershore, Worcestershire WR10 3BL Eckington 495

Open: Monday to Sunday (excluding Friday) 09.00 to 18.00; Friday closed; mail order; catalogue 6p

All lapidary supplies—diamond saws, grinding, polishing and lapping machines (several makes of tumble polisher), faceting heads; an extremely wide range of stones, both rough and cut, chain (made up or by the yard), findings in base metals and silver, books on lapidary, gemology, mineralogy, and geology and a subscription service to American periodicals. Will also undertake custom slabbing. The proprietor used to teach lapidary work in school, has written a book on the craft, and has now retired from teaching to run the shop and, what is more, to live on the premises—so help and advice is always on hand.

EDINBURGH

Scotrocks Craftshops
122 Rose Street, South Lane, Edinburgh Head Office: Helensburgh 3855

Open: Monday to Saturday 10.00 to 17.30; mail order; catalogue 5p

Lapidary specialists where you can buy jewellery fittings in all metals, including precious ones; presentation boxes; precious, semi-precious and imitation stones; jewellers' tools, diamond saws and blades; tumble polishing machines and a complete tumble polishing set; Plasticraft and Enamelcraft kits. Very wide range which includes semi-relevant oddities like metal detectors. There are three shops at the moment (though more are planned). The other two are in Glasgow and Paisley. If you want a catalogue, send 5p and a large stamped addressed envelope.

ENFIELD

Pebblegems
71 St Mark's Road, Bush Hill Park, Enfield, Middlesex   01 366 7636

Open: Monday to Saturday 09.00 to 17.30; mail order; catalogue

Lapidary specialists who sell semiprecious stones; chain and findings in nickel, gilt and silver; tumble polishing machines and grits and rough rock. Their tumbling kits—including machine, grits, polishes and rock—cost from £9.00 to £12.00.

EPSOM

O W Annetts and Sons (see page 16)

Lindsay's Handicrafts and Decor (see page 141) Sheet copper and pewter

FRINTON-ON-SEA

Frinton Handicrafts and Art Centre (see page 17)

FROME

Marcross Gems and B Mandeville (see page 131)

GLASGOW

Miller's (see page 17)

Scotrocks Craftshops
48 Park Road, Glasgow C4

Same hours and stock as the Edinburgh shop (see page 41)

GLENROTHES

Fife Stone Craft
3 Edison House, Fullerton Road, Queensway Industrial Estate, Glenrothes, Fifeshire, Scotland Glenrothes 3013

Open: Monday to Friday 10.00 to 18.00; Saturday and Sunday 11.00 to 17.00; mail order

Rough gemstones, polished tumbled stones, cut stones, lapidary equipment and tools, chain and findings in base metals and silver. Large stock but no catalogue. Minimum order by mail is £5.00, but there is no minimum if you call in.

GLOSSOP

Homecrafts (see page 18)

GODSHILL

The Island Craft Shop (see page 18)

GORSEINON

Y Gegin Fawr (see page 74)

GRAVESEND

Tumble Kraft
43 The Terrace, Gravesend, Kent Gravesend 51553

Open: Monday, Tuesday and Thursday 10.30 to 18.00; Wednesday closed; Friday 10.30 to 21.00; Saturday 09.30 to 18.00; mail order; catalogue 3p

Fairly new shop specialising in lapidary supplies and unusual craft materials—ebony and ivory offcuts, nickel and silver wire, coloured glass chunks and slabs and antique glass pieces, and lost wax casting accessories. Also chain and findings in base metals, sterling silver, stainless steel and rolled gold, semi-precious stones (rough and polished), jewellers'

tools and tumble polishers; some leatherworking tools; felt squares and soft toy accessories; epoxy and polyester resins, acetate sheet and perspex offcuts; enamelling materials, kilns and copper blanks; modelling clays; materials for building your own potter's wheel; and kits for candlemaking, tie and dye, soft toys, cold and kiln enamelling, Dip-it, lost wax casting and tumble polishing. Keen to build up their stock and supply rare materials as well as those more generally available. Catalogue in preparation at the time of going to press.

GUISBOROUGH

Beecrafts (see page 18)

HARROGATE

Arts and Handicrafts (see page 18)

HARTLEPOOL

H and T Gems and Minerals
31 Rosebury Road, Hartlepool, County Durham

Mail order only; catalogue 3½p (postage)

Mail order supplier of all grades of rough opal—also general lapidary supplies; polishes, grits, tumble polishers and fittings.

HASTINGS

The Stone Corner
42 High Street, Hastings, Sussex Hastings 31318

Open: Tuesday to Saturday 09.00 to 17.30; mail order; catalogue 6p

Has just moved along the High Street from number 21 to number 42. Specialises in mineral specimens and lapidary supplies. Good range of semi-precious stones, both rough and polished and also tumble polishing machines and accessories and chain and findings in silver and gold plate.

HATCH END

John Maxfield (see page 19)

HEMEL HEMPSTEAD

Arts and Crafts (see page 19)

International Craft
PO Box 73, Hemel Hempstead, Hertfordshire

Mail order only; catalogue

Mail order suppliers of lapidary equipment, tumbled gemstones, findings in gilt, rhodium plate, rolled gold or sterling silver and ready-made Chanton jewellery. Also tumble polishing machines.

HITCHIN

Kristalap Limited
Marcon House, 131 High Street, Codicote, Hitchin, Hertfordshire
    Codicote 581

Open: Monday to Friday 09.00 to 17.00; mail order; catalogue

Manufacturers and suppliers of industrial diamond products—which means they have diamond abrasives of various kinds for lapidary work. Generally deal by mail order via their catalogue—but you can visit if you make an appointment first. They have diamond powders and burrs, diamond coated files, diamond carving tools, accessories and related bits and pieces.

HOVE

Handicrafts (see page 19)

HUDDERSFIELD

Arts and Crafts (see page 19)

HULL

Gemstones Limited
44 Walmsley Street, Hull, East Yorkshire
    HU3 1QD   Hull 25722

Open: Monday to Saturday 09.00 to 17.30; mail order; catalogue

Lapidary supplier who stocks jewellery kits, clear cast embedding kits, do-it-yourself lapidary machine parts, semi-precious stones (rough and polished), findings in plated base metals and also silver and gold, jewellers' tools and ready-made tumble polishing machines. Also bits of abalone shell for embedding and jewellery making.

Handycrafts of Hull (see page 20)

HYTHE

Needlecraft and Hobbies (see page 20)

ILMINSTER

Opie Gems
57 East Street, Ilminster, Somerset
    Ilminster 2346

Open: Tuesday to Saturday (excluding Friday) 09.30 to 17.30; Friday 09.30 to 19.00; mail order; catalogue in exchange for s.a.e.

Specialise in the supply of minerals and materials for lapidary work, although they do stock other craft materials as well, and plan to extend their range. They will undertake custom cutting and polishing and can supply beads, findings and chain in base metals, stainless steel, silver and gold, copper blanks, precious and semi-precious stones and tumble polishers. Also enamelling materials and kilns, candlemaking supplies and kits for hand polishing, Plasticraft, Enamelcraft, bead loom work, Dip-it and jewellery casting.

JARROW

Bede-Brown (Metalcraft)
1 Hereford Way, Jarrow, County Durham
    Jarrow 891729

Mail order only; catalogue

Wholesale lapidary specialists who will supply individuals, but by mail order only. Very full range of stainless steel findings and fittings—also pairs of matched gemstones (for cufflinks, etc.), agate slabs, handcut amber, crystal kits, rough gemstones and tumble polishers, polished gemstones, antique gold or silver finish jewellery fittings, adhesives and a fairly comprehensive range of relevant books.

KEGWORTH

Kits 'n' Krafts (see page 75)

KENDAL

Kendal Handicrafts (see page 20)   Beads and findings only

KIDDERMINSTER

Arts and Crafts (see page 20)

KING'S LANGLEY

John Harrison
Lindisfarne House, Rucklers Lane, King's Langley, Hertfordshire
    Hemel Hempstead 54439

Open: By appointment; mail order; catalogue in exchange for s.a.e.

Manufacturers and suppliers to the trade of base metal and stainless steel jewellery findings, copper blanks, sheet silver, precious and semi-precious polished stones. (Especially good on opals and matched semi-precious stones for earrings, cufflinks, etc., but will also retail to the general public. You can call by appointment or buy by mail order against the catalogue (free if you send a stamped addressed envelope).

LANCASTER

Leisure Crafts (see page 21)

LANCING

S J Pearce (see page 158)

LEAMINGTON SPA

A S Blackie (see page 21) Imitation stones

LEATHERHEAD

Handicrafts (see page 21)

LEICESTER

Lythe Minerals
36-38 Oxford Street, Leicester, Leicester-shire LE1 5XW   Leicester 50260

Open: Thursday 10.00 to 15.30; Friday 10.00 to 18.00 and Saturday 10.00 to 16.00; mail order; catalogue

Specialise in minerals and rocks for educational and display purposes—also books on all aspects of geology, and geological survey maps (including a map called Gemstone Sites of the British Isles, scale unknown; they point out that it is not for the serious student, but for the amateur gem collector it might come in quite handy). They also have diamond saw blades, polishing powders, dopping wax, cabochons, precious stones, rough rock, packaged specimens, and jewellery findings in gilt, silver plate or nickel. You must spend £1.50 if you want to order by mail (as most people do), but there is no minimum order if you call in. Duplicated catalogue is free—and the list of relevant books is especially useful.

LONDON E12

Leisurecrafts Limited
570 Romford Road, Manor Park, London E12   01 478 6042

Mail order only; catalogue

Mail order suppliers of 'make it your-self costume jewellery' in traditional styles, using marcasite and imitation stones. Illustrated catalogue is free.

EC1

J Brooks (Lapidaries) Simulated Diamond Stones
45 Hatton Gardens, London EC1N 8EX   01 242 8026

Open: Monday to Saturday 08.30 to 16.30; mail order; catalogue

Specialises, as the name implies, in imitation diamonds. Also stocks gold mounts for jewellery. Will undertake gem cutting for customers.

EC1

Charles Cooper Limited
Wall House, 12 Hatton Wall, Hatton Garden, London EC1N 8JQ   01 405 6083

Open: Monday to Friday 09.00 to 17.00; mail order; catalogue

This is a wholesale, rather than a retail, establishment, but it's all right just to call in. They are suppliers of jewellers', silversmiths' and engravers' tools and materials—and in fact are one of the best known sources of jewellers' tools in the country. Also silver, chain, findings and other useful bits and pieces.

EC1

Crafts Unlimited (see page 22)

EC1

E Gray and Son Limited
12/16 Clerkenwell Road, London EC1   01 253 1174

Open: Monday to Friday 09.00 to 17.00; mail order; catalogue

Wholesale jewellers who also stock tools and equipment for the jewellery, silver-smithing and horological trades. Callers are welcome—or you can order from the catalogue (they specify a very low minimum of £1.50, and that only applies to mail order). As well as all possible kinds of tool they have chain and findings in 9 ct silver and rolled gold.

EC1

Johnson Matthey Metals Limited
81 Hatton Garden, London EC1P 1AE   01 405 6989

Open: Monday to Friday 09.30 to 16.15; mail order; catalogue

Suppliers of silver in sheet, wire and tube form and also of solders and sundries. Minimum order £5.00. Are well aware that it is hard for craftsmen to obtain small quantities of silver and are nego-tiating to make it available through other retail outlets. No details yet.

EC1

Minerals, Stones Limited
92 Hatton Garden, London EC1   01 405 0197 and 5286

Open: Monday to Friday 09.30 to 17.30; mail order; catalogue

Specialists in precious and semi-precious gemstones, minerals, tumble polishing machines and grits, and findings in gold and silver. They will cut and prepare rough stones to customers' own specifications and, as well as opals, amethysts, garnets, turquoise, coral, lapis lazuli, moonstones, etc., they have petrified wood, geodes and fossils. If you order by post you must spend at least £2.00.

EC1
D Pennellier
28 Hatton Garden, London EC1N 8DB
  01 405 4064 and 01 242 4681

Open: Monday to Saturday 09.00 to 17.00; mail order; catalogue

Suppliers of precious metal alloys who will make castings in precious metals for jewellery workers. They have findings, beads and chains in 9 ct, 14 ct, 18 ct and 22 ct silver and they also offer fine gold, fine silver, sterling silver and jewellers' tools. Will fulfil any order by mail.

EC1
J Smith and Sons (Clerkenwell) Limited
St John's Square, Clerkenwell, London
  EC1P 1ER   01 253 1277

Open: Monday to Friday 08.30 to 13.00 and 14.00 to 17.15; mail order; catalogue

Non-ferrous metal stockists who will supply small quantities of anything listed in their catalogue 'provided customers know what they want'. They have metal working tools, copper sheet and wire in various types, brass, aluminium, nickel silver etc. Catalogue/handbook is quite technical. Friendly towards informed amateurs, but don't have time to teach the ignorant.

EC1
A E Ward and Son Limited
9/10 Albemarle Way, Clerkenwell,
  London EC1V 4JB   01 253 4036

Open: Monday to Friday 09.00 to 13.00 and 14.00 to 17.45; mail order

Trade suppliers whose business is chiefly with jewellery manufacturers or retailers, but students and amateur jewellers are welcome to call in during working hours (go up to the second floor). They deal in all classes of precious and semi-precious stones and pearls, and will cut stones to special designs and repolish or recut customers' own stones. Will send by mail but have no catalogue.

N8
Bouette Manufacturing Company Limited
645 Green Lanes, London N8
  01 348 0611

Open: Monday to Friday 09.30 to 12.30 and 14.00 to 16.30; mail order; catalogue 5p

Manufacturers and wholesalers of metal fittings and components for the artificial jewellery trade. The address above is the office and stockroom where customers are welcome to call, but most people order from the catalogue (minimum order £1.00). They have semi-precious and imitation stones and also findings in base metals and silver—generally old-fashioned settings including antique silver-finish pendant and brooch settings, charm bracelets and settings for marcasite animal brooches. Everything supplied complete—brooch with pin, necklet with chain and fastener, stones with adhesive.

NW3
Crafts Unlimited (see page 23)

NW7
John Maxfield (see page 23)

SW3
Gregory Bottley and Company
30 Old Church Street, Chelsea, London
  SW3 5BY   01 352 5841

Open: Monday to Friday 09.30 to 17.15; Saturday 09.30 to 12.30; mail order; catalogue 20p

These people are mineralogists and geologists (established 1850!) who arrange lectures and classes and exhibitions. In their Chelsea showrooms—a wonderland for those who are excited by stone—you can see, and buy, precious ores, stones, geological hammers and lapidary machines. Perhaps rather more useful to the rock-hunter than to the jeweller, but a nice place to know about.

SW10
Hobby Horse (see page 23) Especially beads and findings

SW19
Gemlines
10 Victoria Crescent, London SW19
  01 947 4766

Open: Monday to Saturday (excluding Wednesday) 09.30 to 17.30; Wednesday 09.30 to 13.00; mail order

A shop for amateur jewellers—no catalogue yet because they are still extending their range but already they can offer beads, chain, base metal and sterling silver findings, amethyst ovals and faceted stones, tumble polishing machines, diamond blades and other jewellers' tools, copper blanks and all the necessary for enamelling, including kilns. Also seashells. They have some hand-polishing and jewellery making kits and also candlemaking and plastic embedding kits. Enthusiastic about their stock and keen to extend it.

W1
J Blundell and Sons Limited
199 Wardour Street, London W1
  01 437 4746

Open: Monday to Friday (excluding Wednesday) 09.30 to 16.30; Wednesday closed; mail order; catalogue

Are up to their eyebrows and beyond in orders and had trouble fighting down hysteria at the thought of further orders resulting from this book—but if you are prepared to wait until they can get around to you they can sell you gold and silver in sheet or wire form and also the full range of jewellers' findings in both gold and silver.

W1
Eaton's Shell Shop (see page 161) Beads and stones only

W1
Gould's
68 Berwick Street, Oxford Street, London
  W1   01 437 4191

Open: Monday to Friday 08.30 to 17.30; Saturday 08.30 to 13.00; mail order; catalogue

Can supply tools and accessories for jewellers—mounters, and art metal workers, tweezers, gauges, eyeglasses, snippers, gravers, polishers, scales saws, hammers, the lot. Relatively new firm (successors to Herring, Morgan and Southon) and very helpful.

W1
Hirsh Jacobson Merchandising Company Limited
91 Marylebone High Street, London W1
  01 935 4709

Open: Monday to Friday 10.00 to 17.30; mail order; catalogue 10p

Very important suppliers of all possible kinds of lapidary tools and equipment. They can sell you tumble polishers, abrasives and polishing powders, casting kits, diamond files and saws, faceting machines and heads, gem-maker kits, grinding wheels, kilns, opal slicing equipment (and the opals to use it on), slab saws, trim saws, diamond drills, adhesives and so on and so on. Also findings and fittings in gilt or silver finish and in stainless steel and a very good range of semi-precious stones in the rough—agate, amethyst, citrine, lapis lazuli, onyx, serpentine, zebra opals and so on. And books and journals. Very specialised, very informed, very well stocked. Call in if you can, but the catalogue is helpful, too.

W1
Selfridges (see page 24) Stones only

W8
Crafts Unlimited (see page 24)

WC2
Craftorama (Wholesale) Company
14 Endell Street and 49 Shelton Street,
  London WC2H 9HE   01 240 2745

Open: Monday to Friday 10.00 to 18.00; mail order; catalogue 10p

A rock shop, supplying precious, semi-precious and imitation stones, tumble-polishing machines, rough rock, and chain and findings in stainless steel, brass and silver. The shop is on the corner of Endell Street and Shelton Street, and although they are well-known wholesalers they are open to customers as well. Minimum order they will fulfil by mail is one which costs £1.00. (Incidentally, they are open on Saturdays from 10.00 to 16.00 from September to January.)

LOUGHBOROUGH
Artcraft and Do-it-Yourself (see page 25)

LUDHAM
Timgems
The Old Shop, Ludham, Near Great
  Yarmouth, Norfolk
  Potter Heigham 684

Open: Monday and Thursday to Sunday 10.00 to 18.00; Tuesday and Wednesday by appointment only; mail order; catalogue

Large range of lapidary supplies—not only findings, ring boxes and mountings but a lot of cabochons. You get discounts on large orders and they welcome trade enquiries.

MALVERN
Fearnside and Company (see page 25)

MANCHESTER
Fred Aldous (see page 25)

MIDDLESBROUGH
J Goldstein and Son (see page 26)

Thornhill Crafts
25 Tollesby Road, Middlesborough, Teesside, Yorkshire   Middlesborough 84157

Mail order only; catalogue

Mail order suppliers, although you can call if you make an appointment first. They have lapidary equipment and materials, semi-precious stones, rough gemstones, and tumble-polishing machines. Also beads, chain and findings in most metals, including gold and silver. They offer a complete tumble-polishing kit and a complete gemstone jewellery kit. Will arrange lectures and demonstrations.

MORPETH

Tallantyre Wallpapers (see page 26)

NANNERCH

Craft O'Hans (see page 53)

NEW ASH GREEN

The Hobby House (see page 26)

NEWCASTLE UPON TYNE

Ashbourton Gifts and Crafts (see page 27) Copper and pewter

NEWQUAY

Strata Craft (Newquay) Limited
9a Cliff Road, Newquay, Cornwall
  Newquay 2973

Open: Easter to September seven days a week from 09.30 to 17.30 and 19.30 to 21.00. Winter Monday to Saturday (excluding Wednesday) 10.00 to 17.00; Wednesday closed; mail order; catalogue 20p

Specialists in lapidary and enamelling equipment with a stock of chain, findings in base metals and sterling silver; precious, semi-precious and imitation stones; jewellers' tools; tumble polishing machines to use on the local stones; copper blanks and a full complement of enamelling materials and kilns. Very wide range. Also cold enamelling kits. Can offer informed advice and also a diamond saw slabbing service for customers. The 20p for the catalogue is refundable if you buy goods.

Towan Gems and Mineral Centre
33a Bank Street, Newquay, Cornwall
  Newquay 5877

Open: June to September, seven days a week 10.00 to 20.00; October to May, Monday to Saturday 10.00 to 17.00; mail order; catalogue

Very large range of machines, saws, etc. for lapidary work; also mineral specimens for 'decor and investment', findings and semi-precious stones. They will identify minerals and undertake all kinds of lapidary work—cutting and shaping stones for jewellery and silversmithing. (Can also sell you silver if you want to do your own smithing.)

NEWTON STEWART

Country Crafts (see page 27) Semi-precious stones only

NEW WALTHAM

Joseph Ogle (see page 27)

NORTHAMPTON

Abingdon Handicrafts (see page 27)

Arts and Crafts Shop (see page 28)

NORTH SHIELDS

Rough and Tumble Limited
3 Tyne Street, North Shields, Northumberland North Shields 72559

Open: Monday to Saturday (excluding Thursday) 09.00 to 17.30; Thursday 09.00 to 20.00; mail order; catalogue 25p

Lapidary and mineral dealers, very well stocked—chain, findings in base and precious metals; copper blanks; enamelling materials and kilns; precious and semi-precious stones; minerals of many kinds; jewellers' tools and tumble polishing machines. Only a visit, or a copy of the catalogue (25p, refunded against first order of over £1.00) will give you a proper idea of the range. Also, Plasticraft kits.

NOTTINGHAM

Home Pastimes (see page 28) Tumble polishers only

OLDHAM

The Art and Craft Shop (see page 28)

OXFORD

Colegroves (see page 28)

PAISLEY

Scotrocks Craftshops
Lawn Street, Paisley, Renfrewshire

Same hours and stock as the Edinburgh shop—see page 41.

PERRANPORTH

'Seaway' Gift Shop
10 Beach Road, Perranporth, Cornwall
  TR6 0JL No Telephone

Open: May to September only—Monday to Saturday 10.00 to 18.00; mail order supplies all the year round; catalogue 10p

Lapidary supplies—rocks, minerals, gemstones, chain and findings in base metals (precious metals to order), tools and polishing machines, various jewellery making kits and hand polishing kits and also tropical seashells (for local shells, go to the beach!) and ready made shell-craft. They can equip treasure hunters with metal detectors and divining rods. Some books.

PERTH

Dunn's Art Stores (see page 29)   Limited

PETERBOROUGH

Art and Educational Crafts (see page 29)

PORTSOY

Marbleshop
Portsoy, Banffshire, Scotland

Open: Monday to Saturday 09.00 to 17.00; mail order; catalogue 5p

Lapidary suppliers who offer plated chain and findings, semi-precious polished and rough stones and tumble polishing machines.

PRESCOT

The Art Shop (see page 29)

PRESTWICK

Stones and Settings
54 Main Street, Prestwick, Lancashire
   Prestwick 79476

Open: Monday to Saturday (excluding Wednesday) 09.00 to 17.30; Wednesday 09.00 to 13.00; mail order; catalogue 20p

Means what it says—tumbled gemstones, chain and settings in stainless steel, rolled gold and silver in traditional designs, copper blanks, diamond saw blades, slabs and attachments, hand polishing kits, jewellers' tools and machinery and relevant books. Also the materials for cold and kiln enamelling and for plastic embedding; and shells (cowries, bleeding teeth, sea urchins, mother-of-pearl crumbs, and a lot more).

RAYLEIGH

Mineralcraft
1 The Knoll, Crown Hill, Rayleigh,
   Essex SS6 7HB   Rayleigh 2083

Open: by appointment; mail order; catalogue

Mail order supplier (although you can call in if you make an appointment first) of lapidary, cutting and carving materials who will undertake custom casting. Can supply you with chain and findings in base and precious metals, casting silver,

rough and finished stones (precious and semi-precious) and tumble-polishing machines. Also modelling wax and casting wax.

READING

Inspirations
57 Meadway Precinct, Honey End Lane,
   Tilehurst, Reading, Berkshire RG3 4AA
   Reading 583744

Open: Monday to Saturday (excluding Wednesday) 09.00 to 17.30; Wednesday 09.00 to 13.00

Specialists in gemstone and lapidary supplies who will cut stones to order and repair jewellery. They stock chain and findings in all metals, semi-precious polished stones, tumble polishers and rough rock, jewellers' tools and kilns, colours and copper blanks for enamelling. They also have kits for candle-making, cold enamelling, Plasticraft, plaster casting and batik; felt and kapok; leather offcuts; raffia, seashells and modelling clays.

Reading Fine Art Gallery (see page 29)

REDBOURN

Atelier (see page 29)

REDHILL

Baines Orr (London) Limited
1-5 Garlands Road, Redhill, Surrey
   Redhill 67363

Open: Monday to Friday 09.00 to 15.00; mail order; catalogue 10p refundable against £1.00 purchase

Become quite ecstatic when talking about their Gemsai Jewel Tree Kit, about which they will gladly send you details and which probably represents one of the most unusual ways of working with semi-precious stones. But they can also supply an amazing range of tumbled semi-precious stones—they say they have 3,000,000 stones in stock at any one time—and chain and plated findings for the setting thereof.

RICHMOND

Richmond Art and Craft (see page 30)

ROCHDALE

The Art Shop (see page 30) Tumble polishers only

ST ANNES ON SEA

The Handmaiden (see page 30)

SANDBACH

Norgems
4 Front Street, Sandbach, Cheshire
Sandbach 3871

Open: Monday to Friday (excluding
Tuesday) 14.00 to 17.00; Tuesday closed;
Saturday 09.00 to 18.00; Sunday 10.00
to 12.30; mail order; catalogue 15p

Call—or order by post. Lapidary supplies,
machines, rough stones, polished stones,
base and sterling silver chains and findings, mineral specimens. Nice place for
the amateur jeweller or 'rockhound'.

SHEFFIELD

Johnson Matthey Metals Limited
175 Arnndel Gate, Sheffield, Yorkshire
51 1JY Sheffield 23121

Open: Monday to Friday 09.30 to 16.15
(See London branch for details—page 44)

A Massie and Son
154/158 Burgoyne Road, Sheffield, Yorkshire S6 3QD Sheffield 343511

Open: Monday to Saturday (excluding
Thursday) 09.30 to 13.00 and 14.15 to
17.30; Thursday 09.30 to 13.00; mail
order; catalogue

Stockists of lapidary machines and
materials. They have a lot of books on
minerals and rocks; also the minerals and
rocks themselves, precious and semi-
precious stones, chain and findings in
base and precious metals, jewellers' tools,
tumble polishing machines, enamelling
colours, kilns and copper blanks. Qualified and willing to give advice and information on any aspect of the craft.

H R Whitehead (see page 30) Semi-
precious stones

SHEPTON MALLET

Marcross Gems and B Mandeville
13 Market Place, Shepton Mallet, Somerset Shepton Mallet 2491

Open: Monday to Saturday 09.00 to 17.30
(Evenings and weekends by appointment)

All lapidary supplies—see main branch
in Frome on page 131.

R F D Parkinson and Company Limited
Doulting, Shepton Mallet, Somerset
Cranmore 243

Open: Monday to Friday 09.00 to 17.00;
Saturday 09.00 to 13.00; mail order

Really a supplier of geological specimens
who will identify your own specimens
for you. But also sells silver, gold and
chrome chain and findings, rough gemstones and tumble polishers, grits and
polishes.

SHREWSBURY

Gemini
20d Castle Gates, Shrewsbury, Shropshire

Open: Tuesday to Saturday 09.30 to
17.30

Will make jewellery to order or supply
you with the wherewithall to make your
own; chain and findings in base metals
and silver, copper blanks, precious and
semi-precious stones and tumble polishers
and accessories. They also sell candlemaking kits, Enamelcraft, Ventacraft,
Crystal cast and lost wax casting kits
and an Enamelaire kiln kit. May undertake mail order later on.

SKENE

Lapidary Workshops Company
Garlogie School, Skene, Aberdeenshire,
Scotland Skene 381

Open: Monday to Saturday (excluding
Friday) 09.00 to 17.45; Friday 09.00 to
13.00; mail order

Lapidary specialists who will undertake
custom slabbing, drilling and polishing.
From them you can buy slabs of semi-
precious stone for polishing, tumble
polishers, grits and polishes, mineral
specimens, ready polished stones from
stock, chain and findings in base metals
and silver, silver sheet and wire and
complete stone polishing kits. No minimum order for personal callers, but you
should spend at least £1.00 if you want
materials sent by post.

SLAIDBURN

The Jam Pot
5 Chapel Street, Slaidburn, Near Clitheroe, Lancashire Slaidburn 225

Open: Seven days a week, 10.00 to 17.00

Lapidary supplies—tools, machines,
tumble-polished stones, cabochons, a
large range of base metal findings and
the materials and copper blanks for kiln
enamelling (including the kilns). Will
supply by mail only to known customers.

SOUTHAMPTON

Hampshire Hobbies (see page 31)

Jacinth Gems
10 Highfield Crescent, Southampton,
Hampshire SO2 1SF

Mail order only; catalogue

Chiefly known as mail order suppliers of

jade—both jadeite and nephrite—in 10 gm. parcels which vary in price according to the quality of the contents. Also have a limited quantity of saw tailings, rough jade, etc. But they can also offer amethyst, aquamarine, garnet, tourmaline, spodumene, rose quartz, citrine, topaz and some crystal specimens which can be used, uncut, in jewellery-making. Price list gives clear details of what is offered together with notes on hardness, how to polish, etc.

SOUTHSEA

Solent Lapidary
145 Highland Road, Southsea, Hampshire PO4 9EY   Portsmouth 31436

Open: Monday to Saturday (excluding Wednesday) 09.00 to 17.30; Wednesday 09.00 to 13.00; mail order

Suppliers of lapidary machines, rocks and findings who will undertake sawing of gemstones and silver casting. They have chain and findings in base metal, sterling silver, silver and gold; silver sheet and wire; precious, semi-precious and imitation stones, jewellers' tools, tumble polishing machines and advanced lapidary machines. They plan to extend their range to include other craft materials, and already have Plasticraft, Allcraft, Enamelcraft and Supercast kits, candlemaking supplies, seashells and seed beads. Catalogue in preparation.

SOUTH SHIELDS

Craftorama (North)
29 King Street, South Shields, County Durham   South Shields 66762

Open: Monday to Friday (excluding Wednesday) 09.00 to 17.30; Wednesday 09.30 to 13.00; Saturday 09.00 to 17.30; mail order; catalogue 6p

Lapidary specialists, strongly linked with Craftorama Wholesale in London. Very good range of semi-precious stones—also imitation stones, minerals, tumble polishing machines, chain and findings in sterling silver, gold, gilt and nickel. Plenty of stock. Advice always available.

STOKE-ON-TRENT

W G Ball Limited (see page 54)   Findings

Harrison Mayer Limited (see page 57)

STROUD

The Christmas Tree (see page 31) Findings and beads only

SUDBURY

Art and Craft Shop (see page 31)

SUTTON

O W Annetts and Sons (see page 32)

SUTTON COLDFIELD

Hillside Gems
Terminus Shopping Centre, Wylde Green, Sutton Coldfield, Warwickshire

Open: Monday to Saturday 09.00 to 17.30; mail order; catalogue

Especially concerned with gemstones—both polished and rough—but can also supply findings and fittings, jewellers' tools, tumble polishers and even potters' wheels.

SWANSEA

Arts and Crafts (see page 32)

THORNBURY

Arts and Crafts (see page 32)

TIDESWELL

Tideswell Dale Rock Shop
Commercial Road, Tideswell, Derbyshire   Hope Valley 20304

Open: Thursday to Sunday 09.30 to 17.30; mail order; catalogue

Lapidary and silversmithing supplies and mineral specimens. You can buy all kinds of rocks for tumbling and cutting, including a special selection of British rocks and some semi-precious stones which have been ready polished. Also chain and findings in base metals, silver and gold, jewellers' tools of all kinds, tumbling machines, a £1.00 bag of 'agate tumblemix', geological hammers, face masks to keep out the dust, and books on gems, geology and the history of mining. The price list has drawings and a jokey flavour. Large range of materials.

TRURO

Kernocraft Rocks and Gems Limited
9 Old Bridge Street, Truro, Cornwall   Truro 2695

Open: Monday to Saturday (excluding Thursday) 09.00 to 12.30 and 13.30 to 17.00; Thursday 09.00 to 12.30; mail order (from Lemon St.); catalogue 20p

Specialists in lapidary supplies, jewellery mounts and polished gemstones who will undertake gemstone cutting and polishing. The shop is open to customers, but Kernocraft's main business is conducted by mail order from 44 Lemon Street, Truro, Cornwall TR1 2NT (Truro 2695), with a catalogue that looks like the very best kind of travel brochure. The materials they offer are too numerous to list fully—findings and mounts of all kinds in base metals, stainless steel, silver, rolled gold, 9 carat gold and copper; a wealth of books; all kinds of tools and equipment; and stones upon stones, precious and semi-precious. Also related things, like abalone shell and petrified wood.

TUNBRIDGE WELLS

G B Butler
18b The Pantiles, Tunbridge Wells, Kent Tunbridge Wells 22684

Open: Monday to Saturday (excluding Wednesday) 09.00 to 17.00; Wednesday 09.00 to 13.00; mail order (wholesale only); catalogue 5½p

Wholesalers and retailers, specialising in gemstones, jewellery mounts and castings, chains, mineral specimens and fossils. Supply by mail to wholesale customers only, but the personal shopper can buy small quantities at retail prices. They also have copper blanks, enamelling materials and kilns, candlemaking supplies, lino-cutting sets, all the basic necessities for tie-dye, batik and screen printing, and Plasticraft, Enamelcraft and Enamelaire kits.

TWICKENHAM

M L Beach (Products) Limited
41 Church Street, Twickenham, Middlesex TW1 3NS 01 892 0409

Open: Tuesday to Saturday 10.00 to 17.30; mail order; catalogue

An exciting place for the home jewellery maker and stone-hunter—all kinds of stone polishing machinery and all kinds of stones to polish with it; also chains and findings and fittings in precious metals. They are very willing to chat and advise and they also stock quite a lot of useful books. At the time of going to press they were offering a complete stone polishing kit—polisher, motor, instructions, stones, fittings and glue—for £8.85.

Bits and Bobs (see page 54)

WAKEFIELD

Glenjoy Craft and Lapidary Supplies
19/21 Sun Lane, Wakefield, Yorkshire Wakefield 73786

Open: Monday to Friday (excluding Wednesday) 09.00 to 12.30 and 13.30 to 17.00; Wednesday 09.00 to 12.00; Saturday 09.00 to 17.00; mail order; catalogue 20p

Lapidary and jewellery-making supplies —chain, findings in all metals, copper blanks, semi-precious and precious stones and rough gemstones, jewellers' tools, polishing machines and enamelling materials and kilns. They will cut rough gemstones to size and are qualified to advise on matters lapidary. Also candlemaking supplies, seashells and modelling clays.

WARLEY

A and D Hughes Limited
Popes Lane, Oldbury, Warley, Worcestershire 021 552 4500

Open: By appointment; mail order; catalogue

Manufacturers of trim saws, grinding and polishing units, faceting heads and tumbler units, who distribute through retail lapidary specialists all over Britain. However, you may buy direct—either by making an appointment to call in or by way of the free catalogue.

WATFORD

Allcraft (see page 33)

J Simble and Sons
76 Queens Road, Watford, Hertfordshire Watford 26052

Open: Monday to Saturday (excluding Wednesday) 09.00 to 18.00; Wednesday 09.00 to 13.00; mail order; catalogue 15p

Stock of useful tools—for jewellery work (including tumble polishers and semi-precious stones); for leather-working, for lino-cutting and for picture framing.

WELLING

Crafts Unlimited (see page 33)

WELLINGBOROUGH

Happicraft (see page 33)

WELLINGTON

New Age Handicraft Centre (see page 33)

Sesame Ventures (see page 87)

WELWYN GARDEN CITY

Boon Gallery (see page 34) Copper findings and tumble polishers

R H Hill Promotions Limited
23 Church Street, Welwyn Garden City, Hertfordshire Welwyn 5021

Open: Monday to Friday 09.00 to 17.00; mail order; catalogue

A business rather than a shop, but there

is a small showroom and they welcome visitors to it. They have antique silver finish settings for stones, gilt and silver-coloured findings, stainless steel ring and pendant settings, precious, semi-precious and imitation stones, bags of agate 'bits', tools, cements and tumble polishers. Very willing to advise and comment.

WESTCLIFF-ON-SEA

The Gemstone Centre
114 Station Road, Westcliff-on-Sea, Essex Southend-on-Sea 49785

Open: Monday to Saturday (excluding Wednesday) 09.00 to 12.00 and 13.00 to 18.00; Wednesday 09.00 to 13.00; mail order; catalogue 3p (postage)

As the name implies—lapidary specialists who sell semi-precious stones, rough rock, tumble polishing machines, grits and polishes, diamond saws and drills, grinding machines and base metal chain and findings.

WESTCOTT

Westcott Antiques
2 The Green, Westcott, Near Dorking, Surrey Dorking 81900

Open: Monday to Saturday 09.00 to 17.00; Sunday 09.00 to 13.00

Specialise in rocks, minerals, gemstones and lapidary supplies, including diamond cutting wheels, grits, tumble polishers, polishes and findings in all metals. Offer high discounts on bulk orders of rough lapidary rock. No mail order—go and see the rocks.

WHITEHAVEN

Strathclyde Studio
Windsor House, Harras Moor, White-haven, Cumberland Whitehaven 2371

Open: Monday to Friday 10.00 to 17.30; mail order; catalogue

Wholesalers and retailers of mineral specimens, lapidary equipment and jewellery. Quite prepared to give relevant advice and information if you need it. They have hand polishing kits, sample boxes, precious and semi-precious stones, tumbling machines and accessories, jewellers' tools and chain and findings in various metals, including precious ones.

WINCHESTER

Wessex Gems and Crafts
Longacre, Downs Road, South Won-ston, Winchester, Hampshire Winchester 881522

Open: Monday to Saturday 09.00 to 17.00; mail order; catalogue

Well stocked lapidary suppliers who can sell you semi-precious stones (polished or rough), jewellers' tools, chain and findings in nickel plate, gilt and silver, tumble polishing machines and hand polishing gem kits.

WIRRAL

Arts and Crafts (see page 34)

WOKING

Arts and Crafts Shop (see page 34)

YEOVIL

Draytons Decorations (see page 34)

YORK

Derwent Crafts (see page 35) Two general craft shops which specialise in jewellery-making

3 Enamelling

In ordinary craft shops you can generally buy kits for 'cold' enamelling (and most of these kits actually do permit you to be creative). There are also shops which stock all the necessary for kiln enamelling and who can usually offer help and advice if you would like them to. And there are a few specialists to whom you might appeal for unusual materials, rare colours and so on.

For ease of reference, the chapter is divided into two parts—Specialist Suppliers and suppliers of Kilns only —but you will find that most of the general craft shops in Chapter One stock enamelling materials of one kind or another.

SPECIALIST SUPPLIERS

INVERNESS

East Dene Crafts
6 Ballifeary Road, Inverness, Invernesshire, Scotland   Inverness 32976

Open: Summer, Monday to Saturday 09.00 to 10.00 and 16.30 to 20.00; Winter, Saturday 09.30 to 17.30 or telephone for an appointment after 16.00; mail order; catalogue in preparation

Specialise in enamels, kilns, copper blanks and copper findings with a small stock of silvered findings and marquetry and candlemaking kits. Open long but unusual hours in the summer, short hours in the winter, so do telephone first to check. Enamelling demonstrations are sometimes arranged for local schools on request.

LEEDS

Turner Research Limited
Mail Order Department, Jubilee Terrace, Leeds, Yorkshire LS6 2XH

Mail order only; catalogue

Should you have difficulty in getting hold of an Enamelaire or a Plasticraft kit you may order direct from source— which means Turner Research. They will happily send you leaflets.

LONDON N1

The Pot Shop (see page 22)   Very wide range

WC2
Crafts Unlimited
21 Macklin Street, London WC2 9HE
   01 242 7053

Open: Monday to Friday 10.00 to 18.00; Saturday 10.00 to 16.00; mail order; catalogue 25p plus 12p postage

A London retail outlet for Crafts Unlimited at Nannerch in Flintshire (see separate entry). Specialise in enamelling materials, kilns, findings, copper blanks and so on, and will advise on technical problems. Can also supply the following kits—plaster moulding, plastic embedding, candlemaking, tie-dye, batik, lampshade making, rug-making, brass rubbing, pokerwork, and various bits and pieces like Artstraws, pipecleaners, natural straws, tinfoil and origami paper.

NANNERCH

Craft O'Hans
The Old Mill, Nannerch, Near Mold, Flintshire, North Wales   Hendre 542

Open: Wednesday to Sunday 10.00 to 18.00

Run by Hans Theilade, whose particular interest is enamelling. The Old Mill is a true craft centre, with weekend and evening courses in enamelling, batik and tie-dye, Plasticraft, candlemaking, pottery, lapidary work, silk screen printing and other crafts, and also expert advice for those who just want to call in to buy some materials. Send a stamped addressed envelope for details of the courses—and a stamped addressed envelope marked 'newsletter' to discover what a very active centre this is. Particularly strong on enamelling materials (including the necessary findings, pewter and copperfoil, buttons and buckles for enamelling and so on). Also stock beads, chain, rug-making supplies, Penelope embroidery kits, plastic resins and nuggets for melting, candlemaking and silk screen printing materials and some kits—Plasticraft, cold enamelling and the wherewithall to make wooden mosaics. Very concerned to promote craftwork and consequently very helpful.

STOKE-ON-TRENT

W G Ball Limited
Longton Mill, Anchor Road, Longton, Stoke-on-Trent, Staffordshire ST3 1JW
Stoke-on-Trent 33956

Open: Monday to Friday 08.30 to 17.00; mail order; catalogue

Manufacturers and retailers of materials and equipment for jewellery enamelling. They have a very wide range of enamels, ground ready for use—also crackle enamels, sheet steel enamels, a trial pack, etc. They have sheet steel, silver foil, copper sheet, copper blanks, findings—and they offer two kinds of electric kiln together with all kiln enamelling accessories. If there is any relevant accessory that they don't have they can usually get it for you. They offer technical advice on all aspects of the craft and send out a free catalogue which not only lists their stock but offers various pieces of advice and information. Will supply any quantity.

TWICKENHAM

Bits and Bobs
46 Church Street, Twickenham, Middlesex   01 892 8334

Open: Tuesday to Saturday (excluding Wednesday) 09.30 to 17.00; Monday and Wednesday 09.30 to 13.00

Although quite true to the name, and full of bits and bobs, they regard themselves as specialist suppliers of enamelling materials and have a good range of copper blanks, materials and some kilns. Also kits for candlemaking, Plasticraft, Enamelcraft, and marquetry; chain, findings in gilt, nickel and copper, semiprecious and imitation stones and jewellers' tools; leather and leather-working tools; lino-cutting and brass rubbing accessories; felt, hessian, kapok, foam chippings and teddy bears' noses; tiedye and batik materials; (silk screen printing materials are not in stock but 'can be got'); plastic resins and clear casting resins; seashells; raffia and cane; modelling clays, Das, Superwood, etc. Nice place for browsing and rummaging. Will send by mail order, but prefer not to.

KILNS

These four people supply kilns only—no other enamelling materials.

ALTRINCHAM

Lapidary Abrasives (see page 36)

LONDON SW6

The Fulham Pottery Limited (see page 56)

W1

Hirsh Jacobson (see page 46)

TOLLESBURY

R M Catterson-Smith Limited (see page 60)

GENERAL SUPPLIERS

Most general craft shops also stock enamelling requisites—but read the entry carefully, as some have cold enamelling materials only (see entries in Chapter 1).

See also Stoke-on-Trent (Wengers, Harrison Mayer and Podmore, pages 58 and 57).

4 Pottery

If you live in Stoke-on-Trent or London you have no problems, and probably already know where to go for supplies. But even if you live in the Outer Hebrides, so long as you are prepared to pay carriage costs, you can order the materials and machinery for the craft to be delivered to you. The following are the major suppliers, set out in three sections—General, Equipment and Accessories, and Materials.

GENERAL

These are the specialist suppliers of everything for the craft potter—clays, wheels, glazes, kilns and so on. Also included in list are those craft shops from Chapter 1 who stock, or can get, some equipment and materials.

ANDOVER

Arts and Crafts Centre (see page 10)

AYR

Contour Artists' Materials (see page 10)

BOURNEMOUTH

Moordown Leather and Craft (see page 114)

CANTERBURY

Canterbury Pottery (see page 13)

CARDIFF

Rumney Pottery
Rumney, Cardiff, Glamorganshire,
  Wales   Cardiff 78096

Open: Monday to Saturday 09.00 to 19.00

Will sell prepared clays and glazes and also potters' wheels, kilns, etc. on the premises. Will fulfil any order from 50p to £50. Are also prepared to advise on pottery problems.

South Wales Arts and Crafts Suppliers
110 Bute Street, Cardiff, Glamorganshire,
  Wales   Cardiff 41044

Open: Monday to Friday 09.00 to 17.00; Saturday 09.30 to 13.00; mail order; catalogue

At present specialise in ceramics, with a very good range of clays, glazes, frits, wheels, kilns and so on. Will give advice, arrange for the firing of pots, and deliver by mail or van all over the country. But the intention is to expand the range to cover the whole craft field and even now they are able to supply most craft materials on request. Those in stock at present include copper and steel findings, copper blanks, enamelling colours and kilns, silver, pewter, semi-precious stones and tumble polishing machines, and all kinds of modelling clays. And materials which have already been supplied by special request include lino-cutting materials and tools, tie-dye, batik and screen printing materials, glass, perspex, polyester and PVC. By the autumn these, and other items, should be permanently in stock—especially if they get enough support from customers.

CHATTERIS

A L Curtis (ONX) Limited
Westmoor Laboratory, Chatteris, Cambridgeshire PE16 6AT
  Cambridge 2561

(Opening times not applicable); mail order; catalogue

Wholesale suppliers of clays and minerals for craft pottery—also clay refractories. You can buy direct, but telephone or write for an appointment first (and ask for the free leaflet describing the 50 different clays, minerals, bricks, etc., so that you know what they have to offer before you arrive).

COLNE

The Art Shop (see page 15)

CONWY

Conwy Pottery
8 Castle Street, Conwy, North Wales
 Conwy 3487

Open: Summer—Monday to Saturday 09.30 to 21.30; Winter—Monday to Saturday (excluding Wednesday) 10.00 to 17.00; Wednesday 10.00 to 13.00; mail order; catalogue

As well as hand-made pottery, will sell you clays and glazes and can order kilns, wheels and any other equipment. Will give assistance and advice where possible and will undertake the firing of pots, pottery repairs and so on.

DORCHESTER

Frank Herring and Sons (see page 64)

EDINBURGH

Ceramic Workshop
15/16 Victoria Terrace, Edinburgh EH1
 2JL   031 226 5416

Open: Monday to Friday 09.00 to 17.30; mail order; catalogue

The Ceramic Workshop is a registered charity which is open to membership (for £2.50 a year). They provide facilities and technical advice for artists, potters and students and supply all kinds of clays, glazes, frits, raw materials and tools. The catalogue gives precise details of materials available and they will try to get hold of others that they don't at present stock. They plan to design and sell a craft kit containing clay, basic glaze, colours and tools, designed primarily for schools, and retailing at about £10.00. Check with them for details.

FRINTON-ON-SEA

Frinton Handicrafts and Art Centre (see page 17)

GRAVESEND

Tumble Kraft (see page 42)

HARROGATE

Arts and Handicrafts (see page 18)

HEREFORD

Adams and Sons (see page 137)

HUDDERSFIELD

Arts and Crafts (see page 19)

KEIGHLEY

Conways Arts and Crafts (see page 20)

KENDAL

Kendal Handicrafts (see page 20)

LEEDS

E J Arnold and Son (see page 21)

LEICESTER

Dryad (see page 22)

LONDON EC1

Crafts Unlimited (see page 22)

N1
The Pot Shop (see page 22)   Very full range of materials, tools and equipment

NW3
Crafts Unlimited (see page 23)

SW4
Mills and Hubball Limited
Victoria Rise, North Side, Clapham Common, London SW4 0PB
 01 622 7457

Open: Monday to Thursday 08.30 to 12.30 and 13.15 to 17.30; Friday 08.30 to 12.30 and 13.15 to 15.00; mail order; catalogue

Potters' merchants supplying kilns, wheels and pottery-making materials and tools. Their free and fully illustrated catalogue is also an instruction book which tells you how to care for kilns, why you need a pyrometer, how to prepare glazes, enamels and lustres and how to treat clay. Very good range of colours and glazes; plastic and powdered ball and china clay; also tools, brushes, books, charts, tools, power and kick wheels and accessories, pyrometers, kilns and kiln furniture.

SW6
The Fulham Pottery Limited
210 New Kings Road, London SW6 4NY
 01 736 1188

Open: Monday to Friday 09.15 to 13.00 and 14.00 to 16.45; Saturday 09.00 to 12.00; mail order; catalogue

At the Fulham Pottery (which has been active for three centuries) you can buy everything any potter could desire, and since they undertake mail order throughout the UK (and overseas) you don't have to live in London to be glad to know about it. They have basic materials, prepared clays, frits, glazes, colours, tools, accessories and workroom equipment, wheels, kilns (for enamelling as well as for pottery) and kiln furniture. The beautifully produced catalogue is free and not only does it give full details, accompanied by excellent photographs, of every brush, mop, kiln, wheel or pyrometer, it also has a couple of pages of hints on materials and techniques and, at the back, a chemical analysis of every material. They also stock books and say that 'callers are always welcome at the studio to discuss any matter pertaining to pottery'. What more could you want?

W1
The Craftsmen Potters Shop
William Blake House, Marshall Street, London W1   01 437 7605

Open: Monday to Friday 10.00 to 17.30; Saturday 10.30 to 13.00; mail order; catalogue

They are chiefly concerned with selling the work of craftsmen potters, but they also stock relevant tools and books. Meetings are sometimes arranged in the evenings to discuss the technical aspects of pottery but these are only open to members of The Craftsmen Potters Association. But a good place to go and see and buy quality workmanship—and they're nice people too.

W8
Crafts Unlimited (see page 24)

LOUGHBOROUGH
Artcraft and Do-It-Yourself (see page 25)

PETERBOROUGH
Art and Educational Crafts (see page 29)

PILLING
Pilling Pottery
School Lane, Pilling, Preston, Lancashire
Pilling 307

Open: Monday to Saturday 09.00 to 17.00; mail order; catalogue

The pottery has a retail shop which sells potters' equipment—wheels, kilns and tools, and also raw clay and glazes. You can arrange to have your pots fired here.

RICHMOND
Richmond Art and Craft (see page 30)

SOUTHAMPTON
Ceramic Clays
15 Palmerston Road, Southampton, Hampshire   Southampton 30080

Open: Monday to Saturday 09.00 to 17.30; mail order; catalogue

Mainly pottery materials, but some leather-working supplies also. They offer themselves as a retail outlet for local craftsmen in clay or leather, and will also answer technical questions on pottery. They have a full range of clays, glazes, frits, potters' wheels, kilns and tools and also leather pieces, tools and accessories.

STOKE GABRIEL
Lotus Gallery
Stoke Gabriel, Near Totnes. Devonshire, Stoke Gabriel 303

Open: Monday to Saturday 09.00 to 13.00 and 14.00 to 17.30; mail order; catalogue

Lotus Pottery is a small, active pottery; Lotus Gallery is a craft shop and Lotus Products manufactures and markets the accessories for potters. So far they have only accessories and tools but later they may offer a potter's wheel and even a training scheme.

STOKE-ON-TRENT
Harrison Mayer Limited
Uttoxeter Road, Meir, Stoke-on-Trent, Staffordshire ST3 7PX
Stoke-on-Trent 36111

Open: Monday to Saturday 09.00 to 17.00; mail orders; catalogue

Ceramic and metal enamelling specialists who offer 'a complete service to the craft potter'—prepared clays, frits and glazes, potters' wheels, accessories and tools, kilns and kiln furniture for pottery and enamelling. They also have modelling clays and plaster, copper and gilt findings, copper blanks and jewellers' tools. There is no 'minimum order'—although there is a 50p surcharge on orders under £3.00 unless you collect them.

Podmore and Sons Limited
New Caledonian Mills, Shelton, Stoke-on-Trent, Staffordshire
Stoke-on-Trent 24571

Open: Monday to Friday 09.00 to 17.00; Saturday 09.00 to 12.00; mail order; catalogue

Manufacturers and suppliers of craft pottery materials. They have a sales/ showroom on the premises but also do a lot of business by mail order. Can offer everything for the craft potter—clays, glazes, frits, wheels, kilns, accessories and technical advice not only on the use of materials and equipment but on the layout of craft studios. Can also supply whatever you need for metal enamelling —enamels, kilns, copper blanks and findings and jewellers' tools. No minimum order. Very pleased to help craftsmen in any way possible. Very good catalogue.

Potclays Limited
Brickkiln Lane, Etruria, Stoke-on-Trent, Staffordshire Stoke-on-Trent 29816

Open: Monday to Friday 08.00 to 17.30; Saturday 08.00 to 12.00; mail order, catalogue

Fairly obviously—suppliers of potters' clays and allied materials (glazes, frits, etc.) and also tools, equipment, kilns and so on. Properly speaking they are wholesalers, although casual orders will be accepted from established customers. You should write in, with a firm order, stating whether the goods are to be dispatched or whether you will collect. Not for the beginner but for the potter who knows precisely what he wants.

Wengers Limited
Garner Street, Etruria, Stoke-on-Trent, Staffordshire ST4 7BQ
Stoke-on-Trent 25126

Open: Monday to Friday 08.30 to 16.30; mail order; catalogue

A very full range of materials and equipment for craft pottery—prepared clays, wheels, kilns and tools. Also enamelling materials and kilns, copper blanks and a metal enamelling kit for beginners. Very good catalogue—and they will supply any quantities anywhere.

WELLING

Crafts Unlimited (see page 33)

WOLVERHAMPTON

Ferro (Great Britain) Limited (see page 136)

YORK

Derwent Crafts (see page 35)

EQUIPMENT AND ACCESSORIES

If you can't find the equipment you need with the help of the list above, the list below is made up of designers, manufacturers and purveyors of the relevant machinery and accessories.

ALTRINCHAM

Lapidary Abrasives (see page 36) Small kiln only

BRISTOL

Nu-Way Heating Plants Limited
20 Kellaway Avenue, Bristol BS6 7XR
Bristol 49229

Open: Monday to Friday 08.00 to 17.30; Saturday 08.00 to 12.00; mail order

Useful news for potters—Nu-Way manufacture and supply oil and gas burners. No catalogue, but they will do mail order if you phone or write to sort out exactly what you want.

COLCHESTER

Moler Products Limited
Hythe Works, Colchester, Essex CO2 8JU Colchester 73191

Mail order only

Manufacturers of insulating refactory bricks. They supply many 'hobby' kiln builders with bricks and advice. Write or telephone for an appointment or data sheet.

CROYDON

Pottery Equipment Company
17/18 Progress Way, Croydon, Surrey CR9 4DH   01 688 6067

Open: Monday to Friday 09.00 to 17.00; mail order; catalogue

Manufacturers and suppliers of electric potters' wheels, treadle kick wheels and all the relevant accessories. Callers are welcome at the factory but the catalogue gives precise enough details to encourage you to order by letter or telephone.

KEIGHLEY

Judson and Hudson Limited
Parker Street, Keighley, Yorkshire BD21 5LR   Keighley 2016

Open: Works hours are Monday to Friday 07.50 to 12.10 and 13.10 to 16.50; mail order; catalogue

Don't call in, but place an order at the above address with the help of the free catalogue which gives photographs and specifications of the power driven potters' wheels, kick wheels and accessories available. Suppliers to schools and art colleges throughout the country.

MILTON KEYNES

Kasenit Limited
Denbigh Road, Bletchley, Milton Keynes,
 Buckinghamshire
Milton Keynes 72968

Mail order only; catalogue

Designers and manufacturers of gas
(natural, town or propane) fired pottery
kilns, which are not available ex stock
but are made to customers' orders. The
free leaflet gives precise details of the
kind of kiln they offer.

NEWTON POPPLEFORD

Woodley's Potters Wheel Limited
Newton Poppleford, Devon EX10 0BJ
 Colaton Raleigh 676

Open: Monday to Saturday 08.00 to
17.00; mail order; catalogue

Designers and manufacturers of the
'modified Leach pottery kick wheel'. They
promise that it is simple, reliable, inex-
pensive, hardwearing and easy to take
apart and re-assemble —and also readily
adjustable to the leg length of the user.
If you can't call in, the catalogue gives
very precise details.

NORWICH

A E W Engineering Company Limited
Horizon Works, Dereham Road, Cost-
essey, Norwich, Norfolk NOR 51X
 Norwich 742118

Open: Monday to Friday 08.30 to 17.30;
mail order; catalogue

Manufacturers of electric wheels and
kilns for potters. Will sell direct to the
public. You can call at the works by
appointment, or order from the detailed
catalogue which will come to you free
on request.

STOKE-ON-TRENT

William Boulton Limited
Navigation Road, Burslem, Stoke-on-
 Trent, Staffordshire
 Stoke-on-Trent 85658

Open: Monday to Friday 09.00 to 17.15;
mail order; catalogue

Engineers who produce machinery for
the ceramic industry, including schools
and craft potters. You can call at the
factory, write or telephone to be supplied
with potters' wheels (power or kick), kilns
and kiln furniture.

Firegas Kilns Limited
Sneyd Green, Hanley, Stoke-on-Trent,
 Staffordshire Stoke-on-Trent 23641

Mail order only; catalogue

Will make kilns for craft pottery to
order. Will build in the works and deliver, or will build on site. You can write
or telephone for illustrated literature. As
well as gas fired kilns, they will make
oil fired and electric kilns.

Gosling and Gatensbury Limited
Atlas Works, College Road, Hanley,
 Stoke-on-Trent, Staffordshire ST15
 0AB Stoke-on-Trent 22786

Open: Monday to Friday 08.00 to 12.30
and 13.00 to 16.30; Saturday 08.00 to
12.00; mail order; catalogue

A factory producing potters' wheels and
all relevant accessories. You are welcome
to make a direct approach to the works
to buy the machinery and they are quite
willing to give technical advice. Their UK
marketing agents are Harrison Mayer
Limited, also of Stoke-on-Trent. See
page 57.

Kilns and Furnaces Limited
Keele Street, Tunstall, Stoke-on-Trent,
 Staffordshire ST6 5AS
 Stoke-on-Trent 84642

Open: By appointment; mail order;
catalogue

Manufacturers of kilns (suitable for pottery and enamelling), furnaces and craft
pottery equipment. You can visit the
works by appointment, but should order
what you want via the very explicit catalogue. They have pug mills, a modelling
bench, reversible turning lathe, steel
blunger and jar mills, wad box, spray
booth, electric and kick wheels, kilns,
kiln furniture and all accessories.

Litherland's Elements Limited
Sneyd Street, Burslem, Stoke-on-Trent,
 Staffordshire ST6 2NP
 Stoke-on-Trent 23641/2

Open: By appointment; mail order;
catalogue

Designers and manufacturers of elements
for electric kilns and furnaces who will
supply thermocouples to order. They
mostly deal by mail but do welcome personal callers. If, for instance, a studio
potter is visiting Stoke-on-Trent for the
day he can contact Litherland's first and
they will have a replacement element (or
whatever) ready for collection. Very
pleased to help with any (elementary)
problems

J W Ratcliffe and Sons Limited
Rope Street, Off Shelton New Road,
 Stoke-on-Trent, Staffordshire ST4 6DJ
 Stoke-on-Trent 611321

Open: Monday to Saturday 09.00 to
17.00; mail order; catalogue

Manufacturers and suppliers of all kinds of pottery machinery—wheels, kilns and accessories. They will undertake machinery maintenance by arrangement.

SUTTON COLDFIELD

Hillside Gems (see page 50) Wheels

TOLLESBURY

R M Catterson-Smith Limited
Woodrolfe Road, Tollesbury, Nr. Maldon, Essex CM9 8SE
Tollesbury 342

Open: Monday to Friday 08.00 to 17.00; mail order; catalogue

A factory, not a shop, so write or telephone first if you want to call in. They've been making electric kilns and ovens since 1920 and modifying and improving them all the time. They have a good range of kilns for pottery and enamelling in various sizes and of various types, and they also produce kiln furniture and foot and power-driven potters' wheels. Their free catalogue gives very precise details of what they have to offer, and they will supply anywhere in the UK.

WATLINGTON

Len Huxley (Developments)
30 Pyrton Lane, Watlington, Oxfordshire OX9 5LX   Watlington 2545

Open: Monday to Sunday inclusive 09.00 to 18.00; mail order; catalogue

Specialist woodcraftsmen who sell—or hire—electric potters' wheels, designed by a potter and hand-built by themselves. (You can see over the workshop in Marlow by appointment. Contact the address above.) There are two models and they will send specifications on request. They also supply wheels in kit form, each with a construction plan. If you hire a wheel they undertake full maintenance during the time of the hire at no extra cost.

WIRRAL

Morgan Refractories Limited
Neston, Wirral, Cheshire   051 336 3911

Open: Monday to Friday 09.00 to 17.00

Makers of structural and insulating refractories and suppliers of insulating materials and bricks for kiln construction. You cannot call at the premises but must telephone or send in orders or enquiries by post. Unless you have an account their terms are cash-with-order and there is a £5 surcharge on orders below £10. They will send your order but don't have a catalogue as such, although will supply suggested kiln drawings and some technical data. (Know precisely what you want before contacting.)

MATERIALS

Some suppliers are concerned with various kinds of clays, glazes and materials only. These are the ones who are prepared to deal with individuals.

BURTON-ON-TRENT

Moira Pottery Company Limited
Moira, Burton-on-Trent, Staffordshire DE12 6DP   Swadlincote 7961

Mail order only; catalogue

Deal only by mail—or, rather, via British Road Services. They offer stoneware and terracotta clays for pottery (or for modelling) all extracted from their own clay fields and all supplied with matching glazes. They promise to dispatch orders within 7 to 10 days of receipt. If you want to buy, they send you leaflets with prices, carriage charges, technical data on the materials (including recommended firing temperatures) and instructions on preparing glazes which arrive in powder form.

HAVERFORDWEST

Haverfordwest Pottery
Haroldston House Clay Works, Haverfordwest, Pembrokeshire, Wales
Haverfordwest 2611

Open: Monday to Friday 09.30 to 13.00 and 14.00 to 17.00; Saturday 09.30 to 13.00

Pottery manufacturers who have a shop for selling their products. But they are also prepared to sell pottery materials direct from the workshop; stoneware throwing clay and the raw materials for making glazes.

LONDON SW9

Terrey Brothers
55 Andalus Road, London SW9
01 274 2705

Open: Monday to Friday 08.00 to 17.00

Supply casting plaster in 7 pound bags. Cheaper if you collect. They will deliver, but only within South London. Ask for Mr Terrey.

NEWTON ABBOT

Watts, Blake and Bearne Limited
Park House, Courtney Park, Newton
Abbot, South Devon
Newton Abbot 2345

Open: Monday to Friday 09.00 to 17.30;
mail order; catalogue

Offer plastic clay for pottery in 25 kilo-gram lots, and also basic ball and china clay for those who prefer to prepare their own. Callers are made welcome—or you can order by post or by telephone.

STOKE-ON-TRENT

Lingard Webster and Company Limited
Swan Pottery, 4 Holland Street, Tunstall,
Stoke-on-Trent, Staffordshire
Stoke-on-Trent 87069

Mail order only

Write or telephone first to make an appointment. From the Swan Pottery you can buy clays for craft pottery—although the minimum order they will consider is 56 pounds of clay. Are prepared to give information on firing temperatures and to examine and report on faults. They also have plaster of Paris—not very easy to come by these days.

Mellor Mineral Mills Limited
Etruria Vale, Stoke-on-Trent, Stafford-shire ST1 4DD Stoke-on-Trent 23441

Open: Monday to Friday 09.00 to 17.00;
mail order; catalogue

Producers of pottery bodies and glazes and ceramic colours. Contact by letter or telephone for fuller details. Will supply reasonably small quantities.

Price and Kensington Potteries Limited
Trubshaw Cross, Longport, Stoke-on-Trent, Staffordshire ST6 4LR
Stoke-on-Trent 88631

Open: Monday to Friday 08.30 to 17.00

You can buy any amount of prepared red and white clays from the factory. Telephone your order and arrange to collect. They don't send.

SWANSEA

Arts and Crafts (see page 32) Clays and glazes

5 Modelling

If you want to model with potters' clay, then turn back a chapter for the list of suppliers. But if you want to use plaster or one of the modern self-hardening clays, turn to the list of general craft shops in Chapter 1, most of whom stock modelling materials of one kind or another. Stocks tend to vary very much according to what is available, but most shops will order what you want if they can't supply immediately. The specialist in this field is Alec Tiranti of London.

INGATESTONE

Alan Wiseman and Partners (Darwi Marketing)
PO Box 58, High Street, Ingatestone, Essex Ingatestone 2539

Mail order only; catalogue

These are the UK agents for Darwi modelling compound. They claim that it is so malleable that it can be modelled into a truly complex construction and that it hardens and solidifies without firing. They also offer special paints and varnish which give the finished product all the appearance of ceramic work. It is available throughout the country in art and craft shops, but you can send for their leaflet and buy direct (or telephone your order, in which case you will prob-

ably have to speak to an answerphone, so have your message ready!). Also available is the Darwi Family Sculpture Kit—modelling compound, paints, varnish brush, sculpture tool and instruction leaflet.

LONDON W1

Alec Tiranti Limited
72 Charlotte Street, London W1P 2AJ
01 636 8565

Open: Monday to Thursday 09.00 to 18.00; Friday 09.00 to 17.30; mail order; catalogue 5p

Everything to do with carving and modelling is available at Tiranti's where you will get full technical advice on all tools and materials and free booklets on any tools or materials that you buy. They have sculptors' tools, glass fibre materials and tools, woodcarving tools, moulding rubbers, polyester and embedding resins, polyester pigments, modelling tools, stands and clays, plaster and plaster-working tools, self-hardening clays, lino-cutting tools and materials, and also the very necessary safety equipment—goggles, masks, respirators, barrier and cleansing creams. A range which is far too great to express in the space available, but if you are undertaking serious craftwork with plastics, wood, modelling or moulding materials then Tiranti is an extremely important centre for you.

6 Spinning, Weaving and Rug-Making

Spinning and weaving have been dealt with together because so often the suppliers of yarns for handweaving also offer raw wool or flax for handspinning; the suppliers of spinning wheels also offer handlooms and accessories; and there are even suppliers who offer everything for both crafts, including dyes.

However, there are styles of rug-making that are not really catered for below, so Rug-making has a separate section, beginning on page 69.

SPINNING AND WEAVING

AMMANFORD
Cwmllwchwr Mills (see page 82)   Yarns

BATH
Bath Handicraft Supplies (see page 10) Fleece and dyes

BINGLEY
T Lund and Son Limited
Argyll Mills, Bingley, Yorkshire BD16 4JW   Bingley 2301

Open: By appointment; mail order; catalogue

Visit by appointment, but order what you need from the weighty catalogue. They are manufacturers of reeds, frames, healds and weaving accessories who supply to handweavers both at home and abroad. Some of the equipment is rather heavy and industrial, but most is suitable for home weaving and the range is enormous, so it's worth sending for the catalogue to see precisely what they have to offer.

BRADFORD
British Wool Marketing Board
Oak Mills, Clayton, Bradford, Yorkshire
   Bradford 882091

(Opening times not applicable); mail order; catalogue

Will supply British fleece for handspinning in any quantity. Happy to send samples for approval. Ask for Mr Ballinger who deals with all fleece transactions.

R S Duncan and Co (see page 93)

A K Graupner
Corner House, Valley Road, Bradford, Yorkshire BD1 4AA   Bradford 26706

Open: Monday to Friday 09.00 to 17.00; mail order

Suppliers of yarns and wools suitable for tapestry, knitting, crochet, macramé, handweaving and rug-making—and also wool tops for spinning. Callers should make, and confirm, an appointment—otherwise business is conducted by mail. No catalogue, but free samples are available to established customers. For serious workers with yarns it is well worth while, though not necessarily easy, to become an established customer.

The Multiple Fabric Company Limited
Dudley Hill, Bradford, Yorkshire BD4 9PD   Bradford 682323

Open: Monday to Friday 08.00 to 17.00; mail order; catalogue

Mail order (*only*) suppliers of wool, mohair, camel hair and horse hair yarns for handweaving. Write or telephone for free price list and samples. Minimum order—2 kilos of any one quality of yarn.

Texere Yarns
9 Peckover Street, Bradford, Yorkshire BD1 5BD   Bradford 22191

Open: Monday to Friday 09.00 to 12.30 and 14.00 to 17.30; mail order; catalogue

Famous for all types of yarns—suitable for hand weaving, tapestry, rug-making, knitting, crochet and macramé. Also raffia, cane and lampshade-making supplies. Not a shop, incidentally, but a mail order unit with a warehouse in Bradford. You should either phone in your orders or order by post against the free sample cards which will be sent on request (minimum order of one pound).

BRENTFORD

British Wool Marketing Board
Kew Bridge House, Kew Bridge Road, Brentford, Middlesex   01 560 0551

Open: Monday to Friday 09.00 to 17.00; mail order; catalogue

Buy through the mail order catalogue. You can get raw (British only) wool for spinning—whole fleeces if you wish. Also woollen tweed fabrics and pure wool hand knitting yarns.

BRORA

T M Hunter Limited
Sutherland Wool Mills, Brora, Scotland KW9 6NA   Brora 366/7

Mail order only; catalogue

Old-established mail order supplier of yarns for handweaving and carded rovings for handspinning. Good range of colours, and they will send samples and price lists promptly on request.

BURGHEAD

Moray Firth Designs
The Harbour, Burghead, Moray, Scotland Burghead 341

Open: Monday to Friday 08.30 to 17.30; mail order

A workshop, open to visitors, where you can buy Blackface wool combings for handspinning. Also produce soft toy kits for making a teddy bear, a rabbit or a bunny. No catalogue, but if a descriptive letter is insufficient they will invoice samples.

CHEADLE

William Hall and Company (Monsall) Limited
177 Stanley Road, Cheadle Hulme, Cheadle, Cheshire SK8 6RF 061 437 3295

Mail order only; catalogue

Spinners of processed and fancy yarns in all fibres, natural and man-made—also embroidery, knitting, flax, rug and special effect yarns. Shade cards are free but you pay 25p for the Swedish linen lace yarn card. Also offer raw flax for handspinning. Probably the largest supplier of pure Swedish linen yarn in the country.

CHICHESTER

Chichester Handweavers
Oak Bank, Fordwater Road, Chichester, Sussex   Chichester 527483

Open: Any time by appointment; mail order; catalogue

Orders by post or callers by appointment, please. (A foolscap s.a.e. will bring you sample cards.) Specialist suppliers of handweaving yarns and equipment who also make handwoven goods to order. Second-hand looms (as available), spinning wheels and spindles and yarns for weaving, rug-making and hand knitting. Also short lengths of fancy yarn for embroidery and fleece for handspinning.

CLANFIELD

Crowdys Wood Products Limited
The Old Bakery, Clanfield, Oxfordshire OX8 2P   Clanfield 216

Open: Monday to Saturday 09.00 to 18.00

Primarily woodworkers who create, and sell in the shop, furniture, lamps, tableware, toys, pottery and rushwork—but they also have some handmade spinning wheels for sale and have been able to help some of the members of the Oxfordshire Guild of Weavers and Spinners by turning and creating bits and pieces for the repair of spinning wheels and looms. Will even design 'one off' pieces of furniture for weavers to incorporate original woven fabrics. No catalogue, but if you send for their card you will receive a useful map.

DORCHESTER

Frank Herring and Sons
27 High West Street, Dorchester, Dorset Dorchester 4449

Open: Monday to Saturday (excluding Thursday) 08.30 to 17.30; Thursday closed; mail order; catalogue 15p

Very large stock of art and craft materials tended by a very helpful staff. Especially strong on spinning and weaving equipment. Their catalogue is about 80 pages long, only 15p, and well worth its price. They have copper blanks, enamelling materials and kilns, lino-cutting, brass-rubbing and marquetry tools and materials, Enamelcraft and Plasticraft kits, felt, canvas, hessian, kapok eyes and noses for soft toys, trimmings, tapestry sets, potters' clays and glazes, tie-dye, batik and silk screen printing materials, perspex sheets, candle-making supplies; ample stocks of raffia, cane and basket and lampshade-making materials; modelling clays, Das, plasticine, Newclay, etc.; and, of course, an excellent stock of handweaving looms, spinning wheels and all accessories. They can also supply fleece for handspinners.

DORNOCH

Lawrys of Dornoch
Station Square, Dornoch, Sutherland
  Scotland Dornoch 525

Open: Monday to Saturday 09.30 to 18.00; mail order

Handmade sheepskin goods (rugs, mitts, etc,). Also offer a complete sheepskin-rug-making kit and pure wool for handspinning.

DURHAM

Hugh Mackay and Company Limited
Freemans Place, Durham City, County
  Durham Durham 64444

Open: Monday to Friday 09.00 to 17.00; mail order

Manufacturers of Wilton carpets (who display a 'by appointment' crest on writing paper) from whom you can buy weaving yarns in a range of approximately 300 colours. Minimum order ½ pound. Will supply by mail but don't offer a catalogue. Quality, obviously, high.

DURNESS

Balnakeil Sheepskins (see page 69)
Pure wool for handspinning

EAST PRESTON

Bradley Inkle Looms
82 North Lane, East Preston, Sussex
  Rustington 70108

Open: Any time, but 'phone or write before calling; mail order

The Bradleys work from home and make inkle looms to order. These come complete with tension adjuster and shuttles and are sent out within a week of order via British Rail. They don't have a catalogue but will send you a photograph of a loom in use if you need one. They also supply shuttles, spindles, niddy-noddys, etc. and will give lessons in inkle weaving. You will get personal attention, help and advice and a very good service.

EDINBURGH

The Edinburgh Tapestry Company Limited
Dovecot Studios, Dovecot Road, Edinburgh EH12 7LE   031 334 4118

Open: Monday to Friday 08.30 to 17.00; mail order

The Studio is not in fact a retail shop and you should order materials by post or else telephone for an appointment to call in. Suppliers of cotton twine (suitable for macramé work), warp sold on cones, and vertical tapestry looms and frames which are designed and made to order on the premises. Agents for Stuarts of Musselburgh (who prefer not to supply to individuals). Minimum order—one pound of warp.

The Weavers Workshop
Monteith House, Royal Mile, Edinburgh
  031 556 9010

Open: Monday to Saturday 09.30 to 17.30; mail order; catalogue/price sheet

The Workshop mounts exhibitions, the tapestries from which are for sale, and also has a retail wool and weaving supplies shop. They don't have a catalogue yet, but will send you a price sheet which gives a fairly clear idea of what they have to offer—yarns suitable for weaving, tapestry, rug-making, knitting, crochet and macramé, Scottish fleece for spinners and natural lichen dyes. Also spinning wheels, birchwood Finnish looms, and all the additional bits and pieces—bobbins, rug hooks, raddles, shuttles and so on. Quite happy to supply small quantities, and if you can go there you will probably learn a lot and be inspired to create nice things.

ELLAND

Samuel Lumb and Son Limited
Perseverance Mills, Elland, Yorkshire
  Elland 3434

Open: Monday to Friday 08.00 to 18.00; mail order; catalogue

Write or phone for an appointment to call in or for a set of shade cards. Here you can buy woollen yarns of heavier counts suitable for handweaving and for some types of knitting. Also wool for handspinning. Stocks vary. They are willing to supply quite small quantities if they happen to be to hand.

FRINTON-ON SEA

Frinton Handicraft and Art Centre (see page 17)

GALASHIELS

J Hyslop Bathgate Co.
Island Street, Galashiels, Selkirkshire,
  Scotland   Galashiels 2642

Open: Monday to Friday 09.00 to 17.00;
mail order

Mail order only, although they will sell
to callers. Very well know suppliers of
yarns for handloom weavers including
homespun yarn, mohair, angora, chen-
illes and worsted yarns. Also yarns suitable for knitting, crochet and macramé
and woollen and worsted yarns for
tapestries. The minimum order they will
fulfil is four ounces of yarn—which is
very reasonable.

HAWKHURST

'Harris' Looms
Northgrove Road, Hawkhurst, Kent
  TN18 4AP   Hawkhurst 3396

Open: Monday to Friday 09.00 to 17.00
Saturdays by appointment only; mail
order; catalogue

An excellent stock of handweaving looms
and large tapestry frames—also healds
and reeds, bobbin racks, shuttles etc.
Their catalogue offers a photograph of
every loom available, as well as measurements and prices. Extremely helpful.

HIGH WYCOMBE

Lervad (U.K.) Limited
18 Vernon Building, Westbourne Street,
  High Wycombe, Buckinghamshire
  High Wycombe 32561

Mail order only; catalogue

Importers of Danish beech handlooms
and accessories (threading hooks, warping
frames, reeds, etc.). Most of their looms
they regard as small—for instance, the
largest tapestry loom produces a 100 cm
width. No showroom (which they rather
regret) but they say that most people
ordering looms know what they want.
If you don't know, and really want to
see a particular loom in action, ask and
they will give you the address of a
college or school nearby which has one
(they supply a lot of educational establishments). It's then up to you to ask the
college if you may have a look.

HOLYWELL

Holywell Textile Mills
Holywell, Flintshire, Wales
  Holywell 2022

Open: Monday to Saturday 09.00 to
17.30; mail order

In the mill they create blankets, Welsh
tapestry bedcovers, tapestry tweeds and
Welsh flannel and in the Mill Showroom
you can look at and buy the products.
They will also sell pure wool yarns of
suitable weights for handknitting and
handweaving. No catalogue.

HUDDERSFIELD

Arts and Crafts (see page 20) Small
looms

HULL

Handycrafts of Hull (see page 20)
Small weaving looms

ILKLEY

Uni-dye
PO Box No 10, Ilkley, Yorkshire

Mail order only; catalogue

Manufacturers and suppliers of synthetic
dyestuffs and associated chemicals (dye
fixatives, softeners, accelerants, soda ash,
etc.). They offer special introductory
packs and every order comes with
instructions and notes on the treatment
of specific materials. Will also give advice
on all dyeing problems.

ISLE OF HARRIS

The Craft Shop
Tarbert, Isle of Harris, Outer Hebrides,
  Scotland

Open: Monday to Saturday (excluding
Thursday) 09.00 to 13.00 and 14.00 to
18.00 (during the summer months only);
mail order

This is really an outlet for craftsmen,
selling the finished product, but Mr
Glen will undertake woodturning to order
and produces custom built spinning
wheels and all accessories. No catalogue
as such, but he will send you a photograph and details of work he has produced in the past.

ITCHEN STOKE

Miss Hilary Chetwynd
Spindle Hoo, Itchen Stoke, Near Alres-
  ford, Hampshire

Mail order only; catalogue

Reliable mail order supplier of silk yarn
(minimum order two ounces) for handweaving or embroidery and silk sliver
for handspinning. Will dye silk yarn to
colour of customers' choice (minimum
of eight ounces per colour).

KEIGHLEY

Conways Arts and Crafts (see page 20)
Weaving kits

KEITH

Robert Laidlaw and Sons Limited
Seafield Mills, Keith, Banffshire, Scotland
  Keith 2261/2

Mail order only; catalogue

Woollen manufacturers who will supply, by mail, Cheviot wool yarns for handweaving and rug-making in a very good range of colours. Minimum quantity they will deal in is one pound per colour. Good discount if you buy more than ten pounds, even better discount if you buy more than forty pounds. Shade cards and details free on request (and please return the shade cards when you have finished with them).

KENDAL

Kendal Handicrafts (see page 20)   Small weaving looms

KING'S LYNN

Berol (see page 103)   Dyes

LEICESTER

Dryad (see page 22)

LIVERPOOL

Mersey Yarns
2 Staplands Road, Liverpool, Lancashire
  L14 3LL

Mail order only; catalogue 5p

Warp yarns for rug weaving, unspun flax and jute, loom cord. The price list promises cotton, 2 ply flax, 3 and 5 ply hemp, 3 and 6 ply jute, dressed flax, jute sliver, heddle twine, macramé twine, loom cord, tapestry cotton, sisal and heavy cotton.

LLANWRTYD WELLS

Cambrian Factory Limited (*Royal British Legion*)
Llanwrtyd Wells, Breconshire, Wales
  Llanwrtyd Wells 211

Open: Monday to Friday 08.15 to 17.30; Saturday 08.30 to 12.00; mail order; catalogue

Here you can buy new wool weaving yarns and they also supply raw wool for home spinning, 4 ply knitting yarns and Welsh tweeds for dressmakers. The mill shop is open to customers and extends its Saturday opening hours until 16.30 from May to September. Or there is a free catalogue available if you care to buy by post.

LLANYBYDDER

Rhydybont Mills (see page 84)   Yarns

LONDON E17

The Handweavers Studio and Gallery Limited
29 Haroldstone Road, Walthamstow,
  London E17 7AN   01 521 2281

Open: Tuesday to Saturday (excluding Thursday) 10.00 to 17.00; Thursday 10.00 to 21.00; mail order; catalogue

A relatively new venture which offers a lot to handweavers, spinners and dyers. One of the few places where you can go and choose your weaving yarns from the store, and also your natural or chemical dyes, fleece (they can supply almost any type and colour of British fleece on request), natural fibres, looms, spinning wheels and accessories. They also have macramé yarns and beads. You can hire gallery space to exhibit and sell or studio space and equipment to weave, spin or dye. You can also arrange for tuition. Valuable people to know about if you need advice, studio space, or, indeed, high quality materials and 'tools'. The nice things for sale in the gallery, and the nice atmosphere, make the trip to Walthamstow very well worthwhile.

EC1
Crafts Unlimited (see page 22)

NW3
Crafts Unlimited (see page 23)

SW10
Hobby Horse (see page 23)

W8
Crafts Unlimited (see page 24)   Spinning wheels

MIDDLESBROUGH

Boddy's Bookshop
165 Linthorpe Road, Middlesbrough,
  Yorkshire   Middlesbrough 47568

Open: Monday to Saturday (excluding Wednesday) 09.00 to 17.30; Wednesday closed; mail order catalogue

A general bookshop (with a good craft section) who also stocks looms for handweaving (and all kinds of weaving accessories—warping mills, needles, tapestry frames, etc.), spinning wheels and all the basic necessities for lace making—lace pillows, lace bobbins and Swedish linen thread.

OXFORD

Art Needlework Industries (see page 78)

PETTS WOOD

The Hand Loom Centre
59 Crest View Drive, Petts Wood, Kent
  BR5 1BX   Orpington 23016

Open: By appointment only; catalogue

Specialist supplier of handweaving and
spinning equipment and also remedial
and occupational therapy equipment.
Phone or write for catalogue and details
or to make an appointment to visit. Will
also undertake tuition and willingly give
advice on equipment and technique. The
catalogue is free—but no mail order.

ST DAVIDS

Tom Griffiths and Sons
28 High Street, St Davids, Pembrokeshire, Wales   St Davids 444

Open: Monday to Friday 09.00 to 17.30;
mail order

Have a carpet factory at Middle Hill,
Solva, and, as well as carpets, are prepared to sell weaving yarns from the
factory or the shop (above) to callers.
Will do mail order, but don't have a
catalogue.

STRATHMIGLO

Haldane and Company
Gateside, Strathmiglo, Fifeshire, Scotland   Strathmiglo 469

Open: Monday to Friday 09.00 to 17.00;
mail order; catalogue

Craftmade Scottish spinning chairs,
wheels and accessories. The chairs fold
flat for posting and the wheels arrive
dismantled in a cardboard box with instructions for assembling and a photograph of the hoped-for result. They plan
to produce a 'spinning wheel kit', can
supply machine-carded wool for spinning, and will occasionally undertake
spinning wheel repairs. Woodworkers
should note that they can sometimes
supply beech and oak offcuts.

SYSTON

Mailyarns (see page 95)   Nylostrip

TAUNTON

Yarns
21 Portland Street, Taunton, Somerset
  TA1 1UY   Taunton 86634

(Opening times not applicable); mail
order; catalogue

If you want samples, or to place an
order by telephone or by letter, use the
Taunton address above—but visitors are
welcome at the works at 37 High Street,

Wellington, Somerset, where yarns can
be selected and bought. They specialise
in handweaving, tapestry and knitting
yarns—worsteds, wools, cottons and
manmade fibres for weaving, and 2-
ply Shetland in skeins or on cones for
hand or machine knitting. And for hand
spinners, 4″ staple slivers of nylon, Courtelle, Brightfibro, terylene, cheviot and
silk (when available).

TREFNANT

Craftsman's Mark Yarns
Bronberllen,   Trefnant,   Denbighshire,
  North Wales   Trefnant 639

Mail order only; catalogue 22p

Deal almost solely by mail order. Personal callers will be made welcome, but
you should telephone for an appointment
first (and you will probably hold up
work). Suppliers of natural black, grey
and white yarns for handweaving and
wool and fleeces for handspinning. Yarns
are supplied in hank, scoured. Wool
matchings and carded roving for handspinning are available by the pound. They
also supply dyed rug yarn (in whites,
greys, blacks and brown mixtures) and
linen rug warp. The quality and service
is highly thought of by weavers. Catalogue includes samples.

TREFRIW

Trefriw Woollen Mills Limited
Trefriw, Caernarvonshire, Wales
  Llanrwst 640462

Open: Monday to Friday 07.45 to 16.45;
Saturday 10.00 to 16.00; mail order

As well as blankets, quilts and so on,
you can buy Welsh tapestry and tweed
cloth by the yard, raw wool for handspinning and yarns in weights suitable
for weaving and knitting. You can ask
to see over the mill which has the same
opening hours as the shop except that
it's closed on Saturday.

WELLING

Crafts Unlimited (see page 33)

WINSFORD

Eliza Leadbetter
Granville House, 6 Granville Street,
  Winsford, Cheshire CW7 1DP
  Winsford 52808

Open: By appointment only; mail order;
catalogue

A specialist supplier to handspinners,
weavers and dyers who also undertakes
the restoration and repair of spinning
wheels and other textile equipment; gives

lessons; sells books; and is always happy to buy or exchange dye and fibre plants and seeds. Not a shop but a studio in a house. Telephone for an appointment (at any time) or order by mail (any quantity). Full range of spinning and weaving equipment—spindles, wool and cotton handcarders, niddy-noddys, distaffs, spinning wheels and chairs and a 'learn to spin' kit complete with instruction book; Swedish floor and table looms, frame and inkle looms, raddles, reeds, shuttles, heddles and all other accessories. Also natural and chemical dyestuffs, dye and fibre plants and seeds. And a tremendous range of fibres for handspinning and yarns for handweaving. Also handturned lace bobbins and lace making thread.

YORK

Derwent Crafts (see page 35)

RUG-MAKING

Many of the general craft shops in Chapter 1 will stock what you need, but this is a craft which is very well catered for by your local 'corner wool shop'. Most of these people will sell the materials for cross-stitched and tufted rugs, sometimes in kit form and sometimes loose. The larger department stores generally have a wide range of materials for the amateur rug-maker, and it is also well worth checking the telephone directory to see if you have a Readicut Wool Shop nearby (see page 70).

In addition there are firms who specialise in supplying to rug-makers, often by mail order.

ALEXANDRIA

Anartex (see page 113) Sheepskin pieces

AYR

Northern Wool Company
22 Falkland Road, Ayr, Ayrshire KA8 8LP, Scotland Ayr 62944

Mail order only; catalogue 3½p stamp.

Mail order suppliers of thrums for home rug-making, also all sizes of rug canvas. Offer special terms to Women's Institutes, schools and other like establishments. Please send a stamp if you want samples.

DURNESS

Balnakeil Sheepskins
Durness, Sutherland, Scotland
  Durness 267

Open: Monday to Saturday 09.30 to 17.30; mail order

Sheepskin floor coverings (including fitted carpets!) handmade in any colour, size, shape or design—also full kits so that you can make a sheepskin rug at home, and pure wool for handspinning. No catalogue but they will supply by mail (a minimum order of £50 if you are buying at wholesale prices, but if you buy on retail terms there is no minimum).

HEBDEN BRIDGE

The Rug-Craft Centre
Croft Mill, Hebden Bridge, Yorkshire
  HX7 8AP Hebden Bridge 2634

Open: Monday to Friday 09.00 to 17.00; Saturday 09.30 to 12.00; mail order; catalogue

Specialist suppliers of 6-ply rug wools, weaving yarns, canvases and hessian for pile or smooth-faced rugs, canvas work, church kneelers, wall-hangings, etc. Also knitting yarns. Tremendous colour range in yarns. They offer a complete rug-making kit, kits for church kneelers and tapestry kits. Customers are very welcome to browse and ask for advice should they want it. They also provide a free catalogue and mail materials all over the world.

HEREFORD

Winivere Crafts (see page 74)

Winwood Textiles Limited
70 Commercial Road, Hereford, Herefordshire Burley Gate 291

Open: Monday to Friday 09.00 to 17.30; mail order; catalogue

Specialists in rug kits, complete with carpet thrum wool, and all rug-making requirements—squared canvas, hessian, yarns, rug hooks, etc. If you can't get in to the shop to see the large range you can order by mail from Lysle Avenue, Kidderminster, Worcestershire.

NEWPORT

Lambcraft Products
The Limes, Lilleshall, Newport, Shropshire Lilleshall 343

Mail order only; catalogue 55p

A mail order service for make-it-yourself Lambswool Rugs. For 55p you get a catalogue and sample cuttings. Order the kit, and you get bits of sheepskin in the colour or colours of your choice, adhesive and base (rubberised felt or double hessian). All you do is glue the bits of sheepskin on to the base.

OSSETT

Readicut Wool Shop
Westfield Mills, Ossett, Yorkshire
  Ossett 3651

Open: Monday to Saturday 09.00 to 17.30; mail-order (rug kits only); catalogue

Best known for their widely-advertised rug-making kits, which they will send out by mail order although, if one of their nineteen branches is near you, you can call in and choose. They also stock a comprehensive range of knitting and crochet yarns; wall-hanging and soft toy-making kits; and a certain number of haberdashery items—but to personal shoppers only, not by mail. Branches are in Barnsley, Brighton, Cambridge, Canterbury, Chatham, Clapham, Croydon, Huddersfield, Hull, Leeds, Northampton, Portsmouth, St Albans, Southampton, Wakefield, Welwyn, Wigan and York. Opening times vary from branch to branch, so check first!

WIGSTON

T Forsell and Son Limited (Ryagarn)
Blaby Road, South Wigston, Leicestershire LE8 2SG   Wigston 3095

Mail order only; catalogue

Mail order suppliers of the materials to make tufted rugs. They supply the canvas and the pure Scandinavian-style rug wool (both of which they say are also suitable for needlepoint tapestry). The wool comes in more than 50 colours, and you get instructions for making a huge variety of different rugs.

WILTON

The Weavers Shop
King Street, Wilton, Salisbury, Wiltshire
  SP2 0AY   Wilton 2441

Open: Monday to Friday 09.00 to 12.30 and 13.30 to 17.00; mail order; catalogue 10p

There is a tremendous selection of rug wools in a variety of colours at The Weavers Shop—the same wool that goes into Wilton and Axminster carpets (80% wool and 20% nylon). If you can't get there, send 5p for wool samples and price list, or 10p for the catalogue. Minimum order is half a pound of yarn.

WORCESTER

Winwood Textiles Ltd
15 New Street, Worcester, Worcestershire

Open: Monday to Saturday 09.00 to 17.30; mail order; catalogue

Specialise in rug kits and all rug-making requirements—squared canvas, hessian, yarns, rug hooks, etc. If you can't get in to the shop you can order by mail from Lysle Avenue, Kidderminster, Worcestershire.

7 Needlework

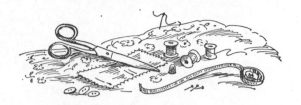

The word 'needlework' has been used to include any work that is accomplished with the aid of a needle—including needlepoint tapestry although not woven tapestry. This chapter is intended to cater for all needs from hat-making and embroidered firescreens to floor cushions, although it will not tell you where to buy ordinary fabrics, zippers, scissors and other things which are very easy to locate in any town.

Branches of John Lewis (see page 76), often trading under other names, but easily distinguished by their green and white paper bags, are excellent for all kinds of needlework supplies. There are branches in Bournemouth (Daniel Neal), Cheltenham (Daniel Neal), Cambridge (Robert Sayle), Edinburgh (John Lewis), Liverpool (George Henry Lee), London SW1 (Peters Jones), Newcastle upon Tyne (Bainbridge) (The Silk Shop), Nottingham (Jessop & Son), Reading (Heelas), Sheffield (Cole Brothers), Southampton (Tyrrell and Green), Southsea (Knight and Lee), Watford (Trewin Brothers) and Windsor (Caleys).

For ease of reference the chapter is divided into sections. The first, General, is made up of shops which stock all kinds of different needlework materials, including those dealt with more specifically in the later sections —sewing machines, fabric, felt and hessian, buttons and button covering, trimmings, upholstery, tapestry and embroidery, millinery, fillings and soft toy making.

GENERAL

ABERDEEN
The Craft Centre (see page 9)

ALEXANDRIA
Anartex (see page 113)   Kits for sheepskin gloves and mittens

ALTRINCHAM
The Handicraft Shop (see page 9)

BEDFORD
Bedford Wool Shop Limited
5/6 The Arcade, Bedford, Bedfordshire
   Bedford 55385

Open: Monday to Saturday (excluding Thursday) 09.00 to 17.30; Thursday 09.00 to 13.00; mail order; catalogue

Specialise in needlework and knitting. Can sell you canvases and tapestry wools, fur fabric, toy fillings and accessories, rug canvases and wools (and kits), Penelope tapestry and embroidery kits, a good range of knitting yarns and embroidery silks. Also suède oddments and large suède skins—and twenty-four kinds of lampshade frame and Raffene to cover them with. Very fully stocked.

BEESTON
The Handicraft Shop (see page 11)
Especially soft toy making

BISHOP AUCKLAND
Auckland Studio (see page 11)

BISHOPS STORTFORD
Galaxy (see page 12)   Embroidery kits and soft toy making materials

BOLTON
Bolton Handicrafts (see page 12)

BRADFORD
R W Copley Limited (see page 96)
Especially for upholstery work or soft toy making

BRAINTREE

Braintree Wool Shop
32/34 Rayne Road, Braintree, Essex
   Braintree 893

Open: Monday to Saturday (excluding
Thursday) 09.00 to 17.15 Thursday 09.00
to 12.30

Same stock as the main branch in Bedford—see separate entry on page 71.

BRIGHTON

Handicrafts (see page 12)

BRISTOL

Bristol Handicrafts (see page 12)

Hobbies and Crafts (see page 12)

Midland Educational (see pages 13, 11)
Soft toy making and tapestry kits

BRIXHAM

Bartlett and Cox
59/61 Bolton Street, Brixham, Devon
   TQ5 9DJ   Brixham 2131

Open: Monday to Friday (excluding
Wednesday) 09.00 to 13.00 and 14.00 to
17.30; Wednesday and Saturday 09.00 to
13.00; mail order

A needlework shop where you can buy
felt, canvas and tapestry wools, kapok,
buttons, knitting and crochet yarns, soft
toy accessories and general haberdashery
items.

BURNLEY

Northern Handicrafts Limited (see page
13)

CANTERBURY

Needlecraft and Hobbies (see page 13)

CARDIFF

Handicrafts and Dressmakers' Aids (see
page 14)

Winifred Ward Limited
11 Royal Arcade, Cardiff, Glamorganshire, Wales   Cardiff 28942

Open: Monday to Saturday (excluding
Wednesday) 08.45 to 17.30; Wednesday
08.45 to 13.00; mail order

Specialists in needlework including Penelope kits and their own embroidery
designs; wide range of embroidery fabrics and silks; felts; hessian in many
colours; kapok and synthetic stuffing
materials; accessories for soft toy making; tapestry canvases and wools, knitting
crochet and macramé yarns; lampshade
frames and raffia and, as an extra, candlemaking supplies. Will send anything
through the post except, understandably,
the lampshade frames.

CHADDERTON

Rose Mill Textiles
Rose Mill, Coalshaw Green Road, Chadderton, Lancashire   061 681 7175

Open: Monday to Saturday 09.00 to
17.00; Friday 09.00 to 13.00; Sunday
10.00 to 13.00; mail order

Very good stock of various kinds of fur
fabric—also felts, acrylic fillings, soft toy
patterns, eyes, noses and masks, hessian,
trimmings and braids and knitting yarns.
No minimum order if you call in, but
if you want goods sent by mail you must
spend £15. No catalogue.

CHEADLE

William Hall (see page 64)

CHELTENHAM

The Christmas Tree (see main entry on
page 14)

Cotswold Craft Centre
59 Little Herberts Road, Charlton Kings,
   Cheltenham, Gloucestershire

Mail order only; catalogue in return for
s.a.e.

Materials for embroidery, collage and
macramé—by mail order only. Lots and
lots of beads in all colours and most substances, sequins, tumbled gemstones in
mixed packs, embroidery yarns and cottons, metal threads, fabric remnants suitable for embroidery, collage, patchwork,
cushion covers, etc., squares of hessian,
gold and silver kid (both real and plastic),
suède pieces (sold by the square inch),
half pound bags of suède and leather offcuts, natural beeswax, net by the half
yard, acetate by the strip ($12'' \times 4''$) or
in packs of mixed colours, wood shavings
(natural and dyed) and macramé cotton
twine in several colours (5p for a shade
card).

CHIPPING CAMPDEN

The Campden Needlecraft Centre
High Street, Chipping Campden, Gloucestershire GL55 6AG

Open: Monday to Saturday (excluding
   Evesham 840583

Thursday) 09.30 to 13.00 and 14.15 to 17.30; mail order; catalogue

Stockists of fabrics, threads and wools for embroidery and tapestry work and useful materials for toy-making, collage and other needlework projects. They have evenweave linens, cottons, bincarette, gold and silver fabric and gold and silver kid, felt, hessian, Royal Paris canvases, kapok, crochet and macramé yarns, DMC wools and cottons, metallic threads and needlework and soft toy making kits. They will undertake the stretching, framing and making up of canvases and embroidery pictures, patchwork cushions and bedspreads. They offer a price list rather than a catalogue.

CHRISTCHURCH

J C Handicrafts
417a Lymington Road, Highcliffe, Christchurch, Hampshire BH23 5EN
    Highcliffe 6776

Open: Monday to Saturday (excluding Wednesday) 09.00 to 17.30; Wednesday 09.00 to 13.00; mail order

Mostly concerned with needlework and rug-making. Can supply dressmaking fabrics, felt, tapestry canvas and wools, embroidery fabrics and threads, felt, washable fillings for toys (and eyes, noses, etc.), buttons, buckles, trimmings, notions, knitting and crochet yarns, lampshade frames and coverings and canvases and wools for rug-making

CLITHEROE

Hartleys Fabrics
12 Market Place, Clitheroe, Lancashire
    Clitheroe 23346

Open: Monday to Saturday (excluding Wednesday) 09.00 to 17.00; Wednesday 09.00 to 13.00

See Skipton branch, page 85.

COLNE

The Art Shop (see page 15)

Hartleys Fabrics
John Street, Colne, Lancashire
    Colne 3222

Open: Monday to Saturday (excluding Tuesday) 09.00 to 17.00; Tuesday 09.00 to 13.00

See Skipton branch, page 85.

CONGLETON

Dortex Handcrafts
Bromley Road, Congleton, Cheshire
    Congleton 295 or 5972

Mail order only; catalogue

Will supply, by mail order only, packs of fabric oddments—either a soft furnishing fabric pack or a braid and trimmings pack—useful for cushions, lampshade trimming, toy making, etc.

COVENTRY

Midland Educational (see pages 15, 11)
Soft toy making and tapestry kits

CREWE

Arts and Crafts (see page 15)

CULLOMPTON

Crafts 'n Creations
9 Exeter Hill, Cullompton, Devon EX15 1DJ   Cullompton 3474

Open: Monday to Saturday 09.00 to 18.00; mail order; catalogue 10p

Geared to mail order, they specialise in felts, fur fabrics and accessories for soft toy making and have an extremely wide range, including kits, patterns, masks, eyes, hair, bells and stuffing materials. They also act as a dolls' hospital. They have embroidery linens, fabrics, transfers, hoops, needles and shears, threads, trimmings (including sequins and beads); tapestry kits, charts, wools, canvases and needles; crochet hooks and cottons; plastic foam sheeting, raffia, Raffene, Rotacane and basket-making kits; lampshade frames, materials, trimmings and kits; rug canvas and hessian, wools and hooks; chains, findings, stones and accessories for jewellery making; whole skins for leather-work and also leather and suède offcuts, thongs, needles, fittings and kits; moulds, paints and cold glaze for 'pottery without firing', and plaster of Paris. Roneo'd catalogue also offers books and leaflets on all the crafts catered for.

DARTFORD

Jaybee Handicrafts (see page 16)

DEWSBURY

Marc Time (see page 16)   Tapestry and soft toys

DONCASTER

Busy Bee
19/21 Netherhall Road, Doncaster, Yorkshire   Doncaster 3270

Open: Monday to Saturday (excluding Thursday) 09.00 to 17.30; Thursday 09.00 to 13.00

Chiefly concerned with art needlework,

knitting wools and general haberdashery items. They have evenweave linens, threads, felt, tailor's canvas, hessian, stuffing materials, buckles, buttons, trimmings, notions, tapestry and knitting wools, crochet and macramé yarns, rug canvases and wools, raffia, cane, lampshade frames and trimmings, basketry materials, toy kits, collage kits and macramé kits.

DORCHESTER

Frank Herring and Sons (see page 64)

EPSOM

Lindsay's Handicrafts and Decor (see page 141) Soft toy-making and curtaining

EXETER

Handicrafts and Lampshades (see page 142)

The Handicraft Shop (see page 17)

FARNWORTH

The Sewing Box
37 Market Street, Farnworth, Bolton, Lancashire Farnworth 73888

Open: Monday to Friday (excluding Wednesday) 09.15 to 17.30; Wednesday closed; Saturday 09.30 to 17.15

Mainly concerned with haberdashery items and dressmaking fabrics—but they also have felt, soft toy accessories, tapestry canvases and wools, evenweave fabrics and embroidery silks.

FRINTON-ON-SEA

Frinton Handicraft and Art Centre (see page 17) Tapestry and soft toy materials

GLASGOW

Miller's (see page 17)

FAREHAM

The Wool Shop (see page 94)

GLOSSOP

Homecrafts (see page 18)

GORSEINON

Y Gegin Fawr
77 High Street, Gorseinon, Glamorganshire, Wales Gorseinon 2651

Open: Monday to Saturday (excluding Thursday) 09.00 to 13.00 and 14.00 to 17.30; Thursday 09.00 to 13.00

Specialise in Welsh goods and offer all needlework materials for dressmaking and embroidery, including a large range of Penelope tapestry and needlework kits. Also fur fabric, Irish (!) linen, hessian, rug canvas, Welsh tapestry fabrics, kapok, haberdashery items, masks, lampshade frames and coverings and trimmings; raffia, cane and basketry supplies; mosaic tiles and powder; jewellers' tools, tumble polishing machines and copper and pewter sheeting; rubber moulds and modelling compounds. Craft materials are all mixed up with craft books, greetings cards, Welsh novelties, toys and costume jewellery and a fancy dress hire service.

GUISBOROUGH

Beecrafts (see page 18)

HARROGATE

Arts and Handicrafts (see page 18)

HEREFORD

Winivere Crafts
22 Union Street, Hereford, Herefordshire HR1 2BT Hereford 4098

Open: Monday to Saturday (excluding Thursday) 09.00 to 17.00; Thursday 09.00 to 13.00; mail order

Specialise in knitting, tapestry and rug wools and canvases, embroidery threads, linen, felt, hessian, notions (including zips for anoraks), trimmings, buttons, buckles and soft toy accessories. Also sell finished crafts. Small stock of gilt and nickel findings, some leather-working tools, fabric dyes, lampshade and candle-making kits and raffia, cane, and basket bases.

HITCHIN

Homecrafts (see page 19)

HOVE

Handicrafts (see page 19)

HUDDERSFIELD

Arts and Crafts (see page 19)

HULL

Handycrafts of Hull (see page 20)

HYTHE

Needlecraft and Hobbies (see page 20)

KEGWORTH

Kits 'n' Krafts
6 Nottingham Road, Kegworth, Derbyshire DE7 2EH   Kegworth 2876

Open: Monday to Friday (excluding Wednesday) 09.00 to 12.30 and 14.00 to 17.30; Wednesday 09.00 to 12.30; Saturday 09.00 to 12.30 and 14.00 to 16.30; mail order; catalogue in exchange for s.a.e.

Specialists in embroidery fabrics, threads, tapestry canvases, wools and Penelope kits who also have a few other craft materials. They have felt and hessian; foam, kapok and terylene fillings; trimmings, buckles, buttons, notions and soft toy accessories; yarns and twines for knitting, crochet and macramé; kits for lino-cutting and marquetry; leather and a small range of tools for working it; beads, chain, findings and copper blanks; candlemaking supplies; thrums for rugmaking; lampshade frames; raffia, seagrass, cane and basket-making materials. They will undertake picture framing, tapestry stretching and the reseating of chairs and stools with seagrass.

KEIGHLEY

Conways Arts and Crafts (see page 20)
Tapestry and soft toys

Spinning Jenny
Bradley, Keighley, Yorkshire BD20 9DD
   Cross Hills 32469

Open: Monday to Friday (excluding Thursday) 09.00 to 17.00; Thursday closed; Saturday 14.00 to 17.00; mail order; catalogue in return for s.a.e.

Specialists in tapestry, embroidery, soft furnishings and upholstery fabrics, and will make up soft furnishings to customers' own specifications. Ring before calling because if both the Whitakers are out on furnishing work the showroom will be closed. Stockists of tapestry and crewel wools suitable for all kinds of canvas work, including needlemade rugs, the canvases themselves, silk embroidery threads (and also gold and silver threads), all kinds of needles and tacks (including upholstery skewers, gimp pins and so on), a very wide range of upholstery and embroidery fabrics and parcels of fabric pieces (no piece less than 18" × 48") for £2.47 post paid for those who can't manage a visit to look through the rummage baskets. Also tapestry and embroidery kits and relevant books.

KENDAL

Kendal Handicrafts (see page 20) Soft toy and tapestry kits

KIDDERMINSTER

Arts and Crafts (see page 20)

LANCASTER

Leisure Crafts (see page 21) Felt and tapestry

LEEDS

E J Arnold and Son (see page 21)

Headrow Gallery (see page 21)
Strongest on soft toy making

LEICESTER

Dryad (see page 22)

Midland Educational (see pages 22, 11)
Soft toy making and tapestry kits

LONDON N9

The Art and Craft Centre (see page 23)

SW1

Watts and Company Limited
7 Tufton Street, London SW1 P3QB
   01 222 7169

Open: Monday to Friday 09.30 to 17.00; mail order

Probably best known as church furnishers and suppliers of Victorian wallpapers and fabrics. They are ecclesiastical embroiderers, craftsmen who will make up gold, silver and brassware to customers' own specifications, designers and suppliers of woodwork who will repair antique furniture, specialists in the carving of coats of arms who have their own workrooms on the premises where embroidery, metal and antiques are all repaired. They also sell a great range of fringes, braids, cords, tassels and Victorian fabrics. You can even get hessian and kapok here. No minimum order, and they will supply you by mail.

SW3

Harrods
Brompton Road, London SW3
   01 730 1234

Open: Monday to Saturday (excluding Wednesday) 09.00 to 17.00; Wednesday 09.00 to 19.00; mail order

Harrods has always claimed that it can supply anyone with anything—from a funeral to an elephant—so I see no reason why you shouldn't put them to work on the odd tjanting, handweaving loom or raw fleece. But among the things regularly stocked are various craft kits and accessories, especially for kiln enamelling and candlemaking (go to the Toy

Department). And like most large stores they can offer fabrics, trimmings, haberdashery items, knitting wools and, in their needlework department, a good range of tapestry and embroidery fabrics, wools, threads, kits and accessories.

SW11
Leisure Crafts (see page 23)

SW17
Homecraft Supplies (see page 24)

W1
Bourne and Hollingsworth
Oxford Street, London W1　01 636 1515

Open: Monday to Saturday (excluding Thursday) 09.30 to 18.00; Thursday 09.30 to 20.00; mail order

As a large department store, they are able to offer a very wide range of dress and furnishing fabrics. They also have a well-stocked haberdashery counter (at which you can make enquiries about their button-holing and belt-covering services) and knitting and crochet yarns in the wool department.

W1
Louis Grossé Limited
36 Manchester Street, London W1
　01 486 9802

Open: Monday to Friday 09.00 to 17.00; mail order; catalogue

Specialists in church fabrics and vestments which means they can offer a wonderful array of fabrics, trimmings and even gold and silver kid. The list sounds rich and luxuriant—Japanese gold and silver threads, metal threads, embroidery threads, red and green wet look leather, gold, silver and lurex cords, rayon cords, hand woven fringes in rayon or pure silk, rayon or silk tassels, brocades, damasks, velvet and velours, lurex, interlinings, linens and terylenes. They say they will weave, make or produce other lines on request. Their bundles of remnants cost £1, £2 or £3. You can have linings only, or fabrics, modern or traditional. For embroiderers they also have instruction booklets from the Embroiderers' Guild.

W1
John Lewis
Oxford Street, London W1A 1EX
　01 629 7711

Open: Monday to Friday (excluding Thursday) 09.00 to 17.30; Thursday 09.00 to 20.00; Saturday 09.00 to 13.00; mail order

Fifteen branches of the John Lewis Partnership (not always called John Lewis see page 71) stock some handicraft materials. They have, of course, a wide range of furnishing and dress fabrics (including fur fabric) and, like most large stores, haberdashery items (zips and scissors), trimmings, wools, buttons, buckles etc. But they also have soft toy kits, felt, kapok, eyes on stalks and plastic noses, raffia and lots of lampshade frames (and suitable covering materials and trimmings), rug-making canvases, wools and needles—mostly in the needlework, knitting and trimming departments. But ask if you get lost.

W1
The Needlewoman Shop
146/148 Regent Street, London W1
　01 734 1727

Open: Monday to Friday 09.00 to 17.30; Saturday 09.00 to 13.00; mail order; catalogue 20p

The Needlewoman Shop says it is 'for those who embroider, crochet, knit or sew', which about sums it up. They have Penelope embroidery packs, traced panels and cushion covers from Sweden supplied complete with threads and instructions, Danish folk designs, counted and cross stitch embroidery and tableware ready to embroider. Also evenweave and embroidery fabrics, all kinds of embroidery threads, sewing accessories (baskets, needles, scissors, etc.), a lot of books, kits for soft toy making and also separate bits and pieces, macramé boards, books and twine, knitting accessories, patterns and wools, everything necessary for needlework tapestry in a great many different designs, and cross-stitch rug and cushion kits. Also some unexpected odds and ends, like a candle-making kit, two marquetry kits, a plastic embedding kit and everything you need for Indian bead loom weaving (including natural beeswax by the block, which has other applications in craftwork). If you want mail order service you must spend £3.00, but if you go to the shop you can spend what you like.

W1
Selfridges (see page 24)

LOUGHBOROUGH
Artcraft and Do-It-Yourself (see page 25)

LYTHAM
Lytham Woodcraft Limited (see page 25)

MAIDSTONE
The Workbasket
82 Bank Street, Maidstone, Kent
　Maidstone 53098

Open: Monday to Saturday (excluding Wednesday) 09.00 to 17.30; Wednesday 09.00 to 13.00

The place to go for embroidery linens and silks, tapestry canvases and wools, felt, and also lampshade frames, Raffene, rug-making materials and yarns for hand knitting and crochet.

MANCHESTER

Fred Aldous (see page 25)

Arts and Crafts
120/122 Elliott Street, Tyldesley, Manchester, Lancashire M29 8FJ
Atherton 2017

Open: Monday to Friday (excluding Wednesday) 09.00 to 18.00; Wednesday 09.00 to 13.00; Saturday 09.00 to 17.00

At the moment the shop specialises in dressmaking fabrics, felt, canvas, hessian, kapok, buttons, buckles, trimmings, general haberdashery items, needlepoint tapestry materials, macramé yarns and soft toy accessories with a certain amount in the way of leather offcuts, beads and lampshade frames—but the plan is to expand the range to take in basketry materials, marquetry and anything else in which customers show an interest.

MIDDLESBROUGH

J Goldstein and Son (see page 26) Felts, trimmings and soft toy materials

MORPETH

Tallantyre Wallpapers (see page 26)
Felts and stuffing materials

NELSON

J W Coates and Co Limited
Albert Street Warehouse, Nelson, Lancashire Nelson 65577

Mail order only; catalogue

Coates offer remnant parcels at 'straight-from-the-factory prices'. Some of the pieces are quite large (skirt and dress lengths, for instance) and all are offered with a 'money back if not satisfied' guarantee. They have suitings, tweeds, Winceyette, taffeta, tartan, Crimplene, sailcloth, corduroy, nylons of various kinds, jersey, drill, net, felt, cotton, towelling, linen, furnishing fabrics, and a lot more. You can also buy threads, scissors, pins, hooks and eyes, binding, trimmings, ribbons and needles far more cheaply than in most haberdashery departments.

Walter Thomason Sewing Centre Limited
43 Scotland Road, Nelson, Lancashire
Nelson 62122

Open: Monday to Saturday (excluding Tuesday) 09.00 to 18.00; Tuesday 09.00 to 12.30; mail order; catalogue

Stock domestic sewing machines (and will undertake their repair), fashion fabrics, piece goods and remnants, and most haberdashery items. Often have bargain lines for sale by mail or on the spot—synthetic fabric lengths, ribbons, lace edgings, and Nytrim (for knitting or crocheting into shopping bags, bath mats etc.) in bumper bundles of assorted colours.

NEW ASH GREEN

The Hobby House (see page 26)

NEWCASTLE UPON TYNE

Ashbourton Gifts and Crafts (see page 27)

The Do it Yourself Foam Centre (see page 27)

Thomas Hunter Limited
16 Saville Row, Newcastle upon Tyne,
Northumberland
Newcastle upon Tyne 27056

Open: Monday to Saturday (excluding Thursday) 09.00 to 17.30; Thursday 09.00 to 18.30; mail order

Specialists in hand knitting and art needlework supplies (including a very large range of tapestries). Can supply all the materials necessary for art needlework, knitting, crochet, macramé, soft toy making, rug-making and lampshade making. Embroidery fabrics, felt, canvas, hessian, kapok, buttons, buckles, trimmings, beads, notions, yarns and twines, eyes for soft toys, frames and fabrics for lampshades, etc. Very old established firm. Do not do mail order as such, but will send out parcels of materials to any value so long as you pay postage and packing.

NEWTON STEWART

Country Crafts (see page 27)

NORTHAMPTON

Abingdon Handicrafts (see page 27)

Arts and Crafts Shop (see page 28)

Midland Educational (see pages 28, 11)
Soft toy making and tapestry kits, mainly

NORTHWICH

Country Crafts (see page 28)

NOTTINGHAM

John Lees of Nottingham
216/217 Drury Walk, Broadmoor Centre,
Nottingham, Nottinghamshire
Nottingham 50906

Open: Monday to Saturday (excluding Thursday) 09.00 to 17.30; Thursday closed

Same stock as the Bedford Wool Shop (who recently took them over) see page 00. The only difference is that John Lees do not stock lampshade materials but are especially hot on rug-making with plenty of carpet thrums and loose cut thrums.

OLDHAM

The Art and Craft Shop (see page 28)
Soft toys and tapestry

OXFORD

Art Needlework Industries Limited
7 St Michael's Mansions, Ship Street, Oxford, Oxfordshire

Open: Monday to Saturday (excluding Thursday) 08.45 to 16.45; Thursday 08.45 to 12.30; mail order; catalogue 50p

If you are concerned with knitting, spinning, weaving, tapestry, macramé, rug-making or embroidery you should investigate the incredible range of materials offered by these people—who will also advise, inform and offer booklists and leaflets on the history and development of all these crafts. All materials are natural (no synthetic fibres or mixtures). They have opened a new department for macramé which stocks all weights and types of cord. They have truly beautiful wools in all weights, an unbelievable range of colours and very high quality for knitting, crochet and tapestry; they have natural yarns for weaving; fleece for hand spinning; rug-making canvases, wools and rug kits; linen embroidery materials; and a tremendous range of ideas for tapestries together with the materials to carry them out. The emphasis is on natural materials and traditional (and sometimes highly complex) designs.

PERTH

Dunn's Art Stores (see page 29)

PORTHCAWL

Fabrics Galore
24 New Road, Porthcawl, Glamorganshire, Wales

Open: Monday to Saturday 09.00 to 17.45; mail order

Wide range of dress fabrics—also beads, trimmings, buttons, buckles, notions, knitting and crochet yarns, felt and the accessories for soft toy making. Will supply by mail order, but don't have a catalogue.

PORT TALBOT

Cliffords (Port Talbot)
5/9a Cwmavon Road, Port Talbot, Glamorganshire, Wales   Port Talbot 2321

Open: Monday to Saturday (excluding Thursday) 09.00 to 17.30; Thursday 09.00 to 13.00

Sewing and knitting machine specialists who sell materials for most of the armchair crafts—felt, canvas, kapok, buttons, buckles, trimmings, tapestry canvases and wools, knitting, crochet and macramé yarns, soft toy accessories, lampshade frames, raffia, cane, basketry supplies, and also kits for embroidery, collage, soft toy making, tapestry and rug-making.

PRESCOT

The Art Shop (see page 29)

PRESTON

The Arts and Crafts Shop (see page 29)
Soft toys and tapestry

RICHMOND

Richmond Art and Craft (see page 30)

ST ANNES ON SEA

The Handmaiden (see page 30)

SALFORD

J & A Forrester
384a Great Cheetham Street East, Salford, Lancashire M7 OUH   Salford 3440

Mail order only; catalogue

Mail order suppliers of a tremendous range of zip fasteners, metal and nylon, long, medium and short, in lots of colours. Also buttons—polyester coloured buttons, imitation leather football buttons, blazer buttons and anchor buttons in 'gold' and 'silver', medallion buttons and dome buttons. And braid—heavy gold, black and white, royal and red. And Sylko sewing thread in all colours, elastic, bias binding, Petersham, press studs, hooks and eyes, tape measures, straight pins, curtain hooks, and gold and silver lurex threads. Minimum order £2.00, and if you buy from the 'clearing line' list you have to take up to 50 assorted zips in whatever colours you are given.

SALISBURY

Mace and Nairn (see page 99)

SHREWSBURY

W M Freeman (see page 30) Chiefly soft toy making

SOLIHULL

Midland Educational (see page 31) Soft toy making and tapestry kits

SOUTHAMPTON

Betty Veal
Waterloo Buildings, London Road, Southampton, Hampshire
Southampton 22010

Open: Monday to Saturday 09.00 to 17.30; mail order

Specialists in materials for tapestry and embroidery, rug-making, knitting and crochet. They will mount tapestry and embroidery pictures and panels and cushions and make up handbags. They have tapestry, embroidery, collage, and rug-making kits; all grades of embroidery fabrics from coarse to fine, felt, hessian, tapestry canvas, threads and wools, knitting yarns, crochet cotton, rug canvases and wools. No catalogue

STONEHAVEN

Christine Riley
53 Barclay Street, Stonehaven, Kincardineshire, Scotland   Stonehaven 3238

Open: Monday to Saturday (excluding Wednesday) 10.00 to 17.30; Wednesday 10.00 to 13.00; mail order; catalogue

Everything (fabrics, threads, books etc.) connected with needlework and embroidery. You should really call in or send for the price list to understand the full extent of the stock—canvas, tapestry wools, Glenshee fabrics, hessian, felt; a tremendous range of threads and silks including Retors d'Alsace for lace-making; crochet cotton which is also suitable for tatting and lace making; gold, silver and metal thread and cord; and also books, charts, transfers, needles, thimbles, embroidery frames, beads, sequins, wooden lace bobbins and washable stuffings for soft toys. Especially wide range of colours and types of embroidery silks and tapestry wools.

STRATFORD-UPON-AVON

Midland Educational (see page 31)
Soft toy making and tapestry kits

STROUD

The Christmas Tree (see page 31)

STURMINSTER NEWTON

Clarkes Handicraft Supplies (see page 31)
Soft toys and tapestry

SUDBURY

Art and Craft Shop (see page 31)

SWANSEA

Arts and Crafts (see page 32)

Homecrafts
10 Victoria Avenue, Swansea, Glamorganshire, Wales   Swansea 52297

Open: Monday to Saturday 09.00 to 17.30; mail order

Can sell you most of the things you need for sewing, knitting, tapestry or embroidery—machine embroidery threads, lurex threads, knitting wools, tapestry canvases and wools, soft toy accessories, knitting and tapestry kits. They also sell and repair sewing machines and can offer a certain amount of raffia, some seashells and Das modelling clay.

TAUNTON

The Spinning Wheel
22 Billet Street, Taunton, Somerset
Taunton 3094

Open: Monday to Saturday (excluding Thursday) 09.15 to 13.00 and 14.15 to 17.30; Thursday closed; mail order

Primarily a needlework shop, although the proprietor says she will give advice on all crafts (and will also stretch tapestries and embroideries). She has embroidery and tapestry fabrics and canvases, threads, silks and wools; lampshade frames, raffia, covering fabrics, braids and fringes; macramé yarns; felt, Nu-stuffing and soft toy accessories and kits; and also embroidery, tapestry and marquetry packs.

TELFORD

The Wool Shop (see page 95)

THORNBURY

Arts and crafts (see page 32)

TOTNES

Dart Handicrafts
66 High Street, Totnes, Devon
Totnes 2828

Open: Monday to Saturday (excluding Thursday) 09.30 to 17.30; Thursday 09.30 to 13.00; mail order; catalogue

Chiefly needlework materials—furnishing

remnants, felt, canvas and tapestry wools, trimmings, knitting and crochet wools, cotton stuffing, notions, eyes and noses for teddy bears and rug-making packs. But also balsa wood aircraft kits, Plastercraft and Plasticraft, marquetry kits, raffia, cane and lampshade frames.

TRURO

The Hobby House (see page 33)

WALSALL

Make and Mend
64 Princes Street, Chase Terrace, Walsall, Staffordshire   Leacroft 253

Open: Monday to Saturday (excluding Thursday) 09.00 to 17.30; Thursday closed

A needlework shop which has begun to stock handicraft materials (and hopes to extend the handicraft side if local demand warrants it). Dress and lightweight tweed fabrics, felt, canvas, hessian, kapok, buttons, buckles, trimmings, soft toy accessories, rug-making equipment, lampshade frames and covering fabrics. Also kits for tapestry panels and pictures, embroidery and collage, rug-making, and wall hangings, and cushion-making packs.

WARE

Fresew
58a High Street, Ware, Hertfordshire   Ware 61164

Open: Monday to Saturday (excluding Thursday) 09.00 to 17.30; Thursday 09.00 to 13.00; mail order; catalogue

Embroidery and needlepoint tapestry specialists who will undertake the covering of buttons and also give talks on 'creative embroidery', with slides, within a limited area (fees and dates by arrangement). They do have embroidery and tapestry kits, but also evenweave fabrics, linens, embroidery and tapestry canvases; threads (natural and synthetic) including lurex thread, embroidery cotton, crewel and tapisserie wools; accessories such as needles, thimbles, tapestry frames and so on; felt, hessian, crash, wadding and kapok mixture, soft toy accessories; haberdashery items like bias and seam binding, elastic, Petersham, buttons, hooks and eyes; and trimmings such as braid, metallic cord, bugle beads, rocaille, pearls, sequins and wooden and plastic beads. Also crochet and macramé yarns, Raffene, lampshade frames and trimmings, tie-dye and batik materials. Catalogue is free but please send postage.

WELLINGBOROUGH

Happicraft (see page 33)   Tapestry kits and soft toy making

WELLINGTON

New Age Handicraft Centre (see page 33)

WELWYN GARDEN CITY

Boon Gallery (see page 34)   Especially toy making

WICKFORD

Homecrafts
24 London Road, Wickford, Essex   Wickford 5387

Open: Monday to Friday (excluding Wednesday) 09.00 to 13.30 and 14.30 to 17.30; Wednesday 09.00 to 13.30; Saturday 09.00 to 17.30

Specialists in 'soft crafts' who sell knitting and crochet yarns, embroidery and tapestry materials, felt, soft toy accessories and fillings (kapok, acrylic and polyester), buttons, buckles and notions.

WIRRAL

Arts and Crafts (see page 34)

WOLVERHAMPTON

Midland Educational (see pages 34, 11) Soft toy making and tapestry kits

WOOLER

Glendale Crafts
10 Church Street, Wooler, Northumberland   Wooler 682

Open: Monday to Saturday 10.00 to 19.30; mail order

Agents for button and buckle covering who can offer quite a lot to the needleworker—dressmaking and furnishing fabrics, felt, canvas, hessian, various stuffing materials, buttons and buckles (of course), trimmings, soft toy accessories, tapestry kits, and rug-making equipment and wools. Also semi-precious and imitation stones; leather offcuts and tools; veneers for marquetry and mouldings for picture framing; raffia, cane and basketry materials; lampshade frames, raffia, Raffene, fabrics, trimmings and so on—and seashells.

WORCESTER

Midland Educational (see page 34) Soft toy making and tapestry kits

WORKINGTON

Kathleen Davies (Crafts)
45c South William Street, Workington,
Cumberland   Workington 3322

Open: Monday to Saturday (excluding
Thursday) 09.30 to 12.30 and 13.30 to
17.15; Thursday closed

Kathleen Davies specialises in all forms
of needlecrafts and is willing and able
to give advice. Stock includes felt, canvas,
hessian, foam, kapok, buttons, buckles,
beads, trimmings and ribbons, notions,
tapestry canvases and wools, soft toy
accessories, knitting, crochet and macramé yarns. Also marquetry and candlemaking supplies, lampshade frames,
fabrics and fringes, various kinds of
raffias, canes and basket bases.

YEOVIL

Draytons Decorations (see page 34)

SEWING MACHINES

There are shops selling sewing machines all over the country. Most of the
major 'makes' have retail outlets in
each town, and most large department
stores stock (and possibly demonstrate) machines as well. Look in the
yellow pages under 'Sewing machines—retail and repairs'. Always try to
buy a machine from a specialist re-
tailer near at hand because that way
you get better after-sales service.
  If you are stuck, most of the major
sewing machine manufacturers offer
a consumer advisory service. Contact
them and they will tell you where your
nearest stockist is, how to go about
buying new needles and other replacement parts, and where to get your
machine repaired or serviced. Here's
whom to contact:

Bernina Sewing Machines
50/52 Great Sutton Street, London EC1
01 253 1198

Also have a small shop in Swiss Centre,
Leicester Square, London WC2 where
they offer tuition to new owners and
advice to prospective customers, but they
don't sell machines. All sales go through
their stockists.

Elna Sewing Machines (GB) Limited
Queens House, 180/182 Tottenham
Court Road, London W1P 0HY
01 323 1187

Will give you addresses of stockists and
information on how to sew certain
fabrics, how to achieve particular results
on an Elna machine, etc. If you already
have an Elna machine you can call at
the above address for free lessons from
Tuesday to Friday each week. If you
are thinking of buying a machine a
demonstration will be arranged.

Jones Sewing Machine Company Limited
Shepley Street, Guide Bridge, Audenshaw, Manchester, Lancashire
061 330 6531

Sell through major department stores and
specialist retailers where tuition and
advice are always available. Apply to
the above address for your nearest stockist. Also make knitting machines (see
relevant chapter).

Necchi (Great Britain) Limited
Titchfield House, 69/85 Tabernacle
Street, London EC2   01 253 2402

Will tell you where their accredited
stockists are, where to get spare parts,
etc. Run training schemes for their dealers, mechanics and demonstrators.

Pfaff (Britain) Limited
Domestic Street Industrial Estate, 22
Croydon Street, Leeds LS11 9RT
Leeds 20645/6

Will give you addresses of stockists,
demonstrations and after-sales service and
also offer a mail order service for replacement needles, bobbins, etc.

Singer Company (UK) Limited
Consumer Products Division, 255 High
Street, Guildford, Surrey GU1 3DH
Guildford 71144

There are 300 Singer shops in Britain,
but you can discover your nearest from
the address above. They have new and
second-hand machines and they will
arrange for lessons on a particular
machine and for dressmaking lessons.
Many of the Singer shops are also
fabric centres and sell threads, needles,
scissors, etc. Also, you can contact the
Fashion Advisor at the above address
(Guildford 33221) who will help with
sewing and fashion problems.

Toyota
Alfran Limited, Unit 32, Rich Industrial
Estate, Crayford Road, Crayford, Kent
Crayford 22256/7

Will send addresses of nearest stockists
and also useful leaflets. Do knitting
machines as well (see relevant chapter).

FABRIC

Every town has a shop or shops specialising in fabrics—dressmaking fabrics, upholstery fabrics, soft furnishing fabrics or whatever. It would be an impossible task to list them all. So the people listed here are the unusual suppliers you might not know about—people who can supply Welsh tapestry fabrics, Scottish tweeds, exotic materials or, at the other end of the scale, people who sell oddments for dolls' dresses or patchwork, and mills which sell direct to the public at low cost, generally by mail order.

As most suppliers listed deal by mail order, it is well worth reading the whole section.

AMMANFORD

Cwmllwchwr Mills
Ammanford, Carmarthenshire, Wales
Ammanford 2503

Open: Monday to Friday 08.00 to 16.45; mail order

Will supply by mail, but you can visit the mill and buy direct—which is more interesting. Mainly concerned with producing Welsh woollen tapestry quilts and cloth, but they will also sell wool yarns for knitting and handweaving.

BARNOLDSWICK

Hartleys Fabrics
41 Albert Road, Barnoldswick, Yorkshire
Barnoldswick 3083

Open: Monday to Saturday (excluding Tuesday) 09.00 to 17.00; Tuesday 09.00 to 13.00

See Skipton branch, page 85.

BENBECULA

D Macgillivray and Company
Muir of Aird, Benbecula, Outer Hebrides, Scotland   Benbecula 304

Open: Monday to Saturday 09.00 to 18.00 (and until 22.00 in the summer months); mail order; catalogue 3½p

Primarily suppliers of ready-made clothes, they also make and knit clothes to order in the size and style you choose. But they sell fabric lengths, too—Harris tweeds, tartans, suitings and dress fabrics. Not only Harris tweed manufacturers but also distributors for the Hebridean Crofter Weavers, so you can buy Scottish fabrics at a reasonable price and support cottage industry at the same time, which is important. Money back 'quality' guarantee on all purchases—but it is unlikely they would ever be asked to keep that promise.

BRADFORD

R S Duncan and Co (see page 93)
Tweeds by the yard

Kiwi Wool Company (see page 93)
Tweed and polyester

BRIGHOUSE

Marsland Textiles
Jubilee Mount, Brighouse, Yorkshire HD6 3BY   Brighouse 4935

Mail order only; catalogue 25p

Mail order suppliers of dressmaking fabrics, both wholesale and retail. There's a £50 minimum quantity stipulated on wholesale orders, but no minimum for retail. Specialise in Crimplene, synthetics and Yorkshire tweeds but can also sell you bargain packs of remnants—some large enough for children's clothes, some small for patchwork or toymaking. Also zips and thread. The 25p for the catalogue is deducted from the total of your first order.

DINAS MAWDDWY

Merion Mill Shop (see page 94)   Welsh tapestry cloth

DYSERTH

Pandy Garments
Pandy, Dyserth, Flintshire   Dyserth 240

Open: Monday to Friday 09.30 to 17.00; Saturday 09.00 to 12.30; mail order

A cottage industry specialising in wool tweeds, and in leather and fur trimmed garments. But you can also buy Welsh tapestry for home sewing, in person or by mail.

FISHGUARD

Workshop
Lower Town, Fishguard, Pembrokeshire, Wales   Fishguard 2261

Open: Seven days a week from 10.00 to 18.00 from Easter to mid-October; mail order; catalogue

The place to go if you want to see what is probably the largest variety of finished craft products under one roof in the whole of Wales. But perhaps of more interest to home craftsmen is the variety of Welsh woollen fabrics. You can buy half a yard, a skirt length, or as much more as you can afford and carry.

GADDESBY

Patricia Ann Fabrics
3 Barrow Crescent, Gaddesby, Leicestershire

Mail order only; catalogue

Mail order supplier of fabrics suitable for flower-making, collage work and soft toys—nylon velvet, brushed nylon and locknit nylon, and also nylon fillings. Samples and lists are free on request.

GALASHIELS

Abbotsford Mills
Huddersfield Street, Galashiels, Selkirkshire, Scotland   Galashiels 3364

Open: Monday to Friday 09.00 to 17.15; Saturday 10.00 to 16.30; mail order

If you are in the area you can buy woollen furnishing and fashion fabrics direct from the mill at straight-from-the-mill prices—also yarns suitable for hand-weaving and knitting. They will send orders (any quantity) but don't offer a catalogue so, unless you call in, making your selection will not be easy.

HASLEMERE

B Shew
Two Ways, Hedgehog Lane, Haslemere, Surrey

Mail order only

A small supplier of cotton patchwork hexagons at 10p for 50. Stocks fluctuate, but an order will be fulfilled if at all possible.

HAVERFORDWEST

Tregwynt Woollen Mill
Tregwynt Factory, Letterston, Haverfordwest, Pembrokeshire, Wales
St Nicholas 225

Open: Monday to Friday 09.00 to 17.00; mail order

The Mill Shop sells gifts, Welsh tapestry bedcovers, clothes made from Welsh wools and so on—but they also deal in Welsh woollen materials, and they don't stipulate a minimum quantity. Although they will supply by mail they don't have a catalogue.

HOLYWELL

Holywell Textile Mills (see page 00)
Welsh tapestry cloth and tweeds

HUDDERSFIELD

Pennine Textiles
Bridge Lane, Holmfirth, Huddersfield, Yorkshire HD7 1AN

Mail order only; catalogue 3½p

Mail order suppliers of Yorkshire woollens and worsteds at straight-from-the-mill prices. Also Crimplene, brushed denim and nylon. Send a stamp for a set of patterns, and state which fabric you are after.

KEIGHLEY

Fashion Fabrics Limited
PO Box 27, Keighley, Yorkshire

Mail order only; catalogue

Offer Crimplene and jersey dress fabrics for home sewing, by mail order only. Reasonable prices—catalogue free.

KIRKBURTON

Willie Shaw
7 Cinder Hill, Kirkburton, Near Huddersfield, Yorkshire (Telephone to be installed)

Mail order only; catalogue

Mail order suppliers of felts and fur fabrics (minimum quantity ¼ of a yard, which is a very reasonable offer!). They have wool fur fabrics, mohair, poodle cloth, short and deep pile nylon fur fabrics, long haired acrilan, and wool felts, all in various colours. Also two pounds' worth (in weight) of mixed fur fabric strips.

LEIGH

The Mill Shop
Mill Lane Textiles Limited, 161 Chapel Street, Leigh, Lancashire   Leigh 3242

Open: Monday to Friday (excluding Wednesday) 09.00 to 17.00; Wednesday 09.00 to 13.00; Saturday 09.00 to 16.00; mail order; catalogue

Manufacturers and suppliers of dressmaking fabrics (mostly man-made) and bonded brushed nylon furnishing fabrics, vinyls for seat covers, etc. Often have bargain parcels of remnants available at about £5.00 a time. Will send free samples on request and are happy to fulfil small orders.

LINGFIELD

Annette Stirling
12 Orchard Cottages, St Piers Lane, Lingfield, Surrey   Lingfield 2125

Mail order only; catalogue in exchange for s.a.e.

An unusual mail order service which aims to offer materials for children to use creatively in packs designed for individual children—or in special sizes and at special rates for schools or groups. And adults find the packs invaluable for doll-dressing and even home-dressmaking. The Pretty Pack has ribbons, sequins, braid and lace. Fancy Dress Packs have filmy materials and large sequins and the Fairy Wings Pack includes bands to hold the wing tips to the fingers. There is also a collage pack and a pre-Christmas pack designed to give children ideas and materials to make presents.

LLANDYSSUL

John Jones Limited
Derw Mills, Pentrecwrt, Llandyssul, Cardiganshire, Wales　Llandyssul 3361

Open: Monday to Saturday 09.30 to 17.30

Call at the mill shop for gift sets of tapestry table mats and hand made clothes—or for pure new wool Welsh tapestry cloth and worsted flannel.

LLANTWRTYD WELLS

Cambrian Factory Limited (see page 67)
Welsh tweeds

LLANYBYDDER

Rhydybont Mills
Llanybydder, Carmarthenshire, Wales　Llanybydder 285

Open: Monday to Friday 09.00 to 16.00; mail order; catalogue in preparation

Weavers of 100% wool Welsh tapestry cloth which they sell by the yard from the mill shop or make up into garments by order. They also sell yarns suitable for knitting and handweaving—in small quantities if you wish it. Everything direct from the mill.

LONDON E1

Pater Textiles Limited
Rampart Street, London E1 2LD
　01 790 1937

Mail order only; catalogue

Claim to be the largest 'direct to cus-tomer' mail order textile service in the country. They buy from the mills and you buy from them. Fashion fabrics of all kinds, soft furnishings, simulated furs, mock leathers and suèdes.

NW1

D Cutler Limited
271 Eversholt Street, London NW1 1BA
　01 387 1312

Open: Monday to Friday 09.00 to 16.00; Saturday 09.00 to 12.00; mail order; catalogue

Manufacturers and wholesalers of chil-drens' clothes who sell fabrics and rem-nants of fabrics (mostly man-made) at rock bottom prices. They have Crimplene, brushed and woven nylon, cotton prints, polyester cotton and taffeta. They will deal by mail, but if it's light clothing materials you are after you're more likely to pick up a bargain if you call in.

NW3

Emil Adler
23 Hillfield Court, London NW3
　01 794 2082

Open: Monday to Friday 09.30 to 17.00; mail order

The shop in Mortimer Street has been sold, but if you telephone Mr Adler at his home address (above) he will arrange an appointment for you to call. He still deals in cotton, cambrics and fine silks and will supply by mail if you can't get along there.

W1

S Borovick and Company
16 Berwick Street, London W1
　01 437 0520

Open: Monday to Friday 09.00 to 17.00
This is where you go for exotic and unusual materials—things like silks, vel-vets, metallised fabrics. Definitely for after-6 wear!

Dace Textiles and Company
Bolsover House, 5/6 Clipstone Street, London W1P 7EB　01 323 1249

Open: Monday to Friday 09.00 to 17.00; mail order; catalogue

Synthetic fur and fleecy fabrics in at least twelve colours (subject to avail-ability). Will do small quantities. Callers very welcome, but they're mainly geared to mail order and will send you a card of sample clippings and a promise that if you are not satisfied with your order when it arrives they will exchange it for the money you paid.

Kantex (Fabrics) Limited
22 Rathbone Place, Off Oxford Street, London W1P 1DF　01 580 6910

Open: Monday to Friday 09.30 to 17.30; Saturday closed

Suppliers of unprimed artists' canvas in pure linen; also natural flax, cotton duck and natural hessian. Paper backed hes-sian for wall coverings.

Liberty and Company Limited
Regent Street, London W1R 6AH
　01 734 1234

Open: Monday to Saturday (excluding Thursday) 09.00 to 17.00; Thursday 09.00 to 19.00; mail order

Although they are not suppliers of craft materials, Liberty cannot be left out of the needlework chapter because of the famous Liberty Printed Fabrics—Liberty Printed Varuna Wool, Tana Lawn, Worsted Wool and Lantana (50% cotton and 50% wool).

MANCHESTER

Donald B Shaw Limited
2 Beaver Street, Manchester M1 6NA
    061 236 1700

Open: Monday to Friday 09.00 to 16.00; mail order; catalogue

Textile manufacturers who create down-proof cambric, cassock and surplice materials and cotton poplins. They will deal with small orders—chiefly by post—and often have materials left over from export orders which are perfect but very cheap.

NELSON

Bradley Mail Order (Textiles) Limited
Brook Street Mill, Brook Street, Nelson,
    Lancashire BB9 9QE
    Nelson 68191/2/3

Open: Monday to Friday 08.00 to 17.00; mail order; catalogue

Customers by appointment only, please. They deal almost exclusively by mail. They offer a forty-eight hour postal service of unbleached calicos for tie-dye, silk screen printing and batik—also novelty toy-making packs (made up from remnants and including stuffing materials). Their main trade is in low-priced polyester jersey, nylon, terylene and Crimplene fabrics—sometimes offered in special 'dressmaking packs' (two Crimplene dress lengths plus zips for less than £2.00, for instance). On request they will send catalogues, order forms and reply envelopes. (If you want samples, they charge 5p per range, which is deducted from future orders.)

The Lidsey Textile Market
21/23 Gisburn Road, Newbridge, Barrow-
    ford, Nelson Lancashire BB9 8NU

Mail order only; catalogue

Offers Lancashire textiles and Yorkshire fabrics, post free, at straight-from-the-mill prices. No samples because stock continually changes, but they will send you price lists and a 'money back if not satisfied' guarantee. They have cottons and tweeds, jerseys and nylons, natural and man-made fabrics, dress fabrics and furnishing fabrics—and special £1.00 bargain parcels.

60 Plus Textiles
Barley, Nelson, Lancashire

Mail order only; catalogue in exchange for s.a.e.

Aim to supply home sewers with good quality fabrics at low prices. Send a stamped addressed envelope for samples and order form. No minimum order. Wide range of dressmaking fabrics and speedy service.

PURLEY

E J Woodley
106 Old Lodge Lane, Purley, CR2 4DH
    01 660 5747

Mail order only

Mail order supplier of half pound bags of mixed fabric snippets—useful for toy making, patchwork, collage and so on.

PYLE

Welsh Textiles Limited
Llantwit Mill, Pyle, Glamorganshire,
    Wales   Kenfig Hill 740172

Open: Monday to Friday 09.00 to 17.00; mail order; catalogue 50p

Weavers of woollen cloth and manufacturers of garments from whom you can buy Welsh woollen cloth. Call at the mill shop or order by mail. They will charge you 50p for the catalogue and samples, but you get 50p knocked off your first purchase.

SKIPTON

Christina Fabrics
Union Mills, Skipton, Yorkshire
    Skipton 4918

Mail order only; catalogue

Dress and furnishing fabrics by the yard (and by mail) straight form the mills and mostly man-made, and also remnant parcels, some containing lengths of up to five yards. They have brocades and cretonnes for furnishing, cushions and curtains; duster pieces; suiting; blanket remnants; bundles of small pieces for dressing dolls; Winceyette; linings; cotton prints; fur fabric pieces; printed nylon; corduroys and needlecord; polyester; Crimplene; lurex; tweeds; dress velvet; sheeting; gingham and brushed nylon. There is a money-back guarantee and they promise that 'special enquiries are always welcome'.

Hartleys Fabrics
6 Swadford Street, Skipton, Yorkshire
    Skipton 3866

Open: Monday to Saturday (excluding Tuesday) 09.00 to 17.00; Tuesday 09.00 to 13.00; mail order; catalogue

Wholesalers, retailers and mail order suppliers of a wide range of fabrics, by the yard or in economy packs. They have downproof fabrics, hessian, quilt fillings and covers, wools, cottons, man-made fibres, curtaining and ribbons. Stocks change constantly so it's best to send for the list. There are three other branches—at Clitheroe, Barnoldswick and Colne (see separate entries for addresses and opening times).

SUTTON COLDFIELD

Streetly Toys
63 Quescett Road East, Streetly, Sutton Coldfield, Warwickshire   021 353 3802

Open: Monday to Friday 09.00 to 17.00 for telephone calls; mail order; catalogue 25p

Mail order only. The 25p for the catalogue is refundable on first order (or on return of catalogue in good condition). Suppliers of fabrics for soft furnishings and also fur fabric, felt, acrylic stuffing materials and soft toy accessories (eyes and grunters, noses and squeakers).

FELT AND HESSIAN

Most craft shops sell one or the other—or both—and most of the people listed earlier in this chapter (under General and Fabrics) can supply them. The following are specialists who stock nothing else in the way of fabrics. For the widest possible range of weights and colours see The Felt and Hessian Shop in EC1

BOLTON

Gent
709 Blackburn Road, Bolton, Lancashire
    Bolton 53642

Mail order only; catalogue

Mail order suppliers of felt squares (about 6″ by 4″) in various colours. They promise 'wholesale prices for the individual' and can also sell you cut out and ready-to-make felt pictures for nursery walls.

KING'S LANGLEY

Warriner Warehouses Limited
Station Road, King's Langley, Hertfordshire   King's Langley 66877

Open: Monday to Friday 09.00 to 17.30; mail order; catalogue

Suppliers of felt, canvas, hessian, kapok

and PVC—their retail shop (The Felt and Hessian Shop) is at 34 Greville Street, London EC1, see page 86—but you may buy direct from the warehouse at retail prices if it is more convenient for you. Particularly wide colour range in felt and hessian. Minimum order they will fulfil by mail is £2.00

LONDON EC1

The Felt and Hessian Shop
34 Greville Street, London EC1
    01 405 6215

Open Monday to Friday 09.00 to 17.15; mail order; catalogue 35p

The Felt and Hessian Shop means just what it says. Almost no minimum quantity—well, they stipulate ¼ yard of felt and ½ yard of hessian, but you are unlikely to want less in any case. Truly enormous colour range—at least 40 hessian colours and 108 different felt colours. As well as the handicraft felts they have floor felt, extra-superfine felt, feltettes, underfelt, PVC and flame proofed muslin and casement.

Russell and Chapple Limited
23 Monmouth Street, London WC2H
    9DE   01 836 7521

Open: Monday to Friday 08.30 to 17.30; mail order; catalogue

Wholesalers and retail suppliers of hessian in great quantities and a variety of colours Also unprimed artists' canvas, linen, jute and cotton.

BUTTON AND BUCKLE COVERING

If your local department store or your nearest Singer shop can't arrange to cover buckles and buttons for you, the following people almost certainly can.

EPPING

Harlequin
258 High Street, Epping, Essex
    Epping 4400

Open: Monday to Saturday (excluding Wednesday) 09.00 to 17.30; Wednesday 09.00 to 12.30; mail order; catalogue

Stockists of almost everything connected with dressmaking—dress fabrics, tailoring canvas, notions and things. Perhaps most useful for their speedy postal service of button, buckle and belt covering in your own fabric. Free catalogue relates to this service only.

LONDON NW5

Minival Limited
1st Floor, Spring House, Spring Place,
  Kentish Town, London NW5 3BH
  01 267 3816/7

Open: Monday to Friday 09.00 to 17.30;
Saturday 09.00 to 13.00; mail order; catalogue

Wholesale merchants, so write in for a
price list or telephone for an appointment. Specialists in trimmings and haberdashery items of all kinds, they will also
undertake the dyeing and covering of
buttons for customers.

W1

Benedict Buttons London Limited
118-120 Great Titchfield Street, London
  W1   01 580 7853

Open: Monday to Friday 08.30 to 17.00
Closed on Saturday; mail order

Specialises in covered buttons of all kinds
for dressmaking and upholstery work.
Minimum order is one dozen. Will also
undertake the covering of buttons both
in their own and the customer's
materials. No catalogue.

TRIMMINGS

LONDON SW1

Watts and Co (see page 75)

W1

Ells and Farrier
5 Princes Street, Hanover Square, London
  W1   01 629 9964

Open; Monday to Friday 09.00 to 17.30;
mail order

Tiny shop, known as The Bead House,
crammed full of beads, sequins, imitation
stones and all kinds of trimmings. Are
prepared to send by mail but have no
catalogue so you have to know quite
precisely what you want. Well worth a
visit, anyway.

Louis Grosse Ltd (see page 76)

WELLINGTON

Sesame Ventures
Greenham Hall, Wellington, Somerset
  Greenham 672469

Open: Monday to Friday 09.00 to 17.00
(Callers by appointment only); mail
order; catalogue

Buy by mail from the catalogue—and
you have to buy quite a lot; a minimum
of £5.00 worth. They have imitation

stones, flat sequins, cup sequins, fancy
sequins, gold oats, wood beads, bugle
beads, braids, cords, pearls, ring racks,
brooch backs and ear clip backs.

UPHOLSTERY

LONDON E15

Mobilia
44 Henniker Road, Stratford, London E15
  01 534 3614

Mail order only; catalogue

If you want to do some upholstering
Mobilia can supply, by mail, all the
awkward bits and pieces you need and
maybe can't find locally (or can't be
bothered to seek out). Working alpha-
betically through their catalogue you will
see that they can sell you adhesives, upholstery buttons (which can be covered
in the material of your choice so long
as you choose from their range), calico,
castors, chisels, courtelle wadding for
cushions, covers (simulated leather or
cloth), cushions (filled with latex or polyether foam), polyether sheets, cottonfelt
for padding, crumbled foam, dacron,
gimp pins in various colours, hessian,
kapok mixture, piping cords, platform
linings, pressers and points for deep
buttoning, tacks, slipping threads in
various colours, twine, upholstery nails,
webbing (jute or rubber), woodstopper,
extra long zips cut to the length required,
and a special upholstery kit containing
three curved mattress needles, one double
and one single bayonet point upholstery
needle, a dozen upholstery skewers and
a piece of tailor's chalk. Some of these
upholstery materials are also useful for
soft-toy making.

TAPESTRY AND EMBROIDERY

These are the major specialist suppliers.

BATH

The Silver Thimble
33 Gay Street, Bath, Somerset

Open: Monday to Friday (excluding
Thursday) 09.45 to 12.45 and 14.15 to
16.45; Thursday and Saturday 09.45 to
12.45; mail order; catalogue

The Silver Thimble is for needleworkers.
They have canvases and Irish linens,
Penelope packs, Glenshee fabrics, embroidery threads and tapestry wools—
and they will stretch tapestries and make
up cushions and evening bags. They also

have crochet and macramé yarns, felt, kapok and foam chippings. (You must spend 50p if you want to order by mail.)

BELFAST

Copeland Linens Limited
PO Box 95, 6 Murray Street, Belfast
   BT1 6QA   Belfast 21065

Mail order only; catalogue 20p

Mail order suppliers of traced needlework and tapestry packs and linen, coloured and natural, by the yard. All tapestry designs are supplied complete with canvas, numbered colour guide, wool, needle and instructions. Embroidery packs are similarly complete. You can also buy linen table mats, pillow slips, cloths etc. ready traced for embroidery. You must send payment with order, but there is a money-back guarantee.

BOLTON

William Briggs and Company Limited
School Street, Bromley Cross, Bolton,
   Lancashire BL7 9PA   Bolton 52181

(Opening times not applicable)

Manufacturers of the Penelope Needlework Packs, Penelope Tapestry kits and Briggs Hot Iron Transfers. You cannot buy direct, but if you are having trouble locating their wares they will give you the address of your nearest stockist.

BRADFORD

A K Graupner (see page 63) Tapestry wools

Texere Yarns (see page 63) Tapestry wools

BURNLEY

Mrs Joan L Trickett
110 Marsden Road, Burnley, Lancashire
   Burnley 26450

Mail order only; catalogue in exchange for s.a.e.

A mail order supplier of all the necessities for embroidery and/or needlepoint tapestry work—embroidery linens, tapestry canvases, crewel and tapestry wools, embroidery threads and accessories. Please send a stamped addressed envelope for the price list—and state if you want shade cards and patterns as well.

CHESTER

Arts and Crafts Studio
15/16 St Michaels Row, Chester, Cheshire
   0244 24900

Open: Monday to Saturday 09.00 to 17.30; mail order

Specialists in tapestry materials of all kinds—from wools, through needles, to canvases. Good people to ask for advice.

CHICHESTER

Chichester Handweavers (see page 64)
Tapestry yarns

DUNDEE

Helen Minns
75 Tullideph Road, Dundee, Angus,
   Scotland

Mail order only; catalogue for s.a.e.

If you have trouble getting hold of Glenshee embroidery fabrics and evenweave linens from your needlework shop, an order sent to the above address will be dispatched without delay. A stamped addressed envelope will bring you a neat package of patterns.

GALASHIELS

J Hyslop Bathgate Co (see page 66)
Tapestry yarns

HEBDEN BRIDGE

The Rug-Craft Centre (see page 69)
Tapestry wools

IPSWICH

Eva Rosenstand
Claydon, Ipswich, Suffolk 1P6 0EQ
   Ipswich 830340

Open: Monday to Friday 10.00 to 16.00; mail order; catalogue 25p

You can visit the showroom at opening times for kits and packs for embroidery, or order by mail or telephone from the full-colour catalogue. The material, pattern, yarn or silk are all included in the kit but materials for mounting and backing are sold separately (or they will mount finished embroideries for you if you wish it). There are pictures in all sizes including miniatures, wall hangings, tablecloths and napkins, chair backs and cushion covers in a variety of designs, mostly animal or vegetable (dogs, birds, flowers, fish etc.) but also abstract geometrically patterned cushions.

LEEDS

P Chalk
Art Needlework Gallery, 25 Butts Court,
   Leeds, Yorkshire LS1 5JS   Leeds 27810

Open: Monday to Friday 09.30 to 17.30; Saturday 09.30 to 13.00; mail order
Art needlework specialists who offer everything for tapestry, embroidery and

related crafts—fabrics, threads, wools, etc.—and who will make up needlework and tapestries into pictures, stools, screens, chair backs and so on. Range far too wide to express here—British and Continental linens, single and double thread canvas, charts, booklets, transfers, embroidery packs and frames, bag handles, bell pull ends, metal threads and a tremendous range of silks, cottons and wools, needles, painted canvases, etc. etc.

LONDON NW4

Wools and Embroideries Limited (see page 94) Tapestry materials

SW1
The Women's Home Industries Tapestry Shop
85 Pimlico Road, London SW1
    01 730 5366

Open: Monday to Friday 09.30 to 17.00; mail order

Specialists in needlepoint tapestry who will hand paint designs on to canvas to order. They stock canvas and tapestry wools and needles, also tapestry kits and rug-making materials. Good source of advice and encouragement.

SW3
The Ladies' Work Society Limited
138 Brompton Road, London SW3 1HY
    01 589 3557

Open: Monday to Friday 10.00 to 17.00; mail order

Specialists in the supply of materials for needlepoint tapestry. They have canvas by the yard, handpainted and trammé designs and crewel and tapestry wools. They will design a canvas specially for you and, when you have worked it, stretch it and make it up for you. Also have macramé yarns (and another branch in Moreton-in-the-Marsh).

SW3
Seldon Tapestries Limited
c/o 10 Kings Mansions, Lawrence Street, London SW3   01 352 7759

Open: By appointment only; mail order; catalogue

Suppliers of painted canvases for needlepoint tapestry—and of the wools and needles. They have traditional and modern designs in stock, but they will also adapt existing designs, create new designs to suit a mood or colour scheme, turn any picture you give them into a needlepoint design—and even work the tapestry for you! Will advise, stretch canvases, upholster stools and generally help in any way possible. You must make an appointment to call.

W1
B Francis
4 Glentworth Street, London NW1
    01 486 3992

Open: Monday to Friday 09.00 to 17.30; Saturday 09.00 to 13.00; mail order

Specialists in tapestry and art needlework who will execute any special design for you. They sell canvas and tapestry wools and threads and will stretch homemade tapestries, frame them, or mount them as cushions, panels, bags and so on. Their advice and comments are worth having.

MORETON-IN-MARSH
The Ladies' Work Society
Delabere House, New Road, Moreton-in-Marsh, Gloucestershire GL56 OAS
Moreton-in-Marsh 50447

Open: Monday to Friday (excluding Wednesday) 10.00 to 13.00 and 14.00 to 17.00; Wednesday 10.00 to 13.00; Saturday 10.00 to 13.00 and 14.00 to 16.00; mail order

Best known as designers of canvas embroidery who also have a wide knowledge of all fields of embroidery. They will supply canvases designed to special order, canvas by the yard, and crewel and tapestry wools. They also undertake the stretching and making up of tapestries. The London showroom is in SW3 and has a separate entry.

NANNERCH
Craft O'Hans (see page 53)

WEST DRAYTON
Colberre (see page 34) Tapestry kits only

WIGSTON
T Forsell and Son (see page 70) Tapestry canvas and wools

WOLVERHAMPTON
The Wool Shop and The Home Artistic Limited
89/90 Darlington Street, Wolverhampton, Staffordshire   Wolverhampton 21898

Open: Monday to Saturday (excluding Thursday) 09.00 to 17.30; Thursday 09.00 to 13.00; mail order; catalogue

Specialist suppliers of the necessities for hand knitting, tapestry and embroidery. They have evenweave fabrics, tapestry canvases and frames, embroidery frames, stranded cotton, crochet cotton, macramé twine, felt, Raffene, tapestry and knitting wools and the full range of Penelope packs. Also rug-making canvases and wools.

MILLINERY

LONDON W1

Paul Craig Limited
14/15 D'Arblay Street, London W1
  01 437 5467

Open: Monday to Friday 08.30 to 17.00; mail order; catalogue

Although millinery fabrics and trimmings are fairly readily available in department stores and haberdashers, basic hat shapes are no longer easy to find. People who used to stock them have given up because the demand has dropped. But if you want to make a hat, save yourself a fruitless trek around the shops and contact Paul Craig. Although it is a wholesale house they are happy to supply individual hat shapes and even to make a basic shape to your own requirements. They also have materials, trimmings and other relevant bits and pieces.

FILLINGS

Most craft shops—particularly if they cater for the makers of soft toys—can supply fillings suitable not only for toys but for floor cushions or duvets or anything else. But if you've had no luck, here is where to turn.

BINGLEY

Beckfoot Mill
Harden, Bingley, Yorkshire BD16 1AR
  Bingley 3138 and 4575

Mail order only; catalogue

Mail order—though they will sometimes serve callers if you're passing the mill. Their speciality is synthetic, washable fillings for soft toys, pillows, cushions, continental quilts, etc. They will also make up cushions and chair seats to your specifications so that all you have to do is cover them.

LONDON E15

Mobilia (see page 87)

The Kapok Company Limited

Should you have trouble getting hold of a supply of Kapok, contact the manufacturers—The Kapok Company Limited, Selinas Lane, Dagenham, Essex RM8 1ES 01 592 2233. They will not sell to you direct, but will try to put you in touch with their nearest stockist.

SOFT TOY MAKING

The following are either general craft shops whose only 'needlework' offering is the wherewithall to make soft toys, or else specialist suppliers of fur fabrics, growlers or whatever. See also General list, starting on page 9.

ANDOVER

Arts and Crafts Centre (see page 10)

AYR

Contour Artists' Materials (see page 10)

BATH

Bath Handicraft Supplies (see page 10)

BEXHILL-ON-SEA

Sackville Handicrafts (see page 140)

BIRMINGHAM

Midland Educational (see page 11)

BOURNEMOUTH

Moordown Leather and Craft (see page 114)

BRAMPTON

The Handyman's Shop (see page 127)
Fillings and eyes only

BRIGHTON

Minutiques
82b Trafalgar Street, Brighton, Sussex
  BN1 4EB Brighton 681862

Open: Monday to Saturday (excluding Thursday) 10.00 to 17.00; Thursday 10.00 to 12.30; mail order; catalogue 20p

A collectors' shop and dolls' hospital who are best known for their collection of antique dolls and toys, dolls' houses and beautiful dolls' house furniture (things like reproduction miniature Staffordshire ornaments, minute real leatherbound books, minuscule copper saucepans, perfect little rocking chairs, tiny pies and strings of sausages to make Hunca Munca's mouth water, beautiful hand-blown glass decanters $\frac{3}{8}''$ tall)—But, because this is also a dolls' hospital, they can sell you wigs, growlers, 'Mamas', joggle eyes, noses and complete faces for soft toy making. The catalogue is 20p but is solely concerned with the minute handmade antiques. Send a stamped addressed envelope for the list of toy making supplies.

Southern Handicrafts (see page 12)

BRISTOL
Craftwise (see page 38)

BURGHEAD
Moray Firth Designs (see page 64)

CAERNARVON
Black Kettle Crafts (see page 13)

CHANDLERS FORD
Creative Crafts (see page 14)

CHELTENHAM
The Colourman (see page 14)

CHESHAM
The Tiger's Eye (see page 39)   Kits only

COLCHESTER
Briggs Art and Book Shop (see page 15)

DUNOON
Dae-It-Yersel (see page 16)

EASTBOURNE
The Sussex Handicraft Shop (see page 16)

FALKIRK
Modelcrafts (see page 17)

FOLKESTONE
Cameo Handicrafts (see page 142)

Palmer's Mail Order
2 Royal Military Avenue, Folkestone, Kent CT20 3EF   Folkestone 75493

Mail order only; catalogue

Mail order suppliers of fur fabric and simulated fur in yards or offcuts, and also washable and flameproof stuffing materials. Virtually no minimum order.

FORDINGBRIDGE
Caxton Decor (see page 17)

GRAVESEND
Tumble Kraft (see page 42)

HAYWARDS HEATH
Jacobs, Young and Westbury (see page 147)   Glass eyes only

HEMEL HEMPSTEAD
Arts and Crafts (see page 19)

LEAMINGTON SPA
A S Blackie (see page 21)   Kits only

LEATHERHEAD
Handicrafts (see page 21)

LETCHWORTH
The Picture Shop (see page 22)

LONDON N1
The Pot Shop (see page 22)   Doll and toy making and dressing

NW3
Crafts Unlimited (see page 22)

W6
Margrave Manufacturing Company Limited
Humbolt Road, London W6   01 385 3510

Mail order only; catalogue

Wholesale suppliers of soft toy accessories who work by mail order only. They sell glass eyes (specifying dogs', cats', rabbits', blue, green, amber or goo-goo); plastic eyes (in the same categories with the addition of plastic mice eyes on wire, which come in tens); washer fitting lock-in eyes; joggle eyes; noses (black, red, hollow, or rubber); squeakers, chimes, growlers and 6 lb sacks of foam crumbs. Minimum order £1.50

W8
Crafts Unlimited (see page 24)

MILTON KEYNES
Milton Keynes Day Centre (see page 26)

NOTTINGHAM
Home Pastimes (see page 28)

REDBOURN
Atelier (see page 29)

ROCHDALE
The Art Shop (see page 30)

SHEFFIELD

H R Whitehead (see page 30)

SHREWSBURY

Wildings (see page 30)

SITTINGBOURNE

Homecrafts (see page 31)

SKIPTON

Craven Art Centre Limited (see page 31)

SOUTHAMPTON

Hampshire Hobbies (see page 31)

TORQUAY

Forestreet Model Centre (see page 32)

TWICKENHAM

Bits and Bobs (see page 54)

TYNEMOUTH

Dolls Hospital
18 Linthorpe Road, Tynemouth, Northumberland NE30 3QR
North Shields 73678

Mail order only

Phone for an appointment because the business is run at home. All dolls and soft toys and some mechanical toys are repaired. And you can buy the accessories for soft toy making—eyes, noses, growlers, squeakers and so on. There is no minimum order. They will send one eye through the post if necessary.

WATFORD

Allcraft (see page 33)   Kits only

WELLING

Crafts Unlimited (see page 33)

WEYMOUTH

The Art Shop
1a St Mary Street, Weymouth, Dorset
   Weymouth 4389

Open: Monday to Saturday 09.00 to 17.30

The Art Shop specialises in toy making, which means they have a good stock of felt and fur fabric, kapok, foam and terylene stuffing materials, soft toy accessories and leather offcuts. But they also have Plasticraft, Enamelcraft, candlemaking and screen printing kits, linocutting and brass rubbing materials and various kinds of modelling clay.

WOKING

Arts and Crafts Shop (see page 34)

8 Knitting, Crochet and Macramé

As there are so many wool shops in Britain—about 23,000 of them, and too many to cope with here—this chapter has been restricted almost entirely to specialists and mail order suppliers. Your 'corner wool shop' will be able to supply most of your needs, and so will larger department stores. It is also well worth checking the phone book to see whether you have a Readicut Wool Shop (see page 70) in your area. The chapter concentrates then on direct wool suppliers—mills who send out beautiful shade cards so rich in colour and texture that surely even a non-knitter will be inspired to buy, and who sell wools, natural and synthetic, at very reasonable prices indeed; and also on the specialist suppliers of Welsh wools and pure Shetland wools.

The first part of the chapter is about Yarns; the second part is about Knitting Machines; and the third part concentrates on Macramé.

YARNS

BRADFORD

Direct Wool Group
PO Box 46, Bradford, Lancashire BD1 2AN

Mail order only; catalogue 3½p stamp

Wool straight from the mill—and dispatched by a firm who say they are specialists in knitting machine yarns. Mostly synthetic, at prices from 3p an ounce. If you want their shade card and samples, please send 3½p stamp.

R S Duncan and Co
30 Chapel Street, Bradford, Yorkshire BD1 5DP   Bradford 33504

Open: Monday to Friday 09.00 to 17.00;

Saturday 09.00 to 12.00; mail order; catalogue

Mail order warehouse with no showroom, but callers are welcomed. Supply yarns suitable for knitting and handweaving, Knitmaster machines, tweeds by the yard and knitting and dressmaking accessories.

Kiwi Wool Company
32 Rebecca Street, Bradford, Yorkshire BD1 2RY   Bradford 32498

Open: Monday to Friday 09.00 to 17.30; mail order; catalogue

A mail order company—though you can call at the warehouse if you're passing. Natural and synthetic knitting wools in a good range of colours and weights, knitting patterns, buttons to match all yarns and knitting and crochet accessories (needles, wools, scissors, etc). Catalogue shows wool cutting and photographs of the Kiwi fabrics available—Shetland and Cheviot tweed and crimped polyester. No minimum order. Money back if you're not satisfied. And surplus yarn returned in good condition will be accepted for exchange or credited.

Knitting Wools (Bradford) Limited
1 Cater Street, Bradford, Yorkshire BD1 5AN   Bradford 26511

Open: Monday to Friday 08.30 to 17.00; mail order; catalogue

Another mail order supplier of hand knitting wools straight from the mill. Samples and shade cards on request (or you are welcome to call in if you're in the area). Promise a prompt service and good colour range.

Knitwell Wools Limited
116 Sunbridge Road, Bradford, Yorkshire BD1 2NF   Bradford 22290

Open: Monday to Friday 08.30 to 17.00; mail order; catalogue

Chiefly mail order, but they do sell over the counter as well. The free catalogue has photographs of the patterns and knitting bags available and snippets from all the various wools; pure wools, nylon, crêpe, Aran and acrylic wools in various weights and a lot of colours. Catalogue also gives washing instructions and how to remove bilberry and blood stains! You can order as little as one ounce. Prompt service.

St John's Knitting Wool Company Limited
PO Box 55, 39 Well Street, Bradford, Yorkshire BD5 8DZ Bradford 29031

Open: Monday to Saturday 09.00 to 17.00; mail order; catalogue

Another chance to buy wool direct from the mill. You can go to the mill itself (Parkside Mill, Parkside Road—off Manchester Road—Bradford) or order from the catalogue which promises 'same day service' except at weekends. The shade card shows lots of colours in hand and machine knitting wools—tweed wools, baby wools, fingering crêpe, pure wools and synthetic wools; 2-ply, 3-ply, 4-ply and double knitting. They also offer buttons, colour matched to the entire range of wools, and rug-making kits. No minimum order.

DINAS MAWDDWY
Merion Mill Shop
Dinas Mawddy, Machynlleth, Montgomeryshire SY20 9LS, North Wales
Dinas Mawddy 311

Open: Monday to Friday 09.00 to 16.30; mail order; catalogue

Knitting yarns from the Merion Mill and Welsh tapestry cloth in 56" widths. They also sell clothes and tablemats and blankets made from the Merion yarns (which you can watch at an earlier stage walking about the Welsh hillsides).

EDWALTON
Silverknit
Edwalton, Nottinghamshire NG12 4DF

Mail order only; catalogue (2½p for each shade card)

Mail order suppliers of six different kinds of knitting yarn—all on cones for knitting machines. A linen/cotton blend in 21 colours; a 3 and 4-ply knitting cotton in 38 colours; a rayon in 38 colours; 100% pure wool; and their special sparkling Silverknit.

ELLAND
Albert Bailey and Sons Limited
Riverside Mill, Elland, Yorkshire HX5 9DR

Mail order only; catalogue 3½p stamp

Mail order suppliers of 100% pure wool crêpe knitting yarn—in hanks or on cone. Please send a stamp for a shade card.

FAREHAM
The Wool Shop
139 Gosport Road, Fareham, Hampshire PO16 0P2 Fareham 5113

Open: Monday to Saturday (excluding Tuesday) 09.00 to 13.00 and 14.00 to 17.30; Tuesday 09.00 to 13.00

Knitting yarns, but also rug canvases and wools, felt, buttons, buckles, trimmings, notions and embroidery fabrics and silks.

LERWICK
Jamieson and Smith Limited
90 North Road, Lerwick, Shetland Isles
Lerwick 579

Open: Monday to Saturday (excluding Wednesday) 09.00 to 17.00; Wednesday closed; mail order; catalogue

Will supply Shetland knitting yarns by return post on receipt of order and cash. Over 200 shades are always in stock and callers are very welcome.

LONDON NW4
Wools and Embroideries Limited
3-5 Queen's Parade, Hendon Central
London NW4 3AR 01 202 9488

Open: Monday to Saturday (excluding Wednesday) 09.00 to 17.30; Wednesday 09.00 to 12.30; mail order; catalogue

Tremendous stock of knitting wools in natural and synthetic fibres, rug wools, stencilled rug canvases, tapestry canvases, tapestry wools, all the necessary needles and rug hooks and oddments like daisy winders. Will mail goods all over the world. Very busy shop with helpful staff.

LOWESTOFT
Chadds Mail Order Wools Limited
Whapload Road, Lowestoft, Suffolk
Lowestoft 4089

Open: Monday to Friday 09.00 to 17.00; mail order; catalogue

Although this is really a mail order company, they say that visitors are welcomed to the premises in parties, by appointment, or even singly if they happen to be passing. Dealers in knitting yarns and accessories—wools, patterns, rug-making equipment, etc. They will supply as little as one ball of wool or one pattern if necessary.

NEWCASTLE UPON TYNE

Newcastle Wool Company Limited
Newcastle upon Tyne, Northumberland

Mail order only; catalogue 3p

Mail order suppliers of synthetic hand-knitting and rug-making wools—also rug canvases, hooks and so on. If you send for samples please state whether you are interested in the knitting wools or the carpet thrums.

PUDSEY

Taiyarn Knitting Wools
Springfield Mills, Farsley, Pudsey, York-shire   Pudsey 71781

Open: Monday to Friday 09.00 to 17.00; mail order; catalogue 5p postage

Produce knitting wools on 8 ounce cones for use on home knitting machines and also matching accessories—buttons, zips, and even suitings and dressmaking fabrics to match the various colours of yarn. You are welcome to call at the mills—or send 5p postage for the catalogue.

SHIPLEY

Holmfirth Wools Limited
Midland Wool Warehouse, Briggate, Windhill, Shipley, Yorkshire BD18 2BS   Shipley 56943

Open: Monday to Friday 09.00 to 17.30; Saturday 09.00 to 12.30; mail order; catalogue

Mail order suppliers (upon whom you may call if you are passing) of high quality, low price, pure wools (balled for hand knitting or on cones for machines). Wide range of colours and plys, includ-ing angora, bouclé, tweed, etc. Will supply from one ounce upwards by return of post. From time to time they have special offers of limited quantities of wool at extra low prices. Also two pound packs of wool for blanket squares.

SYSTON

Mailyarns
38 High Street, Syston, Leicestershire

Mail order only; catalogue

Mail order suppliers of something called Nylostrip which looks like a narrow strip of coloured stockinette-type nylon fabric and can apparently be knitted or woven into a bathmat or teacosy with great speed. Use ordinary knitting needles or, some say, a handloom. They also offer oddments of wool on cone for machine knitters—enough to make a tank top, sweater for a child, etc.

TELFORD

The Wool Shop
38 Market Street, Wellington, Telford, Shropshire   Telford 2482

Open: Monday to Saturday (excluding Wednesday) 09.00 to 17.30; Wednesday closed

At The Wool Shop you can buy wool, but you can also buy felt, canvas, hessian, kapok, soft toy accessories, buckles, but-tons, trimmings, tapestry and embroidery wools and silks, crochet, knitting and macramé yarns, lampshade-making mat-erials and rug-making equipment.

WAKEFIELD

The Wool Fashion Bureau Limited
PO Box 16, Wakefield, Yorkshire
Wakefield 75465

Mail order only; catalogue

Nylon and pure wool knitting yarn, spun in their own mill and supplied by mail in any quantity (down to one ounce). Will exchange unused wools and offer a money back if not satisfied guarantee. The shade card shows an appealing range of colours—including natural Aran. They also have pattern books, and but-tons to match all wools.

KNITTING MACHINES

It is possible to buy knitting machines by mail order from firms who adver-tise in newspapers and magazines. The price is often appealing and the machines quite probably very reliable —but it isn't generally considered a wise move to buy in this way simply because you don't get a demonstration, or any kind of tuition, and after-sales servicing can be a problem. There are a great many knitting machines on the market, but probably only one or two that are exactly right for your personal needs and abilities. Better to contact one of the major manufact-urers who will tell you where your nearest reputable stockist is and how to go about choosing a machine and arranging lessons. Most firms will give you details of group demonstrations, or even arrange a demonstration in your own home, and all will send very detailed information on the machines they make so that you can get a good idea of what is available and what you might like before you start. Here are the addresses to con-tact:

Jones Sewing Machine Company Limited
Shepley Street, Guide Bridge, Audenshaw, Manchester, Lancashire
061 330 6531

Machines sold through department stores and specialist retailers. Offer a very comprehensive postal course which arrives in the form of an impressive lever arch file containing carefully worked out lessons set out in words and diagrams. With lessons 3, 6 and 9 they send you yarn and you knit sample garments and send them in for examination and comment. Not everyone can learn by mail, but for those who can, Jones offer an excellent service. (Also make sewing machines—see relevant chapter.)

Knitmaster International
30/40 Elcho Street, London SW11 4AX
01 228 9303

Will give you information on stockists, servicing, tuition and, indeed, anything you might want to know about any aspect of the Knitmaster machines and the service Knitmaster provide.

Passap Limited
128/129 High Street, Bordesley, Birmingham B12 0LA   021 772 5600

Sell through a network of dealers and mail order and insist that all customers are given full tuition. Will send leaflets describing machines available, and also sell suitable wools, patterns, etc. Willingly give any information you need.

Singer Company (UK) Limited
Consumer Products Division, 255 High Street, Guildford, Surrey GU1 3DH
Guildford 71144

Will send you a detailed leaflet on their Magic Memory Knitting Machine and the address of your nearest stockist (who arranges a demonstration, servicing, etc.). Better known for sewing machines—see relevant chapter.

Toyota
Alfran Limited, Unit 32, Rich Industrial Estate, Crayford Road, Crayford, Kent   Crayford 22256

Will send details of machines and accessories, pattern books, addresses of stockists and any relevant information you care to ask for. Also make sewing machines—see relevant chapter.

MACRAME

Growing in popularity, which means that quite a lot of craft shops are beginning to stock the necessary materials. Here is a list of the places where you can be fairly sure of getting what you need. (Although when it comes to choosing twines, you don't have to go to a craft shop and accept what they consider to be suitable. It's always worth looking to see what good stationers, yachting suppliers and even hardware stores have to offer.)

ABERDEEN
The Craft Centre (see page 9)

AYR
Contour Artists' Materials (see page 10)

BATH
The Silver Thimble (see page 87)

BEESTON
The Handicraft Shop (see page 11)

BELFAST
Ato-Crafts (see page 11)

BIRMINGHAM
Midland Educational (see page 11)   Kits only

BISHOPS STORTFORD
Galaxy (see page 12) Kits only

BOLTON
Bolton Handicrafts (see page 12) Macramé yarns

BRADFORD
R W Copley Limited
38 Sunbridge Road, Bradford, Yorkshire BD1 2AA   Bradford 23500

Open: Monday to Saturday (excluding Wednesday) 09.00 to 17.30; Wednesday 09.00 to 12.00; mail order

Specialise in ropes, twines and cordage—a good place to look for twines for macramé work. They also have macramé kits (and candlemaking kits). They have leather-working tools, woods, veneers and pokerwork tools; basket and lampshade-making supplies; scrimcloth, felt, canvas, hessian, Modacryl for stuffing, and eyes for soft toys.

BRIGHTON
Southern Handicrafts (see page 12)

BRISTOL
Bristol Handicrafts (see page 12)

Craftwise (see page 38)

Hobbies and Crafts (see page 12)

Midland Educational (see pages 13, 11)
Kits only

BURNLEY
Northern Handicrafts Limited (see page 13)

CAERNARVON
Black Kettle Crafts (see page 13)

CHANDLERS FORD
Creative Crafts (see page 14)

CHELTENHAM
The Colourman (see page 14) Kits only

Cotswold Craft Centre (see page 72)

COLNE
The Art Shop (see page 15)

COVENTRY
Midland Educational (see pages 15, 11)
Kits only

DUBLIN
Gemcraft of Ireland (see page 41) Kits only

EDINBURGH
The Edinburgh Tapestry Company Limited (see page 65)

J Hewitt (see page 121)

EPSOM
Lindsay's Handicrafts and Decor (see page 141) Kits only

EXETER
The Handicraft Shop (see page 17)

FRINTON-ON-SEA
Frinton Handicraft and Art Centre (see page 17)

HARROGATE
Arts and Handicrafts (see page 18)

HUDDERSFIELD
Arts and Crafts (see page 19)

KEIGHLEY
Conways Arts and Crafts (see page 20)

LEICESTER
Midland Educational (see pages 22, 11)
Kits only

LIVERPOOL
Mersey Yarns (see page 67)

LONDON E17
The Handweavers Studio (see page 67)

EC1
Crafts Unlimited (see page 22)

J Hewitt (see page 121)

N9
The Art and Craft Centre (see page 23)

NW3
Crafts Unlimited (see page 23)

SW3
The Ladies' Work Society (see page 89)

SW10
Hobby Horse (see page 23)

SW11
Leisure Crafts (see page 23)

W8
Crafts Unlimited (see page 24)

WC2
Arthur Beale Limited
194 Shaftesbury Avenue, London WC2H 8JP 01 836 9034

Open: Monday to Friday 09.00 to 18.00; Saturday 09.00 to 13.00; mail order; catalogue

Sells yacht fittings and clothing twines—rope, string, nylon cord, and fine twine suitable for macramé work. Is prepared to supply small quantities—over the counter or by mail.

LYTHAM
Lytham Woodcraft Limited (see page 25) Kits only

MALVERN
Fearnside and Company (see page 25)
Kits only

MANCHESTER
Fred Aldous (see page 25)

Arts and Crafts (see page 77)

MIDDLESBROUGH
J Goldstein and Son (see page 26)   Kits only

NEW ASH GREEN
The Hobby House (see page 26)   Kits only

NEWCASTLE UPON TYNE
Ashbourton Gifts and Crafts (see page 27)   Kits only

NORTHAMPTON
Arts and Crafts Shop (see page 28)

Midland Educational (see pages 28, 11) Kits only

PERTH
Dunn's Art Stores (see page 29)   Kits only

REDBOURN
Atelier (see page 29)

SHREWSBURY
Wildings (see page 30)   Kits only

SKIPTON
Craven Art Centre Limited (see page 31)   Kits only

SOLIHULL
Midland Educational (see pages 31, 11) Kits only

SOUTHAMPTON
Hampshire Hobbies (see page 31)   Kits only

STRATFORD UPON AVON
Midland Educational (see pages 31, 11) Kits only

SUDBURY
Art and Craft Shop (see page 31)

SWANSEA
Arts and Crafts (see page 32)

TAUNTON
The Spinning Wheel (see page 79)

WARE
Fresew (see page 80)

WELLING
Crafts Unlimited (see page 33)

WELWYN GARDEN CITY
Boon Gallery (see page 34)

WIRRAL
Arts and Crafts (see page 34)

WOKING
Arts and Crafts Shop (see page 34)

WOLVERHAMPTON
Midland Educational (see pages 34, 11) Kits only

WORCESTER
Midland Educational (see pages 34, 11) Kits only

YORK
Derwent Crafts (see page 35)   Kits only

See also first section of this chapter, on Yarns

9 Lace Making

There are still people with the patience to work handmade lace—rather more now than there were a few years ago. The main snags are that there is a world shortage of cotton and linen thread (and although some people will use very fine crochet cotton, the purists won't) and that genuine old lace bobbins are being sold in antique shops as collectors' items. This is doubly sad: for one thing it tends to price them out of the reach of lace makers, and for another it does not seem right that something made for use, and far from obsolete, should be shut away in someone's glass case among ornaments and knick-nacks. However, if you can't get together what you need from your grandmother's attic, your local haberdasher, and the curio shop round the corner, here are some specialist suppliers who should be able to help you.

BEDFORD

E Braggins
26/36 Silver Street, Bedford, Bedfordshire   Bedford 53292

Open: Monday to Saturday 09.00 to 17.30; mail order; catalogue

A department store in which one department deals in all the materials and accessories for lace making. They have plastic Bedfordshire lace bobbins, wooden Swedish bobbins, bolster-shaped cushions, lace pins, pricking boards, photostats of prickings, beads and relevant books. They also stock linen thread, but as there is a world shortage of all kinds of linen thread they may not be able to fulfil your order straight away. Old established lace maker suppliers.

CANTERBURY

Needlecraft and Hobbies (see page 13)

CHEADLE

William Hall (see page 64)

GREAT MISSENDEN

Mr A A Brown
Woodside, Greenlands Lane, Prestwood, Great Missenden, Buckinghamshire HP16 9QU

Mail order only

Mail order supplier of wooden lace bobbins—beautifully hand-turned. No catalogue but will invoice a sample to you on request.

HENLEY-ON-THAMES

Mrs Barbara Werrell
2 Ellery Rise, Frieth, Henley-on-Thames, Oxfordshire   Henley 881615

Mail order only; catalogue; price list

Now that old bobbins have become collectors' items and the price is rising, it's useful to know of someone who makes, by hand, wooden pillow lace bobbins—Honiton, Thumper, French, South Bucks, etc. Send a stamped addressed envelope for the price list (they cost about 10p each, plus 10p for postage and packing). You can choose from what is available, or Mrs Werrell will copy specific bobbins. Mail order only.

HITCHIN

Homecrafts (see page 19)   Thread

HYTHE

Needlecraft and Hobbies (see page 20)

MIDDLESBROUGH

Boddy's Bookshop (see page 67)   Pillows, bobbins and Swedish linen thread

SALISBURY

Mace and Nairn
89 Crane Street, Salisbury, Wiltshire SP1
2PY   Salisbury 6903

Open: Monday to Saturday (excluding Wednesday) 09.30 to 13.00 and 14.00 to 17.30; Wednesday closed; mail order; catalogue

Everything for embroidery and bobbin lace making—British and Danish fabrics for counted and freehand embroidery, Anchor and DMC threads, Swedish linen threads, French canvas, bobbins and relevant books. Looked to by lace-makers and embroiderers all over the country as their principal source of supply.

SOUTHAMPTON

Hampshire Hobbies (see page 31)

STONEHAVEN

Christine Riley (see page 79)

WINSFORD

Eliza Leadbetter (see page 68)

10 Tie-dye, Batik and Screen Printing

For tie-dye all you really need (apart from things you will have around the house, like rubber gloves and a stick for stirring the dye) are fabrics, dyes and binding threads—of which the only one you are really likely to need help in finding is the dye. (Free advice on patterns, fabrics and dyes is available from the Dylon Advice Bureau, Lower Sydenham, London SE26 5HD.)

Batik and screen printing require rather more in the way of equipment, but a very comprehensive batik kit is available from quite a number of craft shops, and many of them stock back-up materials as well. The specialists on batik tend to be candlemakers' suppliers—on account of the wax. (See Candle Makers Supplies in London W14 who have a very good stock and supply by mail.)

Craft shops and graphics suppliers can generally offer the materials and accessories for screen printing, but there are several major specialists in particular; Polyprint of Belfast; Pronk, Davis and Rusby, Sericol Group, Marler and Selectasine of London; Serigraphics of Maesteg; and Alanden Printing Supplies of Stockport.

The people listed below have supplies relevant to all three crafts unless otherwise stated.

ABERDEEN

The Craft Centre (see page 9) Tie-dye and batik

ANDOVER

Arts and Crafts Centre (see page 10)

ASHFORD

Graphic Art Supplies (see page 10) Screen Printing

AYR

Contour Artists' Materials (see page 10) Tie-dye and batik

BATH

Tridias (see page 10) Kits only

BEESTON

The Handicraft Shop (see page 11) Tie-dye and batik

BELFAST

Polyprint
815 Lisburn Road, Belfast BT9 7GX
  Belfast 666410

Open: Monday to Thursday 09.00 to 17.00; Friday 09.00 to 16.00; mail order; catalogue

Pigments, fabrics and accessories for screen printing and fabric printing. They have cotton, mercerised cotton, polyester lawn, terylene gauze; dyes, binders, frames, squeegees, rubber, gauzes, metallic powders. Will supply any quantity—and also offer a £4.00 school pack and a £22.50 major pack.

BIRMINGHAM

Type and Palette (see page 11) Screen printing

BISHOPS STORTFORD

Galaxy (see page 12) Tie-dye and batik

BRIGHTON

Handicrafts (see page 12) Tie-dye and batik

BRISTOL

The Art Centre (see page 136) Screen printing

Bristol Fine Art
74 Park Row, Bristol BS1 5LE
0272 20344

Open: Monday to Saturday 10.00 to 18.00

This is actually an art shop, stocking paints and artists' materials, but they also have quite a large range of fabric dyes suitable for tie-dye, batik and silk screening. (Believed to be the only suppliers of air-brushes in the West Country!) Their catalogue may be available by the time this book goes to press.

Bristol Handicrafts (see page 12)

Craftwise (see page 38)

Hobbies and Crafts (see page 12) Kits

BURNLEY

Burnley Drawing Office Services Limited
212 Padiham Road, Burnley, Lancashire
0282 28381
   and 39 Hammerton Street, Burnley, Lancashire

Open: Monday to Friday 08.30 to 18.00; Saturday 08.30 to 13.00; mail order; catalogue

Suppliers of artists' materials, modelling compounds, lino-craft materials and fabric printing colours. Everything you need for silk screen printing, tie-dye or batik.

CAERNARVON

Black Kettle Crafts (see page 13) Tie-dye and batik

CAMBRIDGE

The Leigh Gallery (see page 13)

CARDIFF

South Wales Arts and Crafts Suppliers (see page 55)

CHAGFORD

Dolphin Crafts (see page 123)

CHANDLERS FORD

Creative Crafts (see page 14)

CHELTENHAM

The Christmas Tree (see page 14)

The Colourman (see page 14) Screen printing kits

CHESHAM

The Tiger's Eye (see page 39) Batik

CHISLEHURST

Selectasine
65 Chislehurst Road, Chislehurst, Kent
   Chislehurst 8544

Open: Monday to Friday 09.00 to 17.00

The warehouse belongs to the London shop, which specialises in screen printing materials and accessories (see page 104) but they will happily supply customers who call in. They're sometimes open on a Saturday. Telephone and check first.

COLBY

Manninart (see page 40) Tie-and-dye

DORCHESTER

Frank Herring and Sons (see page 64)

DUBLIN

Gemcraft of Ireland (see page 41)

EASTBOURNE

The Sussex Handicraft Shop (see page 16) Fabric dyes

EPSOM

O W Annetts and Sons (see page 16) Fabric dyes

EXETER

The Copyshop (see page 137) Fabric dyes

FFESTINIOG

Celmi Candles (see page 107) Tie-dye and batik

FRINTON-ON-SEA

Frinton Handicraft and Art Centre (see page 17)

GLASGOW

Miller's (see page 17)

GUISBOROUGH

Beecrafts (see page 18)

HEMEL HEMPSTEAD

Arts and Crafts (see page 19)

HEREFORD

Adams and Son (see page 137)

Winivere Crafts (see page 74) Fabric dyes

HOVE

Handicrafts (see page 19) Tie-dye and batik

HUDDERSFIELD

Arts and Crafts (see page 19)

HULL

Handycrafts of Hull (see page 20) Fabric dyes

Sutton's Atelier
4/6 Beverley Road, Hull, Yorkshire

Open: Monday to Saturday (excluding Thursday) 09.00 to 17.00; Thursday 09.00 to 12.30

An artists' supplier who has a good range of fabric dyes suitable for tie-dye and batik.

ILKLEY

Uni-Dye (see page 66) Synthetic dyestuffs

KEIGHLEY

Conways Arts and Crafts (see page 20)

KIDDERMINSTER

Arts and Crafts (see page 20)

KING'S LYNN

Berol Limited
Oldmedow Road, King's Lynn, Norfolk
 King's Lynn 61221

Mail order only; catalogue 20p

Manufacturers and suppliers, via mail order, to schools and colleges throughout the country who will also supply to individuals so long as you spend a minimum of £5.00 and send cash with your order. Specialise in many kinds of paints, dyes, crayons, pencils, art and craft papers and so on. They have Margros Emulsion Printing Ink for screen printing; water and oil based printing inks and all the necessities for linoprinting—rollers, trays, blocks and full kits; water based fabric dyes suitable for all natural fabrics; glass for mosaic work (and cutters, adhesives, 'smalti' mosaics, etc.). Full colour catalogue includes instructions and helpful tips.

LANCASTER

Leisure Crafts (see page 21) Batik only

LANCING

Rogate Printers (see page 121) Screen printing inks

LEAMINGTON SPA

A S Blackie (see page 21) Screen printing

LEEDS

E J Arnold and Son (see page 21)

Headrow Gallery (see page 21)

LEICESTER

Dryad (see page 22)

LONDON E15

Blackwell and Company (Printing Inks) Limited
Sugar House Lane, Stratford, London
 E15 01 534 3061

(Opening times not applicable); mail order; catalogue

Manufacturers of various kinds of printing inks and display colours. Don't call in—but you are welcome to order screen printing inks by telephone or by post. No minimum quantity stipulated. Catalogue and colour guide free on request.

EC1
Crafts Unlimited (see page 22)

N1
Fine Art Supplies (see page 22) Fabric dyes

N7
Pronk, Davis and Rusby Limited
90/96 Brewery Road, London N7 9PD
 01 607 4273

Open: Monday to Friday 09.00 to 17.00; mail order; catalogue

Not a shop but a supply house which nevertheless welcomes telephone enquiries from individual customers and doesn't stipulate a minimum quantity purchase. Can supply absolutely all requirements for screen printing and also offer a screen frame stretching service (quotations on request). Very explicit catalogue.

N9
The Art and Craft Centre (see page 23) Fabric dyes

NW3
Crafts Unlimited (see page 23)

SW6
Sericol Group Limited
24 Parsons Green Lane, London SW6
 4HS 01 736 8181

Open: Monday to Friday 09.00 to 17.00; Saturday 09.00 to 12.00; mail order; catalogue

Suppliers of screen process inks, screen frames, screen fabrics, stencil materials, squeegees and all sundries used in the process. Will mount photographic stencils from customers' artwork, recover customers' frames with new mesh or supply new frames with or without mesh. Very prepared to be helpful with advice and information. Will supply by mail order, but stipulate a minimum order of £2.50

SW10
Hobby Horse (see page 23)

SW19
E T Marler Limited
Deer Park Road, Wimbledon, London SW19   01 540 8531

Open: Monday to Friday 09.00 to 17.00; mail order; catalogue

Manufacturers and suppliers of the full range of screen printing materials and tools. You can call in to browse, buy and ask for help—or buy from the catalogue if you know what you need.

W1
Dylon Colour Centre
1a Crawford Place, London W1
   01 262 9648

Open: Monday to Friday 09.30 to 17.30

Dylon sell through retail outlets all over the country, but if you want to make a personal choice from among the full range, go to their Colour Centre where they have all the dyes and chemicals for tie-dye and batik (and some relevant books) and where they will discuss dye effects with you if you wish. No mail order, but they will probably be able to tell you the address of your nearest stockist if you're out of London.

W1
Hamleys (see page 24)

Selectasine
22 Bulstrode Street, London W1
   01 935 0768

Open: Monday to Friday 09.30 to 15.00 and 15.30 to 17.00; mail order; catalogue

Specialist suppliers of everything for the silk screen printer. They have the fabrics (silk, nylon, terylene and organdie), the paper, inks, and all the equipment and accessories—also three sizes of kit, designed for handcut stencils and comprehensively equipped. They supply any quantity by mail and will undertake various services—stretching, cleaning, stencil-cutting. They say, in fact, they will 'try almost anything!' Ask for Miss Knight—she'll be very helpful.

George Rowney (see page 24) Fabric dyes

W1
Selfridges (see page 24) Fabric dyes

W8
Crafts Unlimited (see page 24)

W14
Candle Makers Supplies (see page 107) Batik only—very good stock

WC1
John T Keep and Sons Limited
15 Theobalds Road, London WC1
   01 242 7578

Open: Monday to Friday 08.00 to 17.00; Saturday 08.00 to 12.00; mail order; catalogue

Manufacturers of paints and silk screen printing inks who have stockists and agents in various parts of the country—but you can buy from source at the address above, in person or by mail. They produce oil colours and poster colours as well as inks and will match paint to pattern in any quantity from 1 litre upwards. In the case of screen inks they deal in quantities from 5 litres upwards.

WC2
Crafts Unlimited (see page 53)

LOUGHBOROUGH

Artcraft and Do-It-Yourself (see page 25)

MAESTEG

Serigraphics
Fairfield Avenue, Maesteg, Glamorganshire, Wales   Maesteg 733171

Mail order only; catalogue

Manufacturers of silk screen equipment and materials who deal chiefly with art schools and colleges but are happy to send to individual customers (though they ask that you send the money with the order). Supply direct by mail and carrier—no personal callers. (They say they are the only specialists in the field and that their equipment and materials are in use from Lands End to the Highlands of Scotland.)

MAIDSTONE

Green's Fine Papers Division (see page 164) Paper for screen printing

MALVERN

Fearnside and Company (see page 25) Batik

MANCHESTER
Fred Aldous (see page 25) Tie-dye and batik

MIDDLESBROUGH
J Goldstein and Son (see page 26)

NANNERCH
Craft O'Hans (see page 53)

NELSON
Bradley Mail Order (see page 85) Tie-dye fabrics

NEW ASH GREEN
The Hobby House (see page 26)

NORTHAMPTON
Arts and Crafts Shop (see page 28)

OLDHAM
The Art and Craft Shop (see page 28) Tie-dye and batik

OXFORD
Brush and Compass (see page 28) Tie-dye and batik
Colegroves (see page 28) Batik and screen printing

PERTH
Dunn's Art Stores (see page 29) Screen printing only

PETERBOROUGH
Art and Educational Crafts (see page 29)

PRESCOT
The Art Shop (see page 29)

REDBOURN
Atelier (see page 29) Tie-dye

READING
Inspirations (see page 48)
Reading Fine Art Gallery (see page 29)

RICHMOND
Richmond Art and Craft (see page 30) Tie-dye

SHEFFIELD
H R Whitehead (see page 30) Fabric dyes

SKIPTON
Craven Art Centre (see page 31) Batik and screen printing

SOUTHAMPTON
Hampshire Hobbies (see page 31)

STOCKPORT
Alanden Printing Supplies Limited
Clare Road, South Reddish, Stockport, Cheshire   061 480 1497 or 3554
Mail order only; catalogue

Can supply the complete range of silk screen printing materials and tools. Orders accepted by post or telephone only. No minimum order stipulated, but postage and packing will be charged on orders under £25.

STROUD
The Christmas Tree (see page 31) Tie-dye and batik

STURMINSTER NEWTON
Clarkes Handicraft Supplies (see page 31)

SUDBURY
Art and Craft Shop (see page 31)

SUTTON
O W Annetts (see page 32) Fabric dyes

SWANSEA
Arts and Crafts (see page 32)

TADWORTH
D E P (see page 155) Rigid Vinyl sheet useful in screen printing

TUNBRIDGE WELLS
G B Butler (see page 51) Tie-dye

TWICKENHAM
Bits and Bobs (see page 54) Tie-dye and batik (Screen printing materials can be ordered)

WATFORD
Allcraft (see page 33)

WELLING
Crafts Unlimited (see page 33)

WELWYN GARDEN CITY
Boon Gallery (see page 34)

WEST DRAYTON

Colberre (see page 34)   Tie-dye

WIRRAL

Arts and Crafts (see page 34)   Tie-dye
and batik

YORK

Derwent Crafts (see page 35)   Tie-dye
and batik

11 Candlemaking

Very well catered for—with almost every craft shop able to offer something, even if it's only a kit, so check for your nearest stockist in Chapter 1. Two specialist shops (both of whom have a very large stock and either of whom will try and get hold of relevant materials for you if they are not to hand) deal extensively by mail order—see The Candles Shop and Candle Makers Supplies, both in London.

FFESTINIOG

Celmi Candles
Cynfal House, Ffestiniog, Merionethshire, Wales   Ffestiniog 675

Open: Monday to Friday 09.00 to 17.30

Specialist suppliers of all the tools and materials and accessories for candlemaking—and also batik and tie-dye. In kit form as well. Good stock, but you must go there because they don't have a catalogue or do mail order.

LONDON NW1

The Candles Shop
89 Parkway, London NW1   01 485 3232

Open: Monday to Saturday 10.00 to 18.30; mail order; catalogue

A tremendous stock of candleholders and hand-made candles—classical, scented, imposing, novelty, all kinds, and they welcome enquiries about particular candles you haven't been able to buy elsewhere. And, more important, everything you need to make your own—paraffin wax, beeswax, microhardener, dyes, wicks and wicking needles, moulds, perfumes (honeysuckle, bayberry, frangipani, mexican lime, cedarwood, etc.) and various extras like thermometers, rub-on paints and poster colours to decorate candles from the outside. Good 'home packed' candle making kit. More than

willing to offer advice and assistance if required and to listen to your views if there is something they don't stock that you feel they should.

Craftco
30 Prince of Wales Crescent, London NW1   01 485 2320

Open: Monday to Saturday 09.30 to 18.00; mail order; catalogue for s.a.e.

Specialises in all kinds of candlemaking supplies—in particular the Craftco Heavyweight Candlemaking Kit. Also has a good range of modelling clays and other modelling materials such as the Spread-on Mouldmaker (no dipping, no spraying, sets at room temperature).

SW13
The Candles Shop
9 The Broadway, White Hart Lane, Barnes, London SW13   01 876 3603

Open: Monday to Saturday 10.00 to 18.30; mail order; catalogue

Same stock as the Parkway branch—see page 107.

W14
Candle Makers Supplies
4 Beaconsfield Terrace Road, London W14   01 602 1812

Open: Monday to Saturday (excluding Thursday) 10.30 to 13.00 and 14.00 to 18.00; Thursday 10.30 to 13.00; mail order; catalogue

The catalogue consists of an enormous poster which makes it fairly clear that Candle Makers Supplies can indeed supply you with whatever you should want. Books on 'how to . . .', kits for beginners, all kinds of moulds, waxes, wax dyes, wicks, perfumes and sundries like transfers, wicking needles and thermometers. They also have an extensive range of hot-water dyes for tie-dyeing and everything you could need for batik—waxes, dyes, batik brushes, three kinds of tjanting, batik frames—even rubber gloves.

The poster-catalogue has a map, which is good because the shop (behind Olympia) is not all that easy to find—but if you can't get there they will mail goods on a cash-with-order basis.

MUSSELBURGH

Carberry Candles
Carberry, Musselburgh, Midlothian EH21 8PZ, Scotland
Musselburgh 5656

Open: Monday to Friday 09.00 to 17.00; mail order; catalogue

Candle manufacturers who will sell you all the necessary materials to make your own candles—and also complete kits. (If you buy your materials from a candle manufacturer you can presumably be assured of very good advice, should you want it.)

12 Brass Rubbing

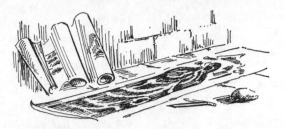

Once upon a time, anyone who wanted to take up brass rubbing was referred to Philips and Page of Kensington Church Street, W8. They remain the only brass rubbing specialists in the country, and the best place to go if you want advice or some special material, but if you live out of London you can almost certainly get what you need from your local craft shop or, more surely, your local art shop. There are even brass rubbing kits available. The following people all have brass rubbing materials for sale—but see page 110 if you still prefer to rely on Philips and Page.

ANDOVER
Arts and Crafts Centre (see page 10)

ASHFORD
Graphic Art Supplies (see page 10)

AYR
Contour Artists' Materials (see page 10)

BATH
Tridias (see page 10)

BEESTON
The Handicraft Shop (see page 11)

BIRMINGHAM
Midland Educational (see page 11)

Type and Palette (see page 11)

BISHOPS STORTFORD
Galaxy (see page 12) Kits only

BOURNEMOUTH
Moordown Leather and Craft (see page 114)

BRIGHTON
Handicrafts (see page 12)

BRISTOL
The Art Centre (see page 136)

Bristol Handicrafts (see page 12)

Hobbies and Crafts (see page 12)

Midland Educational (see pages 13, 11)

CAMBRIDGE
The Leigh Gallery (see page 13)

CARDIFF
Handicrafts and Dressmakers' Aids (see page 14)

CHAGFORD
Dolphin Crafts (see page 123)

CHANDLERS FORD
Creative Crafts (see page 14)

CHELTENHAM
The Colourman (see page 14)

COLCHESTER
Briggs Art and Book Shop (see page 15)

Johae Art Centre (see page 15)

COVENTRY
Midland Educational (see pages 15, 11)

CREWE
Arts and Crafts (see page 15)

DORCHESTER
Frank Herring and Sons (see page 64)

EPSOM
O W Annetts and Sons Limited (see page 16)

EXETER
The Copyshop (see page 137)

FRINTON-ON-SEA
Frinton Handicraft and Art Centre (see page 17)

GLASGOW
Miller's (see page 17)

GLOSSOP
Homecrafts (see page 18)

GODSHILL
The Island Craft Shop (see page 18)

GUISBOROUGH
Beecrafts (see page 18)

HARROGATE
Arts and Handicrafts (see page 18)

HATCH END
John Maxfield (see page 19)

HEMEL HEMPSTEAD
Arts and Crafts (see page 19)

HEREFORD
Adams and Sons (Printers) Limited (see page 137)

HIGH WYCOMBE
Dennis Syrett
28 Castle Street, High Wycombe, Buckinghamshire   High Wycombe 21466

Open: Monday to Saturday (excluding Wednesday) 09.00 to 13.15 and 14.15 to 17.30; Wednesday 09.00 to 13.00

Really concerned with artists' materials and a picture framing service but, like many art shops, also stocks brass rubbing materials and papers and the materials to make your own picture frames. Also modelling clays.

HOVE
Handicrafts (see page 19)

HUDDERSFIELD
Arts and Crafts (see page 19)

HYTHE
Needlecraft and Hobbies (see page 20)

KEIGHLEY
Conways Arts and Crafts (see page 20)

LEAMINGTON SPA
A S Blackie (see page 21)

LEEDS
E J Arnold (see page 21)

Headrow Gallery (see page 21)

LEICESTER
Midland Educational (see pages 22, 11)

LETCHWORTH
The Picture Shop (see page 22)

LONDON EC1
Crafts Unlimited (see page 22)

N1
Fine Art Supplies (see page 22) Kits only

The Pot Shop (see page 22)

N6
E Ploton (see page 131)

N9
The Art and Craft Centre (see page 23)

NW3
Crafts Unlimited (see page 23)

NW7
John Maxfield (see page 23)

SW11
Leisure Crafts (see page 23)

W1
Hamleys (see page 24) Kits only

Paperchase (see page 164)

George Rowney (see page 24)

Winsor and Newton (see page 138)

W8
Crafts Unlimited (see page 24)

Phillips & Page
50 Kensington Church Street, London W8 4DA   01 937 5839

Open: Monday to Friday 10.00 to 18.00; Saturday 10.00 to 14.00 mail order (Norwich address only); catalogue

THE brass rubbing specialists. They supply everything—the paper in various colours and textures (or, if you prefer, brass rubbing book linen), the heelball, the masking tape; erasers for mistakes; and 'Hangits' for suspending the finished product from your picture rail (or wherever). They have a good stock of relevant books and offer a framing and mounting service. They also sell facsimile monumental brasses for the lazy. They are wholesalers as well as retailers which means that even if you get your brass rubbing requisites elsewhere they are likely to have originated at Phillips & Page anyway. The London shop handles the retail side, and you can browse and ask advice. Mail order is dealt with at 40 Elm Hill, Norwich, NOR 7OK (0603 22827) and from here you can get a brass rubbing equipment price list, on request.

WC2
Crafts Unlimited (see page 53)

NEW ASH GREEN
The Hobby House (see page 26)

NEWBURY
Newbury Fine Art Limited (see page 27)

NORTHAMPTON
Arts and Crafts Shop (see page 28)
Midland Educational (see pages 28, 11)

NORWICH
Phillips and Page
This is the mail order branch of the London retail shop. See main entry on page 110.

OXFORD
Brush and Compass (see page 28)
Colegroves (see page 28)

PERTH
Dunn's Art Stores (see page 29)

PETERBOROUGH
Art and Educational Crafts (see page 29)

PRESCOT
The Art Shop (see page 29)

READING
Reading Fine Art Gallery (see page 29)

REDBOURN
Atelier (see page 29)

RICHMOND
Richmond Art and Craft (see page 30)

ROCHDALE
The Art Shop (see page 30)

SALISBURY
The Compleat Artist (see page 125)

SHREWSBURY
W M Freeman (see page 30)
Wildings (see page 30)

SKIPTON
Craven Art Centre Limited (see page 31)

SOLIHULL
Midland Educational (see pages 31, 11)

SOUTHAMPTON
Hampshire Hobbies (see page 31)

STRATFORD UPON AVON
Midland Educational (see pages 31, 11)

STURMINSTER NEWTON
Clarkes Handicraft Supplies (see page 31)

SUDBURY
Art and Craft Shop (see page 31)

SUTTON
O W Annetts and Sons Limited (see page 32)

SWANSEA
Arts and Crafts (see page 32)

THORNBURY
Arts and Crafts (see page 32)

TWICKENHAM
Bits and Bobs (see page 54)

WATFORD
Allcraft (see page 33)

WELLING
Crafts Unlimited (see page 33)

WELWYN GARDEN CITY
Boon Gallery (see page 34)

WEYMOUTH
The Art Shop (see page 92)

WIRRAL
Arts and Crafts (see page 34)

WOKING
Arts and Crafts Shop (see page 34)

WOLLASTON
Trylon Limited (see page 155) Aluminium foil only

WOLVERHAMPTON
Midland Educational (see pages 34, 11)

WORCESTER
Midland Educational (see pages 34, 11)

YEOVIL
Draytons Decorations (see page 34)

13 Leather-working

Leather merchants tend to supply in bulk only—and even if one or two are prepared to sell single skins they tend to want such lapses kept secret in case they are overwhelmed by uneconomically small orders. That, perhaps, is why more and more craft shops are stocking leather—in whole skins and offcuts. Leather from a craft shop will be more expensive than leather from a merchant—but then the craft shop leather is of a consistently good quality, and someone has already established that it is suitable for craftwork. It is also possible to buy leather or suède offcuts by the pound, often from clothing manufacturers, and almost always by mail order. Offcut merchants, craft shops who cater for leather-working, and the few merchants and specialists who welcome small orders are all listed below.

Most of the craft shops below supply tools, dyes and fittings. The basic tools are also available in good hardware shops. Suitable dyes come from the same source and also from chemists, and beeswax comes from some stockists of candlemaking supplies and from most branches of Boots. If craft shops are a bit short on accessories and fittings (buckles, rivets, eyelets, and so on), see; Rose (Fittings) Ltd, Taylor and Co, Batchelor, and Glassner—all of London, and all prepared to mail goods. Also note the new mail order firm called Grainwave Enterprises in London N15—suppliers of just about everything.

ABERDEEN

The Craft Centre (see page 34)

ALEXANDRIA

Anartex

Lomond Industrial Estate, Alexandria, Dunbartonshire, Scotland
Alexandria 52393

Open: Monday to Saturday 09.00 to 17.00; Sunday 10.00 to 17.00; mail order; catalogue

Anartex specialise in made-to-measure sheepskin coats and jackets and have two shops in London and one in Edinburgh. But if you deal direct with the factory (which welcomes callers as well as dealing by mail order) you can buy kits for home sewing of gloves, mittens, children's bootees, etc., and also sheepskin pieces with which to make rugs—or anything else you can think of.

ANDOVER

Arts and Crafts Centre (see page 10)
Tools only

ASHFORD

Davis Sheepskin Products
3 Forresters Place, Torrington Road, Ashford, Kent   Ashford 22539

Open: Tuesday, Thursday and Friday 09.00 to 17.00; mail order

Sheepskins and offcuts (most types, mainly Kent or Romney Marsh)—and leather skins and offcuts. Call, or order by telephone or letter.

AYR

Contour Artists' Materials (see page 10)

BATH

Bath Handicraft Supplies (see page 10)

BECKENHAM

R and A Kohnstamm Limited
4 Croydon Road, Beckenham, Kent BR3 4BD   01 654 3191

Open: Friday 17.00 to 20.00 and Saturday 09.00 to 13.00

This is a factory and warehouse, open for sales to the general public at the above times only. At these times they will sell you leather and leather-working tools. No minimum quantity and a wide range.

BEESTON

The Handicraft Shop (see page 11)

BELFAST

Ato-Crafts (see page 11)

BEXHILL-ON-SEA

Sackville Handicrafts (see page 140)

BIRMINGHAM

W Pond (see page 130) Tools only

BOLTON

Bolton Handicrafts (see page 12) Limited supplies

BOURNEMOUTH

Moordown Leather and Craft
923 Wimborne Road, Moordown, Bournemouth, Hampshire BH9 2BJ
Bournemouth 512048

Open: Monday to Saturday (excluding Wednesday) 09.00 to 17.30; Wednesday 09.00 to 13.00

Sell leather and leather-working tools and accessories and will undertake leather repairs, but also sell other craft materials—base metal findings, tumbled stones, cold enamelling kits, everything for lino-cutting and brass rubbing, marquetry kits, fur fabric, felt, kapok and toys' eyes and noses, prepared clays for pottery and glazes, wheels and kilns, plastic embedding kits, candlemaking supplies, modelling clays, lampshade frames and parchment and raffia and cane.

BRADFORD

R W Copley Limited (see page 96) Tools only

BRAINTREE

Braintree Wool Shop (see page 72)

BRENTFORD

H Band and Company Limited (see page 120)

BRIDGEMARY

Wimhurst's (see page 127) Tools only

BRIGHTON

Southern Handicrafts (see page 12) Tools only

BRISTOL

Craftwise (see page 38) Tools only

Hobbies and Crafts (see page 12)

BURLEY

Leather Workshop
Craft Gallery, Ringwood Road, Burley, Hampshire

Open: Monday to Saturday 09.15 to 13.00 and 14.00 to 17.30; Sunday 14.00 to 17.00; mail order

David Turners' speciality is custom made hand carved leather goods and a leather repair service. He also sells the leather and tools and some accessories (like buckles) to enable you to do it yourself. No minimum order, no catalogue

BURNLEY

Northern Handicrafts Limited (see page 13)

CANTERBURY

Canterbury Pottery (see page 13)

Needlecraft and Hobbies (see page 13)

CHELTENHAM

The Colourman (see page 14) Kits

Cotswold Craft Centre (see page 72)

COLNE

The Art Shop (see page 15)

CULLOMPTON

Crafts 'n' Creations (see page 73)

DARTFORD

Jaybee Handicrafts (see page 16)

EDINBURGH

J Hewit and Sons Limited (see page 121)

Thomas G White and Company Limited
26 Beaverbank Place, Edinburgh EH7 4ET   031 556 7929

Open: Monday to Friday 08.00 to 18.00; mail order

Call at the warehouse or order by post if you are looking for sheepskin, grain leathers, handgrained goatskin or upholstery leathers. No minimum order, but if you spend £10.00 or over they don't charge postage and packing. Will cut leather to shapes for garment and uniform trimming or strengthening.

EXETER
The Handicraft Shop (see page 17)

FALKIRK
Modelcrafts (see page 17)

FOLKESTONE
Cameo Handicrafts (see page 142)

FRINTON-ON-SEA
Frinton Handicraft and Art Centre (see page 17)

GLASGOW
W and J Martin Limited
28 St Andrews Street, Glasgow, Scotland 041 552 0264

Open: Monday to Friday 09.00 to 16.30

Won't send, so you must be in the vicinity. But if you are, you can call in and buy any quantity of clothing, case and bag leather that you choose—all prepared at the Baltic Tannery at Bridge of Weir.

Miller's (see page 17)

GLOSSOP
Homecrafts (see page 18)

GODSHILL
The Island Craft Shop (see page 18)

GOMSHALL
The Tannery Shop
The Gomshall Tanneries Limited, Gomshall, Surrey   Shere 3247

Open: Tuesday to Saturday 10.00 to 17.30; mail order; catalogue

Sheepskin tanners who sell clothing leathers—nappa, suède, woolled sheepskin and washable suède—direct from the tannery shop or by mail. Good range of colours. Free brochure includes instructions on working with leathers and on caring for the finished garments.

Also packets of samples. They say the minimum order they will fulfil by mail is one skin, but they also sell bags of offcuts. Technical sewing and advisory service available to all customers.

GRAVESEND
Tumble Kraft (see page 42)   Tools only

GUISBOROUGH
Beecrafts (see page 18)

HEREFORD
Winivere Crafts (see page 74) Some tools

HIGHAM FERRERS
C and D Hudson
3 Roland Way, Higham Ferrers, Northamptonshire   Rushden 3878

Mail order only; catalogue

Mail order suppliers of leather and leathercloth pieces in bags of mixed colours (you buy by weight). Pieces of upholstery hide, suède, chamois, lambswool, leathercloth and expanded vinyl. They will try to match colours for you and volunteer the information that other types of leather are sometimes available —so state your requirements and see what they can do for you.

HITCHIN
John P Milner Limited
67 Queen Street, Hitchin, Hertfordshire   Hitchin 3618

Open: Monday to Saturday 09.00 to 17.00; mail order; catalogue

Leathercraft specialists. They offer skins suitable for clothes, bags, gloves, etc.— also glove lining materials, tools, threads, thongs and fixtures. What you might call a comprehensive selection. Will also cut leather to size and advise.

HUDDERSFIELD
Arts and Crafts (see page 19)

HULL
Handycrafts of Hull (see page 20)

KEGWORTH
Kits 'n' Krafts (see page 75)

KEIGHLEY
Conways Arts and Crafts (see page 20)

KENDAL
Kendal Handicrafts (see page 20)

KIDDERMINSTER
Arts and Crafts (see page 20)

LANCASTER
Leisure Crafts (see page 21)

LEAMINGTON SPA
A S Blackie (see page 21)

LEATHERHEAD
Handicrafts (see page 21)   Kits

LEICESTER
Dryad (see page 22)

LLANRWST
Snowdonia Taxidermy Studios
Nebo Road, Llanrwst, Denbighshire,
   North Wales   0492 640 664

Open: Monday to Saturday 09.00 to
21.00; mail order

The Taxidermy Studios produce wild-
life models on commission for museums,
schools and naturalists. They also hire
out models for window display, stage
sets and so on. As they are regularly
preparing skins they have varying quantities of trimmings, both of skins and of
prepared leathers, available, which they
will sell by the pound weight. (If you
buy a pound's worth you will have to
take what's going.) Also, they offer a
'home tanning kit' under the name of
K-Tan which contains all the necessary
chemicals and full instructions to enable
you to tan any 'hair on' or wool skin
to the size of a large deer or sheep.

Snowdonia Taxidermy Gallery
Studio 69, Station Road, Llanrwst, Denbighshire, North Wales

Open: Monday to Saturday 10.30 to
17.30; Easter to end of September

The same materials as the Studio above,
with the addition of Winsor and Newton's artists' materials. Seasonal opening
only.

LONDON E1
N Jonas and Sons Limited
148 Shoreditch High Street, London E1
   01 739 5450

Open: Monday to Friday 09.00 to 17.00

Wholesale leather merchants—leather
for clothes, shoes, handbags and belts.
Call in and buy what you want. No
specified minimum quantity. You should
have a fairly good idea of what you're
looking for before you call.

EC1
Alma (London) Limited
Bolton House, 18-30 Clerkenwell Road,
   London EC1M 5PR   01 253 0101

Open: Monday to Friday 09.00 to 12.30
and 13.30 to 17.30; mail order

Suppliers of all kinds of leather—
clothing leathers, craft leathers and bookbinding leathers. Wide range of qualities
and colours and no minimum order. Also
PVC and polyurethane plastics.

Crafts Unlimited (see page 22)

J Hewitt (see page 121)

Rose (Fittings) Limited
337 City Road, London EC1
   01 278 5973

Open: Monday to Friday 08.00 to 17.00;
mail order

Specialists in the accessories and fittings
for leather-work. They stock the leather
itself, tools for working it, and also
buckles, zip fasteners, cotton, thread,
rivets, eyelets, ornaments, chain, locks
and so on. Also PVC and vinyls.

Taylor and Company (Tools) Limited
54 Old Street, London EC1V 9AL
   01 253 2592

Open: Monday to Friday 09.00 to 17.30;
mail order; catalogue

Toolmakers and hardware merchants
who offer a very wide range of leather
craft tools and accessories—all set out
in their fully illustrated free catalogue.
All kinds of tools, knives, creasers, punch
pliers, shears, awls and needles, eyelets,
machines and dies, handles, locks, studs
and more and more. Obviously most of
the tools are relevant to leather bookbinding—but they also offer wood and
cane working tools.

N1
The Pot Shop (see page 22)   Tools and
thonging

N15
Grainwave Enterprises
15 Clifton Gardens, London N15

Mail order only; catalogue 9p

Mail Order only. Send 9p in stamps and
they will send you a list of the leathers,
tools and accessories they have available.
They stock clothing leathers (including
suède, sheepskin, chamois and python);

suède and leather offcuts; handicraft leathers (light and heavy tooling hide, hide sides, skivers and morocco); thonging and belt lengths; hand tools, eyelets, studs, rivets, buckles, purse frames, glue, and patterns for gloves and moccasins. They promise a quick service and, what is more, guarantee to answer every query from anybody regarding leather and tools, whether listed in their catalogue or not.

NW3
J T Batchelor and Company
39 Netherhall Gardens, Hampstead, London NW3 5RL   01 794 8587

Mail order only; catalogue 12p

Mail order supplier of leather, a full range of leather-working tools and fittings (buckles, studs and so on). Leather is supplied either in complete skins or pre-cut (into belt lengths, for example). Also good colour range of aniline leather dyes. Will supply a reasonably priced beginner's kit which contains all the leather, tools, fittings and instructions to enable you to make one belt or two chokers.

Crafts Unlimited (see page 23)

SE1
Demuth Brothers Limited
17 Leathermarket Street, London SE1 3HT   01 407 3080

Open: Monday to Friday 09.00 to 17.00; mail order (c.o.d.)

Leather wholesalers from whom you may buy direct on certain conditions—you must be prepared to spend not less than £50, you must order by telephone, and you must know quite a bit about leather and the type and weight you need because no-one here has time to discuss handstitched purses with small home craftsmen.

J and W Dunn (see page 122)

William Jeffrey and Company Limited
88/90 Weston Street, Bermondsey, London SE1 3QH   01 407 1931/2/3

Open: Monday to Friday 09.00 to 17.00; mail order

A large leather warehouse which is open to customers and offers all types of leather in any quantity, however small—but especially best quality English harness leather, continental modelling leather and genuine Texan 'Latigo' cowboy leather. No catalogue.

G A Roberts and Son Limited
Second Floor, 60 Long Lane, London SE1 4AN   01 407 2960

Open: Monday to Friday 09.30 to 17.00

Sell all types of light leather, suitable for bookbinding, craft leather-work and furniture covering. Will supply any quantity—but over the counter only.

SW10
Hobby Horse (see page 23)   Tools only

SW11
Leisure Crafts (see page 23)

SW17
Homecraft Supplies (see page 24)

SW19
S Glassner
Department SV, 68 Worple Road, Wimbledon, London SW19   01 946 4684

Open: Monday to Friday 09.30 to 17.00 (Callers between 14.00 and 17.00 only); mail order; catalogue

Everything for the maker of small leather goods—all cutting, thonging and boring tools; die punches; accessories like buckles, studs, fasteners and eyelets; synthetic and real leather thonging; suitable adhesives (a rubber paste which will stick almost anything except rubber); a series of 'how to make it' leaflets on handbags, purses and wallets; and leather in various grains and colours sold by the skin. Also two pound packs of leather pieces large enough for purses and comb cases, and two complete leathercraft kits. Note: callers between 14.00 and 17.00 only, unless you specifically make an appointment for the morning.

W1
Louis Grossé Limited (see page 76)
Gold and silver kid

Light Leather Company Limited
18 Newman Street, London W1P 3HD 01 580 3198

Open: Monday to Friday 09.00 to 13.00 and 14.15 to 17.00; mail order

Exporters, wholesalers and retailers of leathers, suèdes and sheepskin suitable for clothing, shoes, belts, etc. You can buy by mail but it's better to go along because there's no catalogue. Minimum quantity you can buy is one whole skin.

Selfridges (see page 24)

W8
Crafts Unlimited (see page 24)

LOUGHBOROUGH
Artcraft and Do-It-Yourself (see page 25)

LYTHAM
Lytham Woodcraft Limited (see page 25)

MANCHESTER
Fred Aldous (see page 25)

Arts and Crafts (see page 77)

MIDDLESBROUGH
J Goldstein and Son (see page 26)

NEW ASH GREEN
The Hobby House (see page 26)

NORTHAMPTON
Arts and Crafts Shop (see page 28)

NOTTINGHAM
Home Pastimes (see page 28)

John Lees of Nottingham (see page 77)

OLDHAM
The Art and Craft Shop (see page 28)

PERTH
Dunn's Art Stores (see page 29)

PETERBOROUGH
Art and Educational Crafts (see page 29)

PRESCOT
The Art Shop (see page 29)

READING
Inspirations (see page 48)

RICHMOND
Richmond Art and Craft (see page 30)

ST ANNES ON SEA
The Handmaiden (see page 30)

SELKIRK
G Tanners Limited
Bridgehaugh Mill, Selkirk, Selkirkshire, Scotland   Selkirk 2216
Mail order only

Contact the factory by writing or telephoning and you can arrange to buy pigskin and deerskin for clothing and for craft leatherwork. If you want to be invoiced you must spend at least £5—if you're prepared to pay cash, there is no lower limit.

SHEFFIELD
Milldale Trading Company
5 Milldale Road, Totley Rise, Sheffield, Yorkshire S17 4HR
Mail order only

Offer 1 pound (approximately) bags of suède and leather offcuts in browns and beiges. Mail order only. 50p per bag when last heard of.

SHEFFIELD
H R Whitehead (see page 30)

SOUTHAMPTON
Ceramic Clays (see page 57)

Hampshire Hobbies (see page 31)

STANMORE
Quality First
27 Court Drive, Stanmore, Middlesex   01 958 7817
Mail order only; catalogue

A fast postal service of modern suède or leather trousers, skirts and waistcoats made to your measurements. They naturally end up with a lot of offcuts and will sell bags of mixed pieces—mostly in dark colours—in good sizes. They are moving to new premises shortly, but mail will be forwarded for two years.

STROUD
Redpath Campbell and Partners Limited
Cheapside, Stroud, Gloucestershire
Mail order only

Mail order suppliers who, from time to time, offer bags of mixed suède and leather pieces in various colours (you must take what you're given!). Suitable for small toys, chokers and so on. You get about $3\frac{1}{2}$ pounds for £2.00 including postage and packing.

SUDBURY
Art and Craft Shop (see page 31)

SWANSEA
Arts and Crafts (see page 32) Tools only

THORNBURY
Arts and Crafts (see page 32)

TWICKENHAM
Bits and Bobs (see page 54)

WATFORD
J Simble and Sons (see page 51) Tools only

WELLING
Crafts Unlimited (see page 33)

WOOLER
Glendale Crafts (see page 80)

YORK
Derwent Crafts (see page 35)

14 Bookbinding

Manufacturers of the materials and tools for binding books tend to supply the trade only, saying that it is not economical for them to sell small quantities—though a few are prepared to deal with schools and adult education institutes where the demand, though low by trade standards, is still quite high. So unless you are attending an evening class, and making use of materials supplied, the search for boards, leathers, gold leaf or whatever can be a little disheartening. The following people are always sympathetic to the binder of single copies. From them you should be able to get whatever you need in the way of materials and tools. The previous chapter on leather may also be relevant, and from the final chapter you should be able to discover where to get hold of unusual endpapers.

ANDOVER

Reckner and Company (see page 163)

BIRMINGHAM

H Goodman (Birmingham) Ltd
Stratford Street North, Birmingham, Warwickshire B11 1BT   021 772 6008

Open: Monday to Friday 09.00 to 13.00 and 14.00 to 17.00 (**By appointment**); mail order

Specialise in bookbinders' hand tools for gilding. No minimum order and they will send anywhere against a pro forma invoice. No catalogue, so you must know what you want. If you decide to call in, please make an appointment first.

BIRMINGHAM

W Pond (see page 130)   Tools

BOLTON

Red Bridge Bookcloth Company Limited
Ainsworth, Bolton, Lancashire
Bolton 22254

Open: Monday to Friday 09.00 to 17.30; mail order; catalogue £2.00

You can call, or write or telephone your order. They are suppliers of bookbinding cloths and your order must be for not less than 20 yards.

BRENTFORD

H Band and Company Limited
Brent Way, High Street, Brentford, Middlesex   01 560 2025

Open: Monday to Friday 09.00 to 15.30; mail order; catalogue

H Band are light leather tanners and dressers and this is not a retail shop but a factory—however callers are welcome so long as they telephone and make an appointment first. Bands are also very willing to send out details and samples of their materials, which are bookbinding vellums, vellums suitable for lampshades, haircalf for fancy leather work, and vellums and parchments handmade to a medieval recipe which are used for writing and illuminating. If you want them to, they will quote you a price for quill pens. Very helpful, offering high quality materials.

BRIGHTON

Handicrafts (see page 12)

BRISTOL

Taylor and Son Limited
2 Asher Lane, Redcross Street, Bristol BS2 0BE   Bristol 291616

(Opening times not applicable)

Suppliers of bookbinding paper, boards, leather, cords and tassels to the *trade only*. You cannot buy direct but, if you are stuck, contact the Handicraft Supplies Department and they will willingly put you in touch with your nearest stockist.

COLNE
The Art Shop (see page 15)

COMPTON CHAMBERLAYNE
Compton Russell (see page 163) Endpapers

EDINBURGH
J Hewit and Sons Limited
Kinauld Leather Works, Currie, Edinburgh EH14 5RS   031 449 2206

Open: Monday to Friday 08.30 to 13.00 and 14.00 to 17.30

Same stock as the London sales office—see page 121.

HOVE
Handicrafts (see page 19)

ILKLEY
Northern Adhesives
11 Parish Ghyll Road, Ilkley, Yorkshire Ilkley 3282

Open: Monday to Friday 08.30 to 18.00; mail order

Specialists in adhesives of all types—suitable for bookbinding, but also for other craftwork which depends on sticking one thing to another. Will accept orders by telephone or by mail—or customers may call in to collect adhesives.

LANCING
Rogate Printers
119 South Street, Lancing, Sussex BN15 8AS   Lancing 5208 and 4963

Open: Monday to Friday (excluding Wednesday) 09.15 to 13.00 and 14.00 to 17.30; Wednesday 09.15 to 13.00; Saturday 09.15 to 13.00; mail order; catalogue 4p (postage)

A Printers' supply service—which means that they offer printers' cards, papers, inks and sundries and can sell you bookbinding materials (paper, boards and some cloth) and also materials (though no tools or accessories) for screen printing. No minimum order.

LEICESTER
Dryad (see page 22)

LONDON EC1
Alma (London) Limited (see page 116)

E3
The Peerless Gold Leaf Company Limited
Fairfield Works, Fairfield Road, Bow, London E3   01 980 4321

Mail order; catalogue

Suppliers of gold leaf and gold and coloured foils. It's a small company so don't call in and overcrowd things. Send for the literature if you need it. If not, simply write in, and please send cash with your order.

EC1
A J Brown Brough and Company Limited
3 Dufferin Street, London EC1Y 8SD   01 638 8085

Open: Monday to Friday 09.00 to 17.00

Business premises, not a shop, but you can call in, write for an appointment, or telephone. They supply hard rolled millboard for bookbinding. Naturally not keen on supplying very small quantities, so the amount must be negotiated. They will undertake the cutting of boards to specified sizes. Also deal in packaging paper, twines and tapes.

J Hewit and Sons Limited
89/97 St John Street, London EC1M 4AT   01 253 1431

Open: Monday to Friday 08.30 to 13.00 and 14.00 to 17.30; mail order; catalogue

Tanners and leather dressers (the works are in Edinburgh—see separate entry). Can supply everything for bookbinding—including machine-cut brass type, buckram, linen, holland, vellum, leathercloth and all types of bookbinding leathers. Also what they call 'sundries', which term covers everything else a bookbinder might need—brushes, numbering ink, knives, gold leaf, type holders, shears, glue pots, adhesives, thread, hemp, rope twine, headbands, cutting boards, finishing presses, etc. etc. Won't send less than a £10 order by mail, but if you call in you can buy as little as you like—and ask advice if you want it. (They also have leathers for other handicrafts and some of the twines are suitable for macramé.)

A Holt and Sons Limited
115 Whitecross Street, London EC1 8JQ   01 606 5676

Open: Monday to Friday 09.30 to 16.30

Manufacturers and suppliers of calico and mull bookbinding cloths. The minimum order they will fulfil is for 50 yards of material, so you need to be keen—or to be a school or organisation engaged on a group project. Telephone your order in and then arrange either to collect the cloth or have it sent by carrier.

Taylor and Company (Tools) Limited (see page 116) Tools

SE1
J and W Dunn Limited
54 Tanner Street, London SE1
01 407 0293

Open: Monday to Friday 09.30 to 16.30; mail order; catalogue

Leather tanners and dressers with a more or less permanent stock of morocco embossed calf and skivers—all suitable for bookbinding. Will supply relatively small quantities of the leathers they have, but will not prepare special skins unless the order is large. Will supply anywhere, but you must pay carriage costs.

A Roberts (see page 117)

W1
George Rowney (see page 24) Brushes

WC1
Frank Grunfeld (see page 164)

SLOUGH

Williams Adhesives Limited
247 Argyll Avenue Trading Estate, Slough, Buckinghamshire
Slough 24343

Open: Monday to Friday 08.30 to 17.30; mail order

Will sell small quantities of all types of gum, glue, paste, rubber solution, natural and synthetic adhesives—particularly suitable for bookbinding. They also run an advisory service on all adhesive problems—what methods to use, which adhesives are best for which materials and where to obtain relevant equipment. You can order by phone or letter, or call in.

SOUTH RUISLIP

George M Whiley
Victoria Road, South Ruislip, Middlesex
01 422 0141

Mail order only; catalogue

Mail order suppliers of any quantity of gold and other metal leaf and/or stamping foil for bookbinding, and also a full range of gilders tools and accessories. If you know just what you want you can telephone or write in your order—if not, ask for the free catalogue.

STAINES

Morane Plastic Company Limited (see page 155)

STOCKPORT

F J Ratchford Limited
Kennedy Way, Green Lane, Stockport, Cheshire SK4 2JX Stockport 8484

Mail order only; catalogue

Suppliers of bookbinding cloths (white back art vellum and quarto quality bookcloth), bookbinding leathers and 'sundries'—herringbone webbing, glue brushes, binding tapes, etc. They are geared to dealing in enormous quantities and say they have never sold small quantities before but will be interested to try it as an experiment. They therefore do not stipulate a minimum quantity at this stage, though they may perhaps be forced to later on. Ask for Mr N S Ratchford, who is a nice man.

SUDBURY

Art and Craft Shop (see page 31)

WITHAM

Mackrell and Company Limited
Industrial Estate West, Colchester Road, Witham, Essex Witham 3431

Open: Monday to Friday 08.00 to 16.30; mail order; catalogue

Mackrells have bookbinders' tools. Although the address above is their factory, callers are welcome, or you can buy by mail or telephone. They will make brass blocks and hand tools to your specifications—and supply type holders and master dies, brass and steel type, colophons, crests, screens and textures, rules, stars, ornamental frames, alphabet hand tools, decorative wheels—in short, they can sell you whatever you need to embellish your freshly bound books.

15 Picture Framing

Shops selling artists' materials can usually supply picture framing kits or mouldings, and also backings and non-reflective glass. Craft shops quite often have kits or mouldings. Hardware and do-it-yourself shops sell the obvious accessories—tools, tacks, hooks and metal corner pieces—and also suitable woods, sometimes trimmed to size, if you're lucky.

The following all carry a reasonable stock of the basic necessities. See especially E Ploton of London if you want to gild your frame, and World of Wood in Mildenhall, Handicrafts of Peterborough, and James Hagerty of Southport who can all supply a very wide range of materials, by mail order if necessary.

ALBRIGHTON

Flexitools Limited (see page 129) Tools only

ALLENTON

Allenton Homecrafts (see page 9)

AYR

Contour Artists' Materials (see page 10)

BEESTON

The Handicraft Shop (see page 11)

BERKHAMPSTEAD

Handyman (see page 145)

BIRMINGHAM

W Pond (see page 130) Tools only

BOURNEMOUTH

Handyman's Treasure Chest
77 Withermoor Road, Winton, Bournemouth, Hampshire
Bournemouth 53298

Open: Monday to Saturday (excluding Tuesday) 09.00 to 17.45; Tuesday 09.00 to 12.30

Run by Mr Domville who has been teaching handicrafts and woodwork for a number of years and is always willing to help anyone. The Treasure Chest is a DIY shop where timber and hardboard are cut to order. Specialise in woods suitable for picture framing, although obviously wood for other purposes is available. Very helpful—no minimum order.

BRAMPTON

The Handyman's Shop (see page 127)

BRIDGEMARY

Wimhurst's (see page 127)

BRISTOL

Doug Lovell and Company
214/216 Church Road, St George, Bristol BS5 8AD   Bristol 556608

Open: Monday to Friday (excluding Wednesday) 09.00 to 13.00 and 14.00 to 17.30; Wednesday 09.00 to 12.30; Saturday 09.00 to 18.00

A general do-it-yourself store which will obtain picture framing materials and tools to order. They say they deal with schools only.

CAMBRIDGE

The Leigh Gallery (see page 13) Kits only

CHAGFORD

Dolphin Crafts
Dolphin House, Mill Street, Chagford, Devon   Chagford 2257

Open: Monday to Saturday 09.00 to 17.30 (From October to March, closed until 14.00 on Monday); mail order

Mainly artists' materials and papers and

picture framing materials, including plain and non-reflective glass. Also a very full stock of craft books, some kits for candle-making and silk screen printing and tools and materials for lino-cutting, brass rub-bing, tie-dye and batik, and a lot of different modelling materials—Newclay, Das, Modroc, etc. They will undertake the mounting and framing of pictures, embroideries and tapestries.

CHELTENHAM
The Colourman (see page 14)   Kits only

CHORLEY
Woodfit (see page 131)

CLITHEROE
Tattersalls (see page 15)   Kits only

COLCHESTER
Johae Art Centre (see page 15)

COLNE
The Art Shop (see page 15)

CREWE
Arts and Crafts (see page 15)

DARTFORD
Jaybee Handicrafts (see page 16)

DUNOON
Dae-It-Yersel (see page 16)

EXETER
The Handicraft Shop (see page 17)

FALKIRK
Modelcrafts (see page 17)

FORDINGBRIDGE
Caxton Decor (see page 17)

FRINTON-ON-SEA
Frinton Handicraft and Art Centre (see page 17)

GLASGOW
Miller's (see page 17)

GLASGOW
Morrisons Artists' Materials
Nithsdale Road Post Office, Glasgow
  G41 4LU 041 423 1280
Open: Monday to Friday 09.00 to 13.00

and 14.30 to 17.30; Saturday 09.00 to 13.00

Mainly artists' materials but also kits and mouldings for picture framing, lino-cutting materials and tools, all types of art and craft paper, a small amount of felt and some modelling materials.

GLOSSOP
Homecrafts (see page 18)

GUISBOROUGH
Beecrafts (see page 18)

HARROGATE
Arts and Handicrafts (see page 18)

HATCH END
John Maxfield (see page 19)

HEREFORD
Adams and Son (Printers) Limited (see page 137)

HIGH WYCOMBE
Dennis Syrett (see page 110)

KEIGHLEY
Conways Arts and Crafts (see page 20)

KIDDERMINSTER
Arts and Crafts (see page 20)

KNUTSFORD
Green's Do It Yourself Supplies (see page 128)

LEAMINGTON SPA
A S Blackie (see page 21)

LEEDS
Headrow Gallery (see page 21)

LETCHWORTH
The Picture Shop (see page 22)

LONDON N6
E Ploton (see page 131) Gilding requisites

N16
General Woodwork Supplies (see page 128)

SW17
Homecraft Supplies (see page 24) Kits only

W1
George Rowney (see page 24)

Selfridges (see page 24)

Winsor and Newton (see page 138)

MALVERN
Fearnside and Company (see page 25)
Kits only

MILDENHALL
World of Wood (see page 128)

MILTON KEYNES
Milton Keynes Day Centre (see page 26)

MORPETH
Tallantyre Wallpapers (see page 26)

NEWCASTLE UPON TYNE
The Do It Yourself Foam Centre (see page 27)

NORTHAMPTON
Arts and Crafts Shop (see page 28)

OLDHAM
The Art and Craft Shop (see page 28)

PETERBOROUGH
Art and Educational Crafts (see page 29)
Kits only

Handicrafts (Peterborough)
New Road, Peterborough, Huntingdonshire PE1 1UD Peterborough 3372

Open: Monday to Saturday (excluding Thursday) 09.00 to 17.30; Thursday closed; mail order; catalogue

Established for thirty years as a mail order house which supplies to schools, hospitals and organisations all over the world. However, they will supply to individuals and you can call in if you want to. They do have raffias, modelling clays and cane, but their specialities are marquetry and picture framing. They have marquetry tools, accessories, kits and instruction booklets and also a very large range of veneers and burrs. You can order by telephone or post and materials will arrive promptly (they promise) C.O.D. For picture framers they offer kits, tools, accessories and ready-mitred mouldings in a wide range of colours

and styles and they will also recommend an instruction book.

READING
Reading Fine Art Gallery (see page 29)

ROCHDALE
The Art Shop (see page 30)

SALISBURY
The Compleat Artist
102 Crane Street, Salisbury, Wiltshire Salisbury 5928

Open: Monday to Saturday (excluding Wednesday) 09.00 to 17.30; Wednesday 09.00 to 13.00

As the name would suggest, they deal in artists' materials, but they also have some craft kits, brass rubbing materials, a good variety of modelling materials and picture framing kits and materials. (Also ready made frames and a framing service.)

SHREWSBURY
W M Freeman (see page 31) Kits only

SITTINGBOURNE
Homecrafts (see page 31) Kits only

SOUTHPORT
James R Hagerty
11/13 Eastbank Street, Southport, Lancashire Southport 56442

Open: Monday to Saturday 09.00 to 18.00; mail order; catalogue

Artists' materials, a picture framing service and picture frame mouldings, machine-mitred ready to join, together with special joining clamps. Also, all the necessary for lino-cutting and candle-making.

STURMINSTER NEWTON
Clarkes Handicraft Supplies (see page 31)

WATFORD
J Simble and Sons (see page 51) Tools only

WELWYN GARDEN CITY
Boon Gallery (see page 34)

WILLENHALL
Jeffrey's (see page 129)

WIRRAL
Arts and Crafts (see page 34)

WOOLER
Glendale Crafts (see page 80)

WOKING
Arts and Crafts Shop (see page 34)

YEOVIL
Draytons Decorations (see page 34)

16 Woodwork, Pokerwork and Marquetry

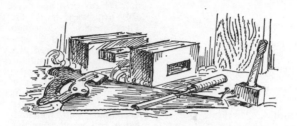

When it comes to woodwork the main problem is, of course, finding the wood. Wood is expensive and in short supply and, among other things, this means that commercial woodworkers who used to throw away offcuts now plan their work so that fewer offcuts result. Those which are inevitable, they are more likely to sell than to give away. In fact there are people who join evening classes not for the tuition or companionship but in order to be assured of a reasonable supply of materials.

It is not possible to list every lumberyard and every do-it-yourself shop in the country, but nevertheless those are the places where you should start. If neither has the material you want, look up Furniture Manufacturers in the yellow pages and see if your nearest small furniture factory can supply you with any useful offcuts.

Another idea, particularly if you are interested in cabinet making, is to go to sales of antique furniture. You may be able to buy, for instance, an enormous mahogany wardrobe—going cheap because people don't like large furniture any more. In that way not only do you get fully seasoned wood, you probably get some old-fashioned brass fittings as well.

Or, of course, you can contact the suppliers listed below. This chapter is divided into General—people with a general stock of wood, tools, fittings and even marquetry kits—Tools, Gilding, Cabinet Fittings, Turning, Pokerwork and Marquetry.

GENERAL

ANDOVER
Arts and Crafts Centre (see page 10)

BERKHAMPSTED
Handyman (see page 145)

BOURNEMOUTH
Handyman's Treasure Chest (see page 123)

BRADFORD
R W Copley Limited (see page 96)

BRAMPTON
The Handyman's Shop
High Cross Street, Brampton, Near Carlisle, Cumberland   Brampton 2739

Open: Monday to Saturday (excluding Thursday) 09.00 to 17.30; Thursday 09.00 to 12.30; mail order (occasionally)

Sell what you would expect to find in a shop of that name, but also some craft materials—Dylon, woods, veneers, marquetry and picture framing materials and tools, basketry supplies, plastic embedding kits, foam fillings and eyes for toys.

BRIDGEMARY
Wimhurst's
178 Nobes Avenue, Bridgemary, Near Gosport, Hampshire   Fareham 80717

Open: Monday to Saturday (excluding Wednesday) 08.45 to 13.00 and 14.15 to 17.30; Wednesday 08.45 to 13.00

A hardware and tool shop which says firmly that it is the only British firm making sheet metal (hand) shrinking and stretching tools. Can also sell you modelling clays, woods, veneers, picture framing woods, mouldings and tools, and tools for leather-working, lino-cutting and woodwork generally.

BRISTOL

Craftwise (see page 38)

CHANDLERS FORD

Creative Crafts (see page 14)

DUNOON

Dae-It-Yersel (see page 16)

FRINTON-ON-SEA

Frinton Handicraft and Art Centre (see page 17)

GLOSSOP

Elliott Brothers
PO Box Number 6, Glossop, Derbyshire

Mail order only; catalogue

Veneer specialists who offer offcuts and full leaves in all popular timbers. Mail order only.

HARROGATE

Arts and Handicrafts (see page 18)

KIDDERMINSTER

Arts and Crafts (see page 20)

KNUTSFORD

Green's Do It Yourself Supplies
The Old Water Tower, Mobberley Road, Knutsford, Cheshire   Knutsford 2031

Open: Monday to Friday 08.00 to 18.00; Saturday 08.00 to 17.00

Make your way to the Water Tower and you can choose from a good range of do-it-yourself supplies which include woods, veneers and picture framing materials and tools. And keep your eye on the enterprise, because the plan is to extend the stock to include more craft materials.

LEEDS

E J Arnold and Son Limited (see page 21)

LONDON EC1

Crafts Unlimited (see page 22)

N16
General Woodwork Supplies
76/80 Stoke Newington High Street, Stoke Newington, London N16   01 254 6052

Open: Monday to Saturday (excluding Thursday) 09.00 to 18.00; Thursday 09.00 to 13.00; mail order; catalogue

Suppliers of imported and British woods which they will cut or plane to your specifications. (They will also sand, dovetail, rebate, turn and carve—but presumably you want to do all that yourself.) They have a wide range of hardwoods and also plywood, veneered plywood, blockboard, veneered blockboard, woods for lathe, carving and turnery work, and softwood. Also hard and softwood mouldings suitable for picture framing. Very keen to help. If you want to call in, send for the catalogue. The map on the back even tells you which bus or tube to catch and which way the one-way traffic system flows.

NW3
Crafts Unlimited (see page 23)

SW17
Homecraft Supplies (see page 24)   Stool frames

SW20
Park Building Supplies
358/374 Grand Drive, Raynes Park, London SW20   01 542 1201

Open: Monday to Saturday 09.00 to 17.30; mail order

A Do-It-Yourself shop where you will find, among other things, casting plasters, liquid latex, and timbers of various types and supplied in any quantity.

W1
Selfridges (see page 24)

Alec Tiranti Limited (see page 62)
Especially for woodcarvers

W8
Crafts Unlimited (see page 24)   Especially strong on marquetry and pokerwork

WC2
Crafts Unlimited (see page 53)

LOUGHBOROUGH

Artcraft and Do-It-Yourself (see page 25)

MILDENHALL

World of Wood
Industrial Estate, Mildenhall, Suffolk   Mildenhall 2550

Open: Monday to Friday 08.00 to 17.30; Saturday 08.30 to 12.30; mail order; catalogue

World of Wood promise that they stock everything for the woodcraftsman—and their 80 page Manual certainly endorses this. They have tools of all kinds, hardwoods of all types and available in any quantity (however small) and a tremendous range of veneers. Everything (materials and tools) you need for woodwork, marquetry, pokerwork and picture framing, including attractive marquetry art sets. A good place for the amateur woodworker to start because even the Manual is an education (though, as always, you will learn far more if you can go in person). Perhaps especially strong on marquetry.

MILTON KEYNES

Milton Keynes Day Centre (see page 26)

NEW WALTHAM

Joseph Ogle (see page 27)

NOTTINGHAM

Fitchett and Woollacott Limited
Popham Street, Nottingham, Nottinghamshire NG1 7JE   Nottingham 53251

Open: Monday to Friday 08.00 to 13.30 and 13.30 to 16.45; mail order; catalogue

Suppliers of timber for woodwork, turning and carving, but right at this moment they have so much work on that they can't possibly fulfil any new orders. If you are not an established customer, approach with caution, and please retire gracefully if they say they cannot help you.

OXFORD

Timbmet Limited
PO Box 39, Chawley Works, Cumnor Hill, Oxford, Oxfordshire OX2 9PP
    Oxford 2223

Open: Monday to Friday 08.00 to 17.30; mail order

Deal in all kinds of hardwoods and will sell fairly small quantities—(minimum order £20). Don't call in, but telephone your order. Would prefer you to collect, but will arange for wood to be delivered if you will pay carriage costs.

SUDBURY

Art and Craft Shop (see page 31)

STRATHMIGLO

Haldane and Company (see page 68)

UXBRIDGE

Mahjacks
27 Windsor Street, Uxbridge, Middlesex
    Uxbridge 32625

Open: Monday to Saturday (excluding Wednesday) 08.30 to 17.30; Wednesday 08.30 to 13.00; mail order

All the basics for the cabinet-making woodworker—a full range of timbers, veneered boards, furniture fittings and hinges, decorative mouldings for use in cabinet work, do-it-yourself tools and materials and also things like formica, whitewood furniture, 'kitchens in boxes', etc.

WELLING

Crafts Unlimited (see page 33)

WESTON-SUPER-MARE

Benmail Supplies
Station Road, St Georges, Weston-super-Mare, Somerset BS22 0XL

Mail order only; catalogue

Mail order suppliers of useful things for woodworkers, including famous-name branded tools, screws, hinges and brackets—all offered at below-retail prices. Illustrated list free, promptly, on request.

WILLENHALL

Jeffrey's
9 Field Street, Willenhall, Staffordshire
    Willenhall 65101

Open: Monday to Saturday (excluding Thursday) 09.00 to 17.00; Thursday 09.00 to 13.00

Well-stocked Do-it-Yourself shop run, suitably enough, by a Mr Wood. They stock various kinds of wood, veneers and picture framing woods and mouldings. Also tools for woodwork and general craft tools.

TOOLS

Most woodworking tools are readily available in hardware and Do-It-Yourself shops throughout the country. But if you have any difficulty, these are the people to contact.

ALBRIGHTON

Flexitools Limited
Albrighton, Shropshire WV7 3PB
    Albrighton 3171

Strictly mail order; catalogue 10p

Flexitools are available through tool retailers, but if you have any difficulty in finding what you need you can buy direct by mail order (send 10p for the catalogue). These tools are for hollow-built wood turnery, picture framing and laminated and shaped woodwork and include cramps and precision saw-jigs and all accessories. They also have hollow-built wood-turning kits and craft sets of tools for laminated and shaped woodwork.

BIRMINGHAM

W Pond and Company Limited
192-194 Corporation Street, Birmingham, Warwickshire B4 6Q5　021 236 6871

Open: Monday to Saturday 09.00 to 17.30; mail order; catalogue

Suppliers of tools and engineering equipment. They have a truly enormous range of both electric and hand tools, many of them suitable for craftwork—especially carpentry and jewellery, but also picture framing, leather-work and bookbinding. The catalogue is really an engineering catalogue for trade use, and is a hefty and expensively produced book which they don't send out lightly—but call, write or telephone if you have special requirements and they will willingly tell you if they can supply (and they probably can).

EAST KIRKBY

Ashley Iles (Edge Tools) Limited
Fenside, East Kirkby, Near Spilsby, Lincolnshire　East Kirkby 372

Open: All day, every day; mail order; catalogue 3p

When asked for their opening hours they said 'we never close'—so I presume you may take them at their word! They deal by direct mail order (although callers are welcome) and specialise in hand forged woodcarving and woodturning tools 'for the connoisseur carver' which are supplied singly or in sets all over the country (and abroad). You can have a very explicit illustrated catalogue in exchange for a 3p stamp.

HODDESDON

Mate Tools Limited
Brewery Road, Hoddesdon, Hertfordshire　Hoddesdon 69626 or 67890

Open: Monday to Friday 08.00 to 18.00; Saturday 08.00 to 12.00; mail order; catalogue

Offer a selection of well-known tools of all kinds at lower-than-shop-prices. (Run by the designer of Lotus Elan Sports Cars and the Black and Decker Workmate, who should know what he's talking about!) All kinds of tools (even garden tools) but for the purposes of this book

the relevant ones are the woodworking and modelling tools. Pride themselves in a 'no quibble money-back guarantee' and prompt service.

HULL

Humbrol Limited
Marfleet, Hull, East Yorkshire

Mail order only

Have produced a range of 'Multicraft Precision Tools'—a variety of blades which have application in woodworking, lino-cutting, plastic cutting, etc. Produce kits and single items and sell through Do-It-Yourself and craft shops. But if you have trouble in locating the tools, contact Humbrol either to buy direct or for the name of your nearest stockist.

LEICESTER

Dryad (see page 22)

LONDON EC1

Taylor and Company (Tools) Limited (see page 116)

N7

Vitrex Florin Limited
457/463 Caledonian Road, London N7 9BB　01 609 0011

(Opening times not applicable)

Supply a good range of hand tools for DIY enthusiasts—including glass cutters. If you can't find what you want in your local hardware shop, contact head office for the name and address of your nearest stockist.

MAIDENHEAD

Black and Decker Limited
Cannon Lane, Maidenhead, Berkshire SL6 3PD　Littlewick Green 2130

(Opening times not applicable)

Will be happy to give you the name and address of your nearest stockist, and to help in any way they can.

NEWARK

D Arundel and Company
Mills Drive, Farndon Road, Newark, Nottinghamshire NG24 4SN Newark 2382

Open: Monday to Friday 08.00 to 17.00; mail order; catalogue 12p

Their business is woodturning lathes and all light woodworking machinery and attachments. Customers may call, but most of the orders are dealt with by mail (or BRS). If you want to inspect the machinery and your only free day is Saturday, you may call by appointment.

SHEFFIELD

Aaron Hildick Limited
Lowther Road, Sheffield, Yorkshire S6 2DR Sheffield 340282

(Opening times not applicable)

Aaron Hildick are manufacturers of woodcarving and light edge tools. They do not sell direct because their tools are available from retail outlets throughout the country—but if you are having trouble locating a supplier, contact them at the above address and they will gladly put you in touch with your nearest dealer. They also supply leaflets which advise on the care of tools.

GILDING

LONDON N6

E Ploton (Sundries) Limited
273 Archway Road, London N6 01 348 0315

Open: Monday to Friday 09.00 to 17.00; Saturday 09.00 to 13.00; mail order; catalogue

Specialists in French artists' materials who can supply gold leaf and all gilding requisites and accessories. They also have modelling clays and brass rubbing and lino-cutting tools and materials.

For other gold leaf suppliers, see Bookbinding chapter.

CABINET FITTINGS

These should not be particularly hard to find in hardware and DIY shops, but there are two mail order firms worth knowing about just in case.

BOLTON

Antique Handles
PO Box 1, Bolton, Lancashire

Mail order only; catalogue 10p

If your woodworking takes the form of cabinet making, Antique Handles can supply you with solid brass reproduction cabinet handles, hinges, fittings and door furniture. Mail order only, but the catalogue is fully illustrated and they don't mind selling single items.

CHORLEY

Woodfit
Whittle Low Mill, Chorley, Lancashire PR6 7HB Chorley 2478

Mail order only; catalogue

Mail order suppliers of all kinds of cabinet hardware—hinges, roller catches, stays and brackets, keyhole plates, bureau and cupboard locks, period brass handles and door knockers, castors, military chest fittings and handles, etc., etc. Wide range at reasonable prices. Plan to offer picture frame mouldings in the very near future.

TURNING

Specialist suppliers of tools, woods and vital accessories (like peppermill mechanisms and so on).

BLAYDON-ON-TYNE

Wood Components Limited
Newburn Bridge Road, Ryton Industrial Estate, Blaydon-on-Tyne, County Durham NE21 4TB Blaydon 4224

Mail order only

These are wood turners and importers who produce precision woodwork to customers' specifications. However, they will sometimes supply amateur turners with wood suitable for turning, round beads, balls, bored wooden cubes, etc. Write, or telephone between 09.00 and 16.00 Monday to Friday.

BURY ST EDMONDS

Country Craft Studio
Lawshall, Bury St Edmonds, Suffolk IP29 4PA Cockfield Green 661

Open: Monday to Friday 09.00 to 18.00; mail order; catalogue

Specialist suppliers of all the necessary tools for wood turners and carvers and also accessories—table-lighter inserts, candlestick eyelets, blades for steak knives and letter openers—and many more. Currently enlarging their stock and working on a new catalogue. Minimum order by mail should cost £1.00.

COLCHESTER

Johae Art Centre (see page 15) Turning tools.

FROME

Marcross Gems and B Mandeville
17 Portway, Frome, Somerset Frome 2375

Open: Monday to Saturday 09.00 to 17.30 (Evenings and weekends by appointment); mail order; catalogue

Lapidary supplies and turning woods. For woodworkers they offer a mail order service of a good range of selected hardwoods suitable for turning and carving, including offcuts and trial parcels of assorted timbers. All wood is guaranteed so long as you return defective pieces immediately and before you begin work on them. There are also chains and findings in stainless steel and other metals, precious and semi-precious stones, jewellers' tools and machines, tumbling machines and accessories, rough rock and a wide range of relevant books. Also gem kits, lost wax casting kits, tumbling kits and crystal glass mosaics. There's another branch in Shepton Mallet.

LITTLE YELDHAM

Peter Child
The Old Hyde, Little Yeldham, Near Halstead, Essex Great Yeldham 291

Mail order only; catalogue

Run by the author of *The Craftsman Woodturner*, who offers residential tuition in woodturning and also a mail order service for woodturning tools, pokerwork machines, suitable woods, waxes and polishes and accessories (like star base hors d'oeuvre dish inserts, arenoid barometer movements and peppermill mechanisms). Also, of course, lathes and safety equipment.

SHEPTON MALLET

Marcross Gems and B Mandeville
13 Market Place, Shepton Mallet, Somerset Shepton Mallet 2491

Open: Monday to Saturday 09.00 to 17.30 (Evenings and weekends by appointment) Woodturning blanks—see main branch in Frome on page 131.

POKERWORK

Not as popular as it once was and quite a few craft shops have stopped supplying. But in addition to all the branches of Crafts Unlimited, the following people can sell you what you need.

FALKIRK

Modelcrafts (see page 17)

GODSHILL

The Island Craft Shop (see page 18)

LEAMINGTON SPA

A S Blackie (see page 21)

LETCHWORTH

The Picture Shop (see page 22)

LITTLE YELDHAM

Peter Child (see page 132)

MILDENHALL

World of Wood (see page 128) Specialist mail order supplier

MANCHESTER

Fred Aldous Limited (see page 25)

PRESTON

Arts and Crafts (see page 29)

SOUTHAMPTON

Hampshire Hobbies (see page 31)

STURMINSTER NEWTON

Clarkes Handicraft Supplies (see page 31)

MARQUETRY

Probably the branch of woodworking which is best catered for. Most craft shops sell kits and some sell separate veneers. World of Wood at Mildenhall (see page 128) is the major supplier, from whom most of the craft shops below get their supplies in the first place.

ABERDEEN

The Craft Centre (see page 9) Kits only

ALTRINCHAM

The Handicraft Shop (see page 9) Kits only

AYR

Contour Artists' Materials (see page 10)

BATH
Bath Handicraft Supplies (see page 10)
Kits only

BEESTON
The Handicraft Shop (see page 11)

BELFAST
Ato-Crafts (see page 11)

BIRMINGHAM
Midland Educational (see page 11)
Kits only

BISHOPS STORTFORD
Galaxy (see page 12) Kits only

BOURNEMOUTH
Moordown Leather and Craft (see page 114) Kits only

BRIGHTON
Handicrafts (see page 12) Kits only
Southern Handicrafts (see page 12) Kits only

BRISTOL
Bristol Handicrafts (see page 12)
Hobbies and Crafts (see page 12)
Midland Educational (see pages 13, 11) Kits only

BURNLEY
Northern Handicrafts Limited (see page 13)

CAERNARVON
Black Kettle Crafts (see page 13)

CANTERBURY
Needlecraft and Hobbies (see page 13)

CARLISLE
Merricrafts (see page 141) Kits only

CHELTENHAM
The Chrismas Tree (see page 14) Kits only
The Colourman (see page 14) Kits only

CHESHAM
The Tiger's Eye (see page 39) Kits only

COLCHESTER
Briggs Art and Book Shop (see page 15)
Kits only

COVENTRY
Midland Educational (see pages 15, 11)
Kits only

CREWE
Arts and Crafts (see page 15)

DARTFORD
Jaybee Handicrafts (see page 16) Kits only

DEWSBURY
Marc Time (see page 16) Kits only

DORCHESTER
Frank Herring and Sons (see page 64)

EASTBOURNE
The Sussex Handicraft Shop (see page 16)

EPSOM
O W Annetts and Sons Limited (see page 16) Kits only
Lindsay's Handicrafts and Decor (see page 141) Kits only

EXETER
The Handicraft Shop (see page 17)

FALKIRK
Modelcrafts (see page 17)

FOLKESTONE
Cameo Handicrafts (see page 142) Kits only

FORDINGBRIDGE
Caxton Decor (see page 17) Kits only

GLASGOW
Miller's (see page 17) Kits only

GLOSSOP
Homecrafts (see page 18)

GUISBOROUGH
Beecrafts (see page 18) Kits only

HITCHIN
Homecrafts (see page 19) Kits only

HOVE
Handicrafts (see page 19) Kits only

HUDDERSFIELD
Arts and Crafts (see page 19) Veneers and cutting tools

HULL
Handycrafts of Hull (see page 20) Veneers

HYTHE
Needlecraft and Hobbies (see page 20)

INVERNESS
East Dene Crafts (see page 53)

KEGWORTH
Kits 'n' Krafts (see page 75) Kits only

KEIGHLEY
Conways Arts and Crafts (see page 20) Kits only

LANCASTER
Leisure Crafts (see page 21) Veneers

LEAMINGTON SPA
A S Blackie (see page 21) Kits

LEEDS
Headrow Gallery (see page 21) Kits only

LEICESTER
Midland Educational (see pages 22, 11) Kits

LETCHWORTH
The Picture Shop (see page 22) Kits

LONDON N9
The Art and Craft Centre (see page 23)

SW11
Leisure Crafts (see page 23) Kits

W1
Hamleys (see page 24) Kits only
The Needlewoman Shop (see page 76) Kits

LYTHAM
Lytham Woodcraft Limited (see page 25)

MANCHESTER
Fred Aldous (see page 25)

MARKET HARBOROUGH
The Hobby Shop (see page 154) Kits only

MIDDLESBROUGH
J Goldstein and Son (see page 26) Kits and packs of veneers

MILDENHALL
The World of Wood (see page 128) Very large stocks

MORPETH
Tallantyre Wallpapers (see page 26) Kits only

NEWCASTLE UPON TYNE
Ashbourton Gifts and Crafts (see page 27) Kits only

NORTHAMPTON
Abingdon Handicrafts (see page 27) Kits only

Arts and Crafts Shop (see page 28)
Midland Educational (see pages 28, 11)

NOTTINGHAM
Home Pastimes (see page 28)

OLDHAM
The Art and Craft Shop (see page 28)

PERTH
Dunn's Art Stores (see page 29) Kits only

PETERBOROUGH
Handicrafts (see page 125) Specialists

PRESCOT
The Art Shop (see page 29) Kits only

PRESTON
The Arts and Crafts Shop (see page 29)

REDBOURN
Atelier (see page 29)

RICHMOND
Richmond Art and Craft (see page 30)
Kits only

ROCHDALE
The Art Shop (see page 30) Kits only

ST ANNES ON SEA
The Handmaiden (see page 30)

SHEFFIELD
H R Whitehead (see page 30) Kits only

SHREWSBURY
Wildings (see page 30) Kits

SITTINGBOURNE
Homecrafts (see page 31) Kits only

SKIPTON
Craven Art Centre Limited (see page 31) Kits

SOLIHULL
Midland Educational (see pages 31, 11) Kits

SOUTHAMPTON
Hampshire Hobbies (see page 31)

STRATFORD-UPON-AVON
Midland Educational (see pages 31, 11) Kits only

STROUD
The Christmas Tree (see page 31) Kits

STURMINSTER NEWTON
Clarkes Handicraft Supplies (see page 31)

SUTTON
O W Annetts and Sons (see page 32) Kits

SWANSEA
Arts and Crafts (see page 32) Kits

TAUNTON
The Spinning Wheel (see page 79) Kits only

THORNBURY
Arts and Crafts (see page 32)

TORQUAY
Forestreet Model Centre (see page 32) Kits only

TOTNES
Dart Handicrafts (see page 79) Kits only

TWICKENHAM
Bits and Bobs (see page 54) Kits

WATFORD
Allcraft (see page 33) Kits

WELLINGTON
New Age Handicraft Centre (see page 33) Kits

WELWYN GARDEN CITY
Boon Gallery (see page 34) Kits

WEST DRAYTON
Colberre Limited (see page 34) Kits

WIRRAL
Arts and Crafts (see page 34) Kits

WOKING
Arts and Crafts Shop (see page 34)

WOLVERHAMPTON
Midland Educational (see pages 34, 11) Kits

WOOLER
Glendale Crafts (see page 80)

WORCESTER
Midland Educational (see pages 34, 11) Kits

WORKINGTON
Kathleen Davies (see page 81)

YEOVIL
Draytons Decorations (see page 34) Kits

YORK
Derwent Crafts (see page 35) Kits

17 Lino-cutting

It is not hard to find the materials and tools for lino-cutting. Kits, back-up materials and accessories (for children as well as for adults) are readily available from most art shops and many craft shops.

ANDOVER
Arts and Crafts Centre (see page 10)

ASHFORD
Graphic Art Supplies (see page 10)

AYR
Contour Artists' Materials (see page 10)

BATH
Tridias (see page 10)

BIRMINGHAM
Midland Educational (see page 11)

Type and Palette (see page 11)

BISHOP AUCKLAND
Auckland Studio (see page 11)

BISHOPS STORTFORD
Galaxy (see page 12)   Kits only

BOURNEMOUTH
Moordown Leather and Craft (see page 114)

BRIDGEMARY
Wimburst's (see page 127)

BRIGHTON
Handicrafts (see page 12)

BRISTOL
The Art Centre
583 Fishponds Road, Fishponds, Bristol
  Bristol 653536

Open: Monday 09.00 to 17.00; Tuesday to Saturday (excluding Wednesday) 09.00 to 18.00; Wednesday 09.00 to 13.00; mail order

Art materials, sign writing materials and picture frames (also picture framing done on the premises)—but a very good stock of lino-cutting tools and materials, brass rubbing and candlemaking supplies, modelling clays and screen printing materials; inks, frames, paper and so on.

Bristol Handicrafts (see page 12)

Hobbies and Crafts (see page 12)

Midland Educational (see pages 13, 11)

BURNLEY
Burnley Drawing Office Services Limited (see page 102)

CAERNARVON
Black Kettle Crafts (see page 13)

CAMBRIDGE
The Leigh Gallery (see page 13)

CARDIFF
South Wales Arts and Crafts Suppliers (see page 55)

CHAGFORD
Dolphin Crafts (see page 123)

CHANDLERS FORD
Creative Crafts (see page 14)

CHELTENHAM
The Colourman (see page 14)

CHESHAM
The Tiger's Eye (see page 39)

COLCHESTER
Briggs Art and Book Shop (see page 15)

COLNE
The Art Shop (see page 15)

COVENTRY
Midland Educational (see pages 15, 11)

CREWE
Arts and Crafts (see page 15)

DEWSBURY
Marc Time (see page 16)

DORCHESTER
Frank Herring and Sons (see page 64)

EASTBOURNE
The Sussex Handicraft Shop (see page 16)

EPSOM
O W Annetts and Sons Limited (see page 16)

EXETER
The Copyshop
95 Fore Street, Exeter, Devon
Exeter 50431

Open: Monday to Friday 09.00 to 17.30; Saturday 09.00 to 13.00; mail order; catalogue

A drawing, art and graphics supplier (who also give a copying service) where you will find plenty of lino-cutting materials and tools and also brass rubbing materials, Rowney sets of fabric dyes, modelling materials and acetate sheets, both clear and coloured.

FALKIRK
Modelcrafts (see page 17)

FRINTON-ON-SEA
Frinton Handicraft and Art Centre (see page 17)

GLASGOW
Miller's (see page 17)

Morrisons Artists' Materials (see page 124)

GUISBOROUGH
Beecrafts (see page 18)

HATCH END
John Maxfield (see page 19)

HEMEL HEMPSTEAD
Arts and Crafts (see page 19)

HEREFORD
Adams and Sons (Printers) Limited
34 Church Street, Hereford, Hereford-shire   Hereford 6381

Open: Monday to Saturday 09.00 to 17.30; Thursday closed; mail order

Artists' materials suppliers who can also supply materials for those crafts which are close to arts—lino-cutting tools and materials, clays for potters and for modelling, glazes, brass rubbing materials and silk-screen printing materials. Also mouldings and kits for picture framing. Minimum order they will supply by post is £2.00. No catalogue

HOVE
Handicrafts (see page 19)

HUDDERSFIELD
Arts and Crafts (see page 19)

HULL
Humbrol Limited (see page 130)   Tools only

KEGWORTH
Kits 'n' Krafts (see page 75)

KEIGHLEY
Conways Arts and Crafts (see page 20)

KING'S LYNN
Berol (see page 103)

LEAMINGTON SPA
A S Blackie (see page 21)

LEEDS
E J Arnold (see page 21)

Headrow Gallery (see page 21)

LEICESTER
Dryad (see page 22)

Midland Educational (see pages 22, 11)

LONDON EC1
Crafts Unlimited (see page 22)

N1
Fine Art Supplies (see page 22) Kits only

The Pot Shop (see page 22)

N6
E Ploton (see page 131)

NW3
Crafts Unlimited (see page 23)

NW7
John Maxfield (see page 23)

SW11
Leisure Crafts (see page 23)

W1
George Rowney (see page 24)

Selfridges (see page 24)

Alec Tiranti Limited (see page 62)

Winsor and Newton Limited
51/52 Rathbone Place, London W1P
  1AB   01 636 4231

Open: Monday to Saturday 09.00 to 17.30; catalogue

The main shop of the well-known artists' materials suppliers. But having dismissed their enormous art range as irrelevant to this book, it's worth noting that they have good stocks of certain handicraft materials—for lino-cutting and brass rubbing. Also picture framing kits and modelling clays and materials.

W8
Crafts Unlimited (see page 24)

MALVERN
Fearnside and Company (see page 25)

MORPETH
Tallantyre Wallpapers (see page 26)

NEW ASH GREEN
The Hobby House (see page 26)

NEWBURY
Newbury Fine Art Limited (see page 27)

NORTHAMPTON
Arts and Crafts Shop (see page 28)

Midland Educational (see pages 28, 11)

OLDHAM
The Art and Craft Shop (see page 28)

OXFORD
Brush and Compass (see page 28)

Colegroves (see page 28)

PERTH
Dunn's Art Stores (see page 29)

PETERBOROUGH
Art and Educational Crafts (see page 29)

PRESCOT
The Art Shop (see page 29)

PRESTON
The Arts and Crafts Shop (see page 29)

READING
Gun Street Gallery
14 Gun Street, Reading, Berkshire
  Reading 51473

Open: Tuesday and Wednesday 09.00 to 17.00; Thursday to Saturday 09.00 to 17.30

Artists' materials, framed reproductions and gifts—but also lino-cutting and candlemaking materials and modelling clays.

Reading Fine Art Gallery (see page 29)

REDBOURN
Atelier (see page 29)

RICHMOND
Richmond Art and Craft (see page 30)

ROCHDALE
The Art Shop (see page 30)

SHREWSBURY
W M Freeman (see page 30)

Wildings (see page 30)

SOLIHULL
Midland Educational (see pages 31, 11)

SOUTHAMPTON
Hampshire Hobbies (see page 31)

SOUTHPORT
James R Hagerty (see page 125)

STRATFORD UPON AVON
Midland Educational (see pages 31, 11)

STURMINSTER NEWTON
Clarkes Handicraft Supplies (see page 31)

SUDBURY
Art and Craft Shop (see page 31)

SUTTON
O W Annetts and Sons Limited (see page 32)

SWANSEA
Arts and Crafts (see page 32)

THORNBURY
Arts and Crafts (see page 32)

TUNBRIDGE WELLS
G B Butler (see page 51)

TWICKENHAM
Bits and Bobs (see page 54)

WATFORD
Allcraft (see page 33)

J Simble and Sons (see page 51) Tools only

WELLING
Crafts Unlimited (see page 33)

WELWYN GARDEN CITY
Boon Gallery (see page 34)

WEYMOUTH
The Art Shop (see page 92)

WIRRAL
Arts and Crafts (see page 34)

WOLVERHAMPTON
Midland Educational (see pages 34, 11)

WORCESTER
Midland Educational (see pages 34, 11)

YEOVIL
Draytons Decorations (see page 34)

18 Lampshades

Some large stores sell lampshade frames—or you may already have a frame that you want to re-cover. Failing that, the following are all places where you can buy them, often by mail order if necessary.

Once you have the frame, you can cover it with raffia or with parchment or with fabric and braid and tassels. The specialist suppliers in this chapter should have a fairly good range of possible covering materials. If the shop where you buy the frame has nothing else to offer (and where this is the case I have indicated it in the text) your local craft shop (see Chapter 1) can almost certainly supply raffia and your nearest fabric shop (see Chapter 7) suitable materials and trimmings. Or look in Chapter 19 for raffia suppliers and Chapter 23 for paper and parchment. Last but not least, try your local branch of the John Lewis Partnership (see page 76), if you have one, as they tend to have particularly good stocks of all kinds of frames and trimmings.

ABERDEEN
The Craft Centre (see page 9)

ALTRINCHAM
The Handicraft Shop (see page 9)

AYR
Contour Artists' Materials (see page 10)

BATH
Bath Handicraft Supplies (see page 10)

BEDFORD
Bedford Wool Shop (see page 71)

BEESTON
The Handicraft Shop (see page 11)

BELFAST
Ato-Crafts (see page 11)

BEXHILL-ON-SEA
Sackville Handicrafts
11 Sackville Road, Bexhill-on-Sea, Sussex   Bexhill 213533

Open: Monday to Saturday (excluding Wednesday) 09.00 to 13.00 and 14.00 to 17.30; Wednesday 09.00 to 13.00

Specialise in lampshade-making supplies —frames, a very large range of trimmings, hard-backed fabric and raffia. Will also make lampshades to order from customers' own fabric, and will re-string beads. But they do stock other craft materials as well—cold enamelling and candle-making kits; leather offcuts; felt, hessian, foam chips and soft toy accessories; rug-making kits; a small amount of knitting and macramé yarns—and Newclay for modelling.

BIRMINGHAM
Midland Educational (see page 11)

BISHOP AUCKLAND
Auckland Studio (see page 11)

BOLTON
Bolton Handicrafts (see page 12)

BOURNEMOUTH
Moordown Leather and Craft (see page 114)

BRADFORD

R W Copley Limited (see page 96)

Texere Yarns (see page 63)

BRAINTREE

Braintree Wool Shop (see page 72)

BRENTFORD

H Band and Company Limited (see page 120) Vellum and parchment

BRIGHTON

Handicrafts (see page 12)

Southern Handicrafts (see page 12)

BRISTOL

Bristol Handicrafts (see page 12)

Midland Educational (see pages 13, 11)

BURNLEY

Northern Handicrafts Limited (see page 13)

CAERNARVON

Black Kettle Crafts (see page 13)

CANTERBURY

Needlecraft and Hobbies (see page 13)

CARDIFF

Handicrafts and Dressmakers' Aids (see page 14)

Winnifred Ward (see page 72)

CARLISLE

Merricrafts
9a Lowther Street, Carlisle, Cumberland
    Carlisle 23853

Open: Monday to Saturday (excluding Thursday) 09.00 to 17.30; Thursday closed

Although they do stock other craft materials, Merricrafts specialise in lampshade materials—frames, fabrics, raffias, tassel trimmings and so on, and in natural canes and general basketmaking supplies. They also have some bits and pieces for jewellery-making—beads, findings and imitation stones; and marquetry kits, and kits for making felt animals (as well as a supply of felt pieces outside kit form).

CHELTENHAM

The Colourman (see page 14)

CHRISTCHURCH

J C Handicrafts (see page 73)

CLITHEROE

Tattersalls (see page 15)   Kits only

COLCHESTER

Briggs Art and Book Shop (see page 15)

COLNE

The Art Shop (see page 15)

COVENTRY

Midland Educational (see pages 15, 11)

CREWE

Arts and Crafts (see page 15)

CULLOMPTON

Crafts 'n' Creations (see page 73)

DARTFORD

Jaybee Handicrafts (see page 16)

DEWSBURY

Marc Time (see page 16)   Frames only

DONCASTER

Busy Bee (see page 73)

DORCHESTER

Frank Herring and Sons (see page 64)

DUNOON

Dae-It-Yersel (see page 16) Frames only

EPSOM

Linday's Handicrafts and Decor
125 High Street, Epsom, Surrey
    Epsom 24343

Open: Monday to Saturday (excluding Wednesday) 09.00 to 17.30; Wednesday 09.00 to 13.00; mail order

Very large range of lampshade frames and of covering materials, braids, tassels, fringes and so on. They also undertake shade covering as a general service so if you get in a muddle they are well qualified to sort you out. Also curtaining materials—tapestry, collage, candle-making, macramé and marquetry kits; a good stock of cane, raffia and seagrass; felt, stuffing materials and soft toy accessories; and, for jewellers, semi-precious and imitation stones and also sheet copper and pewter and the tools to work them with.

EXETER

Handicrafts and Lampshades
128 Sidwell Street, Exeter, Devon
  Exeter 71429

Open: Monday to Saturday 09.00 to 17.30

This shop is chiefly concerned with the making of lampshades and most of the other materials stocked relate to this—frames, silks, satins, georgettes, raffia, trimmings and parchment. Also table lamps that you can buy and then create a frame for. However, they also have tapestry packs and tapestry frames, linens for embroidery and lots of embroidery threads, and rug-making packs. Altogether the place to go if you want to decorate your home with embroidered chair backs and tapestry firescreens, homemade lampshades and rugs.

The Handicraft Shop (see page 17)

FALKIRK

Modelcrafts (see page 17)

FOLKESTONE

Cameo Handicrafts
40 The Old High Street, Folkestone,
  Kent   Folkestone 51025

Open: Monday to Saturday (excluding Wednesday) 09.00 to 17.30; Wednesday 09.00 to 12.30; mail order

Lots of lampshade frames, covering fabrics, trimmings, raffia, etc.—and they will cover lampshades to order on the premises. Also base metal findings—leather offcuts and leather working tools—felts and soft toy accessories—marquetry kits—cane and basket making supplies.

GLASGOW

Miller's (see page 17)

GLOSSOP

Homecrafts (see page 18)

GODSHILL

The Island Craft Shop (see page 18)

GORSEINON

Y Gegin Fawr (see page 74)

GUISBOROUGH

Beecrafts (see page 18)

HARROGATE

Arts and Handicrafts (see page 18) General craft shop which specialises in lampshade-making materials

HEREFORD

Winivere Crafts (see page 74)   Kits only

HITCHIN

Homecrafts (see page 19)

HOVE

Handicrafts (see page 19)

HUDDERSFIELD

Arts and Crafts (see page 19)

HULL

Handycrafts of Hull (see page 20)

KEGWORTH

Kits 'n' Krafts (see page 75)

KEIGHLEY

Conways Arts and Crafts (see page 20)

LEAMINGTON SPA

A S Blackie (see page 21)

LEATHERHEAD

Handicrafts (see page 21)

LEEDS

Headrow Gallery (see page 21)

LEICESTER

Dryad (see page 22)
Midland Educational (see pages 22, 11)

LONDON N9

The Art and Craft Centre (see page 23)

SW6

Wood and Wirecraft Supplies
19a Jerdan Place, Fulham Broadway,
  London SW6   01 385 2910

Open: Monday to Saturday (excluding Thursday) 10.00 to 17.00; Thursday closed

The wood part of the shop has been discontinued but the wirecraft part is full of lampshade frames—also natural parchment and raffia to cover them with, and chair cane when available. Will undertake covering of chairs and lampshades, and the window is full of all kinds of natural straw baskets for all kinds of purposes.

SW11
Leisure Crafts (see page 23)

SW17
Homecraft Supplies (see page 24)

W1
John Lewis (see page 76)

WC2
Crafts Unlimited (see page 53) Kits only

LYTHAM
Lytham Woodcrafts Limited (see page 25)

MANCHESTER
Fred Aldous (see page 25)

Arts and Crafts (see page 77)

MILTON KEYNES
Milton Keynes Day Centre (see page 26)

NEW ASH GREEN
The Hobby House (see page 26)

NEWCASTLE UPON TYNE
Ashbourton Gifts and Crafts (see page 27)

Thomas Hunter Limited (see page 77)

NORTHAMPTON
Arts and Crafts Shop (see page 28)

Midland Educational (see pages 28, 11)

NORTHWICH
Country Crafts (see page 28)

NOTTINGHAM
Home Pastimes (see page 28)

OLDHAM
The Art and Craft Shop (see page 28)

PERTH
Dunn's Art Stores (see page 29) Frames only

PETERBOROUGH
Art and Educational Crafts (see page 29)

PORT TALBOT
Cliffords (see page 78)

PRESCOT
The Art Shop (see page 29)

PRESTON
The Arts and Crafts Shop (see page 29)

RICHMOND
Richmond Art and Craft (see page 30)

ST ANNES ON SEA
The Handmaiden (see page 30)

SHREWSBURY
W M Freeman (see page 30)
Wildings (see page 30)

SITTINGBOURNE
Homecrafts (see page 31)

SKIPTON
Craven Art Centre Limited (see page 31)

SOLIHULL
Midland Educational (see pages 31, 11)

SOUTHAMPTON
Hampshire Hobbies (see page 31)

STRATFORD UPON AVON
Midland Educational (see pages 31, 11)

STURMINSTER NEWTON
Clarkes Handicraft Supplies (see page 31)

SUDBURY
Art and Craft Shop (see page 31)

SWANSEA
Arts and Crafts (see page 32)

TAUNTON
The Spinning Wheel (see page 79)

TELFORD
The Wool Shop (see page 95)

TORQUAY
Forestreet Model Centre (see page 32)
Frames only

TOTNES
Dart Handicrafts (see page 79)

TRURO
The Hobby House (see page 33)

WARE
Fresew (see page 80)

WATFORD
Allcraft (see page 33)

WELLINGBOROUGH
Happicraft (see page 33)

WELLINGTON
New Age Handicraft Centre (see page 33)

WELWYN GARDEN CITY
Boon Gallery (see page 34)

WIRRAL
Arts and Crafts (see page 34)

WOKING
Arts and Crafts Shop (see page 34)
Frames only

WOLVERHAMPTON
Midland Educational (see pages 34, 11)

WOOLER
Glendale Crafts (see page 80)

WORCESTER
Midland Educational (see pages 34, 11)

WORKINGTON
Kathleen Davies (see page 81)

YEOVIL
Draytons Decorations (see page 34)

19 Cane and Raffia

To some people, crafts and basket-work are synonymous. It therefore follows that craft shops are usually fairly well stocked with basket bases, various kinds of cane, natural and synthetic raffia, and willow, with which you can indeed make baskets —though you can also cover lamp-shades with the raffia, seat chairs or stools with the cane or, indeed, do anything you see fit with any of it.

Whines and Edgeler of Dorchester (The Bamboo People) are specialist importers who can probably sell you anything your local craft shop can't, and so can Smit and Co of Guildford, though they're really whole-salers. If corn dollies are your thing and the craft shops can't help, and gleaning gives you backache, turn to David Keighley Crafts of Hitchin or Corn Dollies of Siddington. And if you need help with your willow wattle hurdles, Musgraves of Stoke St Gregory could be useful.

ABERDEEN
The Craft Centre (see page 9)

ALTRINCHAM
The Handicraft Shop (see page 9)

AYR
Contour Artists' Materials (see page 10)

BATH
Bath Handicraft Supplies (see page 10)

BEESTON
The Handicraft Shop (see page 11)

BELFAST
Ato-Crafts (see page 11)

BERKHAMPSTEAD
Handyman
7 London Road, Berkhamstead, Hertfordshire   Berkhamstead 4461

Open: Monday to Saturday (excluding Wednesday) 09.00 to 18.00; Wednesday 09.00 to 13.00

Specialise in basketry and cane work, the re-seating of stools and picture framing —or can sell you the materials and tools to do it yourself. Also offer woods, veneers, woodworking tools and accessories and modelling clays.

BIRMINGHAM
Midland Educational (see page 11)

BISHOPS STORTFORD
Galaxy (see page 12)

BOLTON
Bolton Handicrafts (see page 12)

BOURNEMOUTH
Moordown Leather and Craft (see page 114)

BRADFORD
R W Copley Limited (see page 96)
Texere Yarns (see page 63)

BRAMPTON
The Handyman's Shop (see page 127)

BRIGHTON
Handicrafts (see page 12)
Southern Handicrafts (see page 12)

BRISTOL

Bristol Handicrafts (see page 12)

Craftwise (see page 38) Basketry kits

Hobbies and Crafts (see page 12)

Midland Educational (see pages 13, 11)

BURNLEY

Northern Handicrafts Limited (see page 13)

CAERNARVON

Black Kettle Crafts (see page 13)

CANTERBURY

Needlecraft and Hobbies (see page 13)

CARDIFF

Handicrafts and Dressmakers' Aids (see page 14)

CARLISLE

Merricrafts (see page 141)

CHANDLERS FORD

Creative Crafts (see page 14)

CHELTENHAM

The Colourman (see page 14)

CLITHEROE

Tattersalls (see page 15)

COLCHESTER

Briggs Art and Book Shop (see page 15)

COLNE

The Art Shop (see page 15)

COVENTRY

Midland Educational (see pages 15, 11)

CREWE

Arts and Crafts (see page 15)

CULLOMPTON

Crafts 'n' Creations (see page 73)

DARTFORD

Jaybee Handicrafts (see page 16)

DEBENHAM

Deben Rush Weavers
High Street, Debenham, Stowmarket, Suffolk Debenham 349

Open: Monday to Friday 08.30 to 16.30; mail order; catalogue

Specialists in rush, willow and bamboo work who will repair rush and cane chairs. From them you can buy rushes to do your own work.

DEWSBURY

Marc Time (see page 16)

DONCASTER

Busy Bee (see page 73)

DORCHESTER

The Bamboo People (Whines and Edgeler)
Godmanston, Dorchester, Dorset Cerne Abbas 393

Open: Monday to Saturday 09.00 to 13.00 and 14.00 to 17.00; mail order; catalogue

You can call, but their trade is chiefly conducted by mail order (mainly because they are in such a rural area that not many people can get there). They have a tremendous stock of natural handicraft cane (centre cane) and basket and tray plywood bases. Also seagrass, bamboo, raffia and so on, and a good range of books to tell you how best to deal with it all when you have it. Undertake to fulfil any order, however small.

Frank Herring and Sons (see page 64)

EASTBOURNE

The Sussex Handicraft Shop (see page 16) Basket-making kits

EPSOM

O W Annetts and Sons Limited (see page 16)

Lindsay's Handicrafts and Decor (see page 141)

EXETER

Handicrafts and Lampshades (see page 142) Raffia only

The Handicraft Shop (see page 17)

FALKIRK

Modelcrafts (see page 17)

FOLKESTONE

Cameo Handicrafts (see page 142)

FRINTON-ON-SEA

Frinton Handicraft and Art Centre (see page 17)

GLASGOW

Miller's (see page 17)

GODSHILL

The Island Craft Shop (see page 18)

GORSEINON

Y Gegin Fawr (see page 74)

GUILDFORD

Smit and Company Limited
99 Walnut Tree Close, Guildford, Surrey GU1 4UQ Guildford 71551

Mail order only; catalogue

Importers and wholesalers of all types of natural cane. They are really geared to supplying schools and institutions but if you really cannot get cane, raffia, traybases and basketry supplies elsewhere they will mail goods to you. Rather regretfully they stipulate a minimum order of £10—partly because it is uneconomic to supply smaller quantities and partly because £10 covers the cost of posting a quantity likely to arrive in good condition. (They say they have discovered from experience that a minimum of five traybases will travel well; any smaller quantity invariably means damaged goods.) An old-established and courteous firm.

HARROGATE

Arts and Handicrafts (see page 18)

HAYWARDS HEATH

Jacobs, Young and Westbury Limited
J Y W House, Bridge Road, Haywards Heath, Sussex Haywards Heath 2411

Open: Monday to Friday 08.30 to 12.45 and 14.00 to 17.00; mail order; catalogue

Mail order only. Telephone during working hours, or write for the catalogue. Suppliers of cane, plywood and picture bases, synthetic raffia, beads and glass eyes. (You can make a basket that looks at you!)

HEREFORD

Winivere Crafts (see page 74)

HITCHIN

Homecrafts (see page 19)

David Keighley Crafts
100 Hermitage Road, Hitchin, Hertfordshire SG5 1DG Hitchin 53916

Mail order only; catalogue

David Keighley makes all kinds of corn dollies and favours by hand and markets not only these but also a corn dolly kit and straw grown specially for the work. He is also an adviser on rural crafts who organises lectures and demonstrations. Send s.a.e. for details.

HOVE

Handicrafts (see page 19)

HUDDERSFIELD

Arts and Crafts (see page 19)

HULL

Handycrafts of Hull (see page 20)

HYTHE

Needlecraft and Hobbies (see page 20)

KEGWORTH

Kits 'n' Krafts (see page 75)

KENDAL

Kendal Handicrafts (see page 20)

KIDDERMINSTER

Arts and Crafts (see page 20)

LANCASTER

Leisure Crafts (see page 21)

LEAMINGTON SPA

A S Blackie (see page 21)

LEATHERHEAD

Handicrafts (see page 21)

LEEDS

E J Arnold (see page 21)

Headrow Gallery (see page 21)

LEICESTER

Dryad (see page 22)

Midland Educational (see pages 22, 11)

LETCHWORTH
The Picture Shop (see page 22)

LONDON EC1
Crafts Unlimited (see page 22)

Taylor and Company (Tools) Limited (see page 116) Tools only

N1
The Pot Shop (see page 22)

N9
The Art and Craft Centre (see page 23)

NW3
Crafts Unlimited (see page 23)

SW6
Wood and Wirecraft Supplies (see page 142)

SW10
Hobby Horse (see page 23)

SW11
Leisure Crafts (see page 23)

SW17
Homecraft Supplies (see page 24)

W1
Eaton's Shell Shop (see page 161) Good stock

Hamleys (see page 24)

W8
Crafts Unlimited (see page 24) Raffia only

LOUGHBOROUGH
Artcraft and Do-It-Yourself (see page 25)

LYTHAM
Lytham Woodcraft Limited (see page 25)

MALVERN
Fearnside and Company (see page 25) Raffia and seagrass only

MANCHESTER
Fred Aldous (see page 25)

MIDDLESBROUGH
J Goldstein and Son (see page 26)

MILTON KEYNES
Milton Keynes Day Centre (see page 26)

NEW ASH GREEN
The Hobby House (see page 26)

NEWCASTLE UPON TYNE
Ashbourton Gifts and Crafts (see page 27) Raffia and Raffene

The Do-It-Yourself Foam Centre (see page 27)

NORTHAMPTON
Abingdon Handicrafts (see page 27)

Arts and Crafts Shop (see page 28)

Midland Educational (see pages 28, 11)

NORTHWICH
Country Crafts (see page 28)

NOTTINGHAM
Home Pastimes (see page 28)

OLDHAM
The Art and Craft Shop (see page 28)

PERTH
Dunn's Art Stores (see page 29)

PETERBOROUGH
Handicrafts (Peterborough) Limited (see page 125)

PORT TALBOT
Cliffords (see page 78)

PRESCOT
The Art Shop (see page 29)

READING
Inspirations (see page 48)

ST ANNES ON SEA
The Handmaiden (see page 30)

SHREWSBURY
W M Freeman (see page 30)

Wildings (see page 30)

SIDDINGTON
'Corn Dollies'
The Golden Cross, Siddington, Near Macclesfield, Cheshire SK11 9JP Marton Heath 358

Open: Seven days a week, all day

Raymond Rush is a writer and broadcaster (on farming and village life) and a specialist in handmade corn dollies. He will give demonstrations within a 30 mile radius, and you can call at the farm shop to buy ready-made corn dollies or the straw to make your own. No mail order, but call any time because Mr Rush says 'when we are up, we are open!'

SITTINGBOURNE
Homecrafts (see page 31)

SKIPTON
Craven Art Centre Limited (see page 31)

SOLIHULL
Midland Educational (see pages 31, 11)

SOUTHAMPTON
Hampshire Hobbies (see page 31)

STOKE ST GREGORY
Geoffrey Musgrave and Son
Withy Grove, Stoke St Gregory, Near Taunton, Somerset
  Burrowbridge 218
Open: Monday to Friday 09.00 to 18.00; mail order
In fact, wholesale suppliers of handmade baskets, hampers and willow wattle hurdles, made on the premises (and believed to be one of the oldest crafts of all). However, they are always very happy to welcome visitors and to suggest where you might get hold of basket making supplies (and since they are within easy reach of Sedgemoor and Athelney—the only district in this country where willows are still grown for commercial use—the information should be very practical).

STRATFORD UPON AVON
Midland Educational (see pages 31, 11)

STURMINSTER NEWTON
Clarkes Handicraft Supplies (see page 31)

SUDBURY
Art and Craft Shop (see page 31)

SUTTON
O W Annetts and Sons (see page 32)

SWANSEA
Arts and Crafts (see page 32)

THORNBURY
Arts and Crafts (see page 32)

TORQUAY
Forestreet Model Centre (see page 32)

TOTNES
Dart Handicrafts (see page 79)

TRURO
The Hobby House (see page 33)

TWICKENHAM
Bits and Bobs (see page 54)

WARE
Fresew (see page 80)   Raffene only

WELLING
Crafts Unlimited (see page 33)

WELLINGBOROUGH
Happicraft (See page 33)

WELLINGTON
New Age Handicraft Centre (see page 33)

WELWYN GARDEN CITY
Boon Gallery (see page 34)

WIRRAL
Arts and Crafts (sec page 34)

WOKING
Arts and Crafts Shop (see page 34)

WOLVERHAMPTON
Midland Educational (see pages 34, 11)

WOOLER
Glendale Crafts (see page 80)

WORCESTER
Midland Educational (see pages 34, 11)

WORKINGTON
Kathleen Davies (see page 81)

YEOVIL
Draytons Decorations (see page 34)

YORK
Derwent Crafts (see page 35)

20 Glass and Mosaic-work

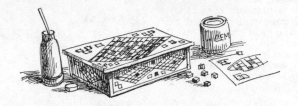

Probably the crafts least well catered for. Whether you want glass and solder for a stained glass window, or glass and tesserae for mosaic-work, or glass to embed in plastic resins to create plaques or panels, the materials are not easy to find (except for the plastic resins, see Chapter 21). This seems to be partly because of the shortage of glass, partly because 'general' craft shops feel glasswork is too specialised to justify their stocking the materials, and partly because the few large companies who can supply the materials are geared to dealing with large orders and find it uneconomic to part with small quantities.

The Pot Shop in Islington has already realised the situation and can supply most needs in this field. Perhaps soon more retail outlets will make the same discovery and become the necessary middleman between the large companies and the craftsmen.

Meanwhile you can either work, as some people do, with broken bottle glass; or telephone your nearest glass factory to ask if you may sort through their breakage pieces (these are generally thrown away, but tend to be very jagged, so take care); or contact one of the following who may well be able to help you.

ANDOVER

Arts and Crafts Centre (see page 10)
Mosaic Kits

BRISTOL

Craftwise (see page 38)

CARDIFF

South Wales Arts and Crafts Suppliers (see page 55)

COLNE

The Art Shop (see page 15)

EDINBURGH

K E S Mosaics
23 Argyle Place, Edinburgh EH9 1JJ
031 229 6464

Open: Monday to Saturday 09.00 to 18.00; mail order; catalogue

K E S Mosaics cater for all aspects of the craft and supply all types of materials, tools, accessories and instruction leaflets to individual craftsmen as well as to schools, hospitals and institutions. (They also have made-up articles—lamps, bowls, trays, jewellery, panels, murals, etc.) They have hobby packs and kits, mosaic stones, cements and bases, glass mosaic, smalti, glazed and unglazed ceramic mosaic, and recommended books on the subject. Will supply any quantity anywhere. Also Plasticraft and Enamelcraft kits and modelling clays.

FALKIRK

Modelcrafts (see page 17)

FROME

Marcross Gems (see page 131)

GRAVESEND

Tumble Kraft (see page 42)

GORSEINON

Y Gegin Fawr (see page 74)

KIDDERMINSTER

Fry's Metals Limited
Worcester Road, Kidderminster, Worcestershire Kidderminster 4931

Open: Monday to Friday 07.30 to 17.00; mail order; catalogue

Manufacturers and suppliers of solder for glasswork. They will supply you direct (minimum order 3 kilograms) either by mail or in person if you care to call at the works. But they are really wholesalers who supply retailers all over the country and would be willing to give you the name and address of your nearest stockist.

KING'S LYNN

Berol (see page 103)

LETCHWORTH

The Picture Shop (see page 22) Mosaic Kits

LONDON E10

The Lonsdale Metal Company
608/632 High Road, London E10
01 539 1222

Open: Monday to Friday 08.00 to 13.00 and 14.00 to 17.30 (by appointment only)

A factory producing window leading which can be used in stained glass work. They are geared to dealing in large quantities but do their best to accommodate craftsmen who only need a few feet of leading. But please know exactly what you want, telephone your order through, and agree a date on which you will collect. They want to help but it is neither economical nor practical for them to send the leading, and if you try to wander round the factory personally selecting a few feet you will hold up work and will not be loved.

N1
The Pot Shop (see page 22) Glass, leading, and stained glass window kits

N7
Vitrex (see page 130) Tools

N9
The Art and Craft Centre (see page 23) Mosaic kits

SW6
Reed Harris
Riverside House, Carnwath Road, London SW6 01 736 7511

Open: Monday to Friday 09.00 to 17.30 (by appointment only)

Importers of glass and ceramic mosaics who are accustomed to selling in large quantities to the building trade and to, or via, architects. Not very enthusiastic about selling small quantities to amateurs, but you may be lucky. Occasionally have boxed lots of discontinued colours. For best results, phone or write in. Don't appear in person without an appointment. If you are successful, you must call and collect your order. They won't send.

SW8
The Mosaic Centre
83/85 Bondway, Vauxhall, London SW8 1SQ 01 735 2821

Open: Monday to Friday 09.00 to 12.00 and 13.00 to 16.45; mail order; catalogue

Specialist suppliers of mosaics and tools for the mosaicist, who will undertake the papering up of vitreous glass mosaic ready for fixing. They sell vitreous glass mosaic (and have a special offer of irregularly shaped vitreous glass mosaics which are rejected for commercial mosaic work but suitable for use in schools, etc.); Byzantine Venetian glass mosaic; gold and silver Venetian glass mosaic; irregular smalti mix; their own mosaic nipper, a serrated fixative hand spreader, and a squeegee grouter (large or small). Minimum order £2.00. Special terms for large orders.

SW17
Homecraft Supplies (see page 24) Mosaic Pebbles and glues

NORTHAMPTON
Arts and Crafts Shop (see page 28)

PERTH
Dunn's Art Stores (see page 29)

SHEPTON MALLET
Marcross Gems (see page 132)

SOLIHULL

Proctor and Lavender Mosaics Limited
Bridge Estate, Lode Lane, Solihull, Warwickshire 021 705 3078

Mail order only

Will sell discontinued lines of glass and ceramic mosaics—generally in hundred pound boxes which cost about £11. Tend to deal with schools quite a lot. You don't get a choice but must take what you're given in the mixed lot.

STOKE-ON-TRENT

Building Adhesives Limited
Federation House, Stoke-on-Trent, Staffordshire

(Opening times not applicable)

Manufacturers and suppliers of adhesives suitable for mosaic-work. Do not supply direct to the public, but will advise on your nearest local supplier if you're stuck.

WEMBLEY

James Hetley and Company Limited
16 Beresford Avenue, Wembley, Middlesex   01 903 4151

Open: Monday to Friday 08.00 to 13.15 and 13.45 to 16.30; mail order; catalogue

Wholesalers of all the necessities for stained glass work. Prefer not to deal with small orders because it isn't economical, but are arranging to reach the public via The Pot Shop in Islington (see separate entry on page 22). They have antique glass, coloured slab glass, soldering sticks, Tungsten hammers for breaking up slabs and a wide range of stains for painting on glass. Can sometimes offer boxed lots of works breakage pieces. If your needs are sufficient to warrant dealing direct, then please send cash with order. (Nice, helpful people, but run off their feet with demands for glass which is, in any case, in short supply.)

WOLVERHAMPTON

Ferro (Great Britain) Limited (see page 156)

21 Plastics

Because plastic comes in so many forms, it has almost endless possibilities in craftwork. According to type, it can be carved or used for mosaics and mobiles and decorative constructions, or you can even make chair covers with it. There is also a vogue just now for embedding seashells, sharks teeth and dried grasshoppers in transparent plastic resins, and most craft shops stock kits or materials to enable you to do just this (although the world shortage of all forms of plastics, especially resins, may limit supplies soon).

In general, plastics can be worked with the same tools you would use on wood—lathes, drills, saws, knives and so on. So see your local hardware shop, or Chapter 16.

The British Plastics Federation (47 Piccadilly, London W1, 01 734 2041) have an Information Bureau which is really intended for the British Plastics industry, but they can, and are very willing to, give some information to individual enquirers. They don't keep records of retail outlets but are in a position to identify trade names, and are also able to provide the names of manufacturers of materials and machinery from whom, in turn, names of retail suppliers might be forthcoming. They also give technical advice—and a list of publications and journals (all concerned with the use of plastics in industry, not in craftwork, but nevertheless possibly relevant for the technical information they contain).

This chapter is divided into three parts—General, Tools and Machinery, and craft shops which stock Embedding Resins only.

GENERAL

BIRMINGHAM

Fox and Offord Limited
Alma Street, Birmingham, Warwickshire
021 359 3214

Mail order only; catalogue

Maybe you should know about these people because they produce plastic moulding equipment designed for educational use. If you want details, send for Sheet POL.2 which describes the Polylab machine which can demonstrate, among other things, injection moulding of thermoplastics, vacuum forming of thermoplastic sheet and the differences in crossbreak strength and tensile strength of various plastic materials. Will supply anywhere on receipt of an official order.

BRENTFORD

Strand Glass
109 High Street, Brentford, Middlesex
01 568 7191

Open: Monday to Friday 09.00 to 17.30; Saturday 09.00 to 13.00; mail order; catalogue

Glass fibre stockists who do things like hiring out canoe moulds, offering a technical information service and holding day and morning lectures on the material. From them you can buy polyester and epoxy resins, polyurethane foam, moulding materials, clear polyester resin casting kits and kits for constructing fibre glass kayaks.

BURNLEY

Northern Handicrafts Limited (see page 13) Perspex sheets and offcuts

CANTERBURY

Needlecraft and Hobbies (see page 13)

CARDIFF
South Wales Arts and Crafts Suppliers
(see page 55)

COLCHESTER
Briggs Art and Book Shop (see page 15)

Johae Art Centre (see page 15)   Acetate

COLNE
The Art Shop (see page 15)

CREWE
Arts and Crafts (see page 15)

DORCHESTER
Frank Herring and Sons (see page 64)

DUNOON
Dae-It-Yersel (see page 16)

EASTBOURNE
Gemstones Limited (see page 41)

EXETER
The Copyshop (see page 137)   Acetate
sheets

FALKIRK
Modelcrafts (see page 17)   Plasticraft
kits and coloured acetate sheets

GRAVESEND
Tumble Kraft (see page 42)

HYTHE
Needlecraft and Hobbies (see page 20)

KIDDERMINSTER
Arts and Crafts (see page 20)   Polyester
casting resins and plastic construction
kits

LEICESTER
Dryad (see page 22)

LEICESTER
*Smith Brothers Asbestos Company
Limited*
Freemans Common Road, Aylestone
   Road, Leicester, Leicestershire
   Leicester 57331

Open: Monday to Saturday 08.30 to
13.00 and 14.00 to 17.30; mail order;
catalogues

A vast and bewildering array of industrial merchandise—asbestos goods, packaging and jointing materials, insulating
materials; masses of rubber things from
carpet underlay to gloves; hoses, elevator
belts, Ferodo brake and clutch linings
and so on and on. But they have industrial plastics—plastic rods, acetate
sheeting, foam, polyester resins, polystyrene ceiling tiles, etc., and they are
prepared not only to supply in small
quantities (5p minimum cash sale—£1
if you want goods sent on credit) but also
to cut materials to size. Their free catalogue gives a clear idea of their staggering range—and only a dedicated crafts-
man-in-plastic could really decide precisely how many of the goods available
have an application in craft work. But
if you want a specific kind of plastic you
are almost certain to find it here.

LETCHWORTH
The Picture Shop (see page 22)

LONDON EC1
Alma (London) Limited (see page 116)

The Felt and Hessian Shop (see page
86)   PVC

Rose (Fittings) Limited (see page 116)
PVC and vinyls

SW20
Park Building Supplies (see page 128)
Liquid latex

W1
Hamleys (see page 24)   Plasticraft kits
and expanded polystyrene

Paperchase (see page 164)   PVC

Alec Tiranti Limited (see page 62)
Tools and materials

MALVERN
Fearnside and Company (see page 25)

MARKET HARBOROUGH
The Hobby Shop
15 Nelson Street, Market Harborough,
   Leicestershire
   Market Harborough 2762

Open: Monday to Saturday (excluding
Thursday) 07.30 to 18.00; Thursday
07.30 to 14.00; mail order

If, as you work with plastics, you decide

that you want to make up plastic models of aircraft, boats and numerous other things from kits, then this is your shop. Wide range of sets and kits—and even marquetry kits.

NANNERCH
Craft O'Hans (see page 53)

NEWCASTLE UPON TYNE
Harper and Company
12/20a Diana Street, Newcastle upon Tyne, Northumberland
Newcastle 22283

Open: Monday to Friday 08.15 to 16.45; Saturday 08.15 to 12.15

Really and truly sign specialists, but they do stock sheet perspex and perspex rod and tubing which they will happily sell to you so long as you don't want less than 50p worth of it. There is a catalogue but they don't do mail order.

NORTHAMPTON
Arts and Crafts Shop (see page 28)

Modern Fittings Limited
4/6 Dunster Street, Northampton, Northamptonshire NN1 3JY
Northampton 35630

Open: Monday to Friday 09.00 to 12.30 and 13.00 to 17.00; mail order; catalogue

Modern Fittings fabricate, mould and supply perspex—also acetate and PVC. You can buy any amount, large or small, though if you want it sent they will obviously charge postage and packing.

RICHMOND
Richmond Art and Craft (see page 30)

STAINES
Morane Plastic Company Limited
Gresham Road, Staines, Middlesex TW18 2AT Staines 51985

Open: Monday to Friday 09.00 to 17.30; mail order; catalogue

Clear and coloured adhesive coated plastic films—very suitable as protective covering in bookbinding. They are wholesalers, but you can write or telephone with your order because they will mail it to you so long as it comes to at least £1.50. Will also undertake laminating of prints and paper.

STANMORE
G H Bloore Limited
480 Honeypot Lane, Stanmore, Middlesex 01 952 2391

Open: Monday to Friday 09.00 to 17.30; mail order; catalogue

Supply rigid industrial plastics—perspex and acetate. Catalogue is free to industrial users but as the minimum order is only £2.00 they are a reasonable source of supply for craftsmen who want to make mobiles, mosaics, or whatever.

TADWORTH
D E P
Frith Park, Walton on the Hill, Tadworth, Surrey Tadworth 3517

Mail order only; catalogue

Manufacturers and mail order suppliers of Astrafoil—rigid vinyl sheet which comes in four main types (clear, polished both sides—clear, one side matt—white opaque, one side polished and one matt—white translucent, one side polished and one matt.) It's specifically made for use in graphic arts and is recommended to replace glass or metal. What you do with it is up to you—but they will supply as little as one sheet; will send detailed technical information leaflets on its properties, reactions to solvents, heat, etc.; and recommend it for use in (among other things) screen printing.

TWICKENHAM
Bits and Bobs (see page 54)

WATFORD
Allcraft (see page 33)

WEST DRAYTON
Colberre (see page 34)

WOLLASTON
Trylon Limited
Thrift Street, Wollaston, Northamptonshire NN9 7QJ Wollaston 275

Open: Monday to Friday 08.00 to 12.15 and 13.30 to 16.45; mail order; catalogue

General plastic suppliers who have spent a great deal of time developing ideas and techniques for the use of plastics by craftsmen. They operate a technical advice service and send out free information leaflets which do not simply tell you what is available but also how best to use it when you have it. They also arrange technical courses and demonstrations (enquire at the address above). They stock clear and opaque resins, sculpting resins, their own 'Trylart artistic plastic kit', an 'embedding pack' for clear casting, glass fibre materials and tools and rubber moulding compounds. They are willing to supply small quantities and are genuinely interested in the products they sell. (They also have cold enamelling materials and aluminium foil for brass rubbing.)

WOLVERHAMPTON

Ferro (Great Britain) Limited
Ounsdale Road, Wombourne, Wolverhampton, Staffordshire
　　Wombourne 4144

Open: Monday to Friday 08.30 to 12.30 and 13.30 to 17.00; mail order; catalogue

You can call in, although they prefer to deal by mail order. This is an enormous concern, with manufacturing plants all over the world, where you can choose from a very large range of plastics—glass fibre, resins, gelcoats, paste colours, lay-up tools, solvents and release agents—and they are prepared to give technical advice and to service kilns and machinery. They also stock jewellers' tools, copper blanks and copper findings; clays, glazes, power wheels and kilns for pottery; modelling clays and plaster of Paris. They have a silastic mould-making kit and, newly on the market, a glass-working kit and a set of organic glass colours.

TOOLS AND MACHINERY

In general, tools come from craft shops and hardware stores, but here are three slightly unusual specialists.

CHIPPENHAM

The Small Power Machine Company Limited
Bath Road Industrial Estate, Chippenham, Wiltshire SN14 OBR
　　Chippenham 50366

Mail order only; catalogue

Suppliers of plastic-moulding, machines, including one small machine widely used in schools. Also moulding materials and prepared moulds. Send for the literature or call by appointment to view the machines. There is also an advisory service on injection moulding.

HULL

Humbrol Limited (see page 130) Tools only

HUNTINGDON

M L Shelley and Partners Limited
St Peters Road, Huntington, Huntingdonshire PE18 7HE
　　Huntingdon 53651/2/3

Mail order only; catalogue

Manufacturers of machinery for vacuum forming of plastic materials. The small machine has been produced especially for use in schools.

EMBEDDING RESINS

These craft shops sell embedding resins and no other form of plastic—quite often the resins come in kit form, and when they do they tend to be accompanied by that which you should embed.

ABERDEEN

The Craft Centre (see page 9)

ALDEBURGH

The Beachcomber (see page 36)

ALLENTON

Allenton Homecrafts (see page 9)

ALTRINCHAM

The Handicraft Shop (see page 9)

ANDOVER

Arts and Crafts Centre (see page 10)

AYR

Contour Artists' Materials (see page 10)

BATH

Tridias (see page 10)

BECKENHAM

Bondaglass-Voss
158/164 Ravenscroft Road, Beckenham, Kent　01 778 0071

Open: Monday to Friday 09.00 to 17.00; Saturday 09.00 to 12.00; mail order; catalogue

Manufacturers of Polyester resins whose free, illustrated leaflet describes the product and gives quite precise instructions on how to use it. Almost any object can be embedded in a clear block of resin, either for purely decorative purposes or to preserve specimens which can be clearly seen but are at the same time protected from excessive handling. Bondaglass-Voss are manufacturers whose products may very well be available in your local craft shop. However they do have a retail outlet at the above address where you can buy even small quantities and they will also supply by mail order— but they do emphasise that they are primarily suppliers to the trade rather than to individuals.

BEESTON
The Handicraft Shop (see page 11)

BELFAST
Ato-Crafts (see page 11)

BIRMINGHAM
Midland Educational (see page 11)

Type and Palette (see page 11)

BISHOP AUCKLAND
Auckland Studio (see page 11)

BISHOPS STORTFORD
Galaxy (see page 12)

BOURNEMOUTH
Moordown Leather and Craft (see page 114)

BRAMPTON
The Handyman's Shop (see page 127)

BRIGHTON
Handicrafts (see page 12)

BRISTOL
Craftwise (see page 38)
Midland Educational (see pages 13, 11)

BROADSTAIRS
Gemset (see page 38)

CAERNARVON
Black Kettle Crafts (see page 13)

CAMBRIDGE
The Leigh Gallery (see page 13)

CHANDLERS FORD
Creative Crafts (see page 14)

CHELTENHAM
The Christmas Tree (see page 14)
The Colourman (see page 14)

CHESHAM
The Tiger's Eye (see page 39)

CHICHESTER
Rockcraft (see page 40)

CLITHEROE
Tattersalls (see page 15)

COLBY
Manninart (see page 40)

COVENTRY
Midland Educational (see pages 15, 11)

DEWSBURY
Marc Time (see page 16)

EASTBOURNE
The Sussex Handicraft Shop (see page 16)

EAST KESWICK
Westby Products (see page 16)

EDINBURGH
K E S Mosaics (see page 150)

EPSOM
O W Annetts and Sons (see page 16)

FRINTON-ON-SEA
Frinton Handicraft and Art Centre (see page 17)

GLASGOW
Miller's (see page 17)

GLOSSOP
Homecrafts (see page 18)

GODSHILL
The Island Craft Shop (see page 18)

HATCH END
John Maxfield (see page 19)

HEMEL HEMPSTEAD
Arts and Crafts (see page 19)

HITCHIN
Homecrafts (see page 19)

HORSHAM
Annetts and Sons (see page 19)

HOVE
Handicrafts (see page 19)

HULL
Gemstones Limited (see page 43)

ILMINSTER
Opie Gems (see page 43)

KEIGHLEY
Conways Arts and Crafts (see page 20)

KENDAL
Kendal Handicrafts (see page 20)

LANCASTER
Leisure Crafts (see page 21)

LANCING
S J Pearce
121 South Street, Lancing, Sussex BN15
8AS
Mail order only; catalogue for s.a.e.

Illustrated lists always available if you
send a stamped addressed envelope.
Specialise in plastic embedding kits and
accessories (including shells and other
embeddables) and the materials for gemstone jewellery making—chain and findings in gilt and silver finish and semi-
precious stones.

LEEDS
E J Arnold (see page 21)

Turner Research Limited (see page 53)

LEICESTER
Midland Educational (see pages 22, 11)

LONDON NW7
John Maxfield (see page 23)

SW10
Hobby Horse (see page 23)

SW19
Gemlines (see page 45)

W1
The Needlewoman Shop (see page 76)

WC2
Crafts Unlimited (see page 53)

MANCHESTER
Fred Aldous (see page 25)

MIDDLESBROUGH
J Goldstein and Son (see page 26)

MORPETH
Tallantyre Wallpapers (see page 26)

NEW ASH GREEN
The Hobby House (see page 26)

NEWCASTLE UPON TYNE
Ashbourton Gifts and Crafts (see page 27)

The Do-It-Yourself Foam Centre (see page 27)

NORTHAMPTON
Abington Handicrafts (see page 27)

Midland Educational (see pages 28, 11)

NORTH SHIELDS
Rough and Tumble Limited (see page 47)

NORTHWICH
Country Crafts (see page 28)

NOTTINGHAM
Home Pastimes (see page 28)

PERTH
Dunn's Art Stores (see page 29)

PETERBOROUGH
Art and Educational Crafts (see page 29)

PRESCOT
The Art Shop (see page 29)

READING
Inspirations (see page 48)

Reading Fine Art Gallery (see page 29)

REDBOURN
Atelier (see page 29)

SHEFFIELD
H R Whitehead (see page 30)

SHREWSBURY
W M Freeman (see page 30)

Wildings (see page 30)

SKIPTON
Craven Art Centre Limited (see page 31)

SOLIHULL
Midland Educational (see pages 31, 11)

SOUTHAMPTON
Hampshire Hobbies (see page 31)

SOUTHSEA
Solent Lapidary (see page 50)

STRATFORD UPON AVON
Midland Educational (see pages 31, 11)

STROUD
The Christmas Tree (see page 31)

SUTTON
O W Annetts and Sons (see page 32)

SWANSEA
Arts and Crafts (see page 32)

THORNBURY
Arts and Crafts (see page 32)

TRURO
The Hobby House (see page 33)

TUNBRIDGE WELLS
G D Butler (see page 51)

WELLINGBOROUGH
Happicraft (see page 33)

WELWYN GARDEN CITY
Boon Gallery (see page 34)

WEYMOUTH
The Art Shop (see page 92)

WIRRAL
Arts and Crafts (see page 34)

WOKING
Arts and Crafts Shop (see page 34)

WOLVERHAMPTON
Midland Educational (see pages 34, 11)

WORCESTER
Midland Educational (see pages 34, 11)

YEOVIL
Draytons Decorations (see page 34)

YORK
Derwent Crafts (see page 35)

22 Shells

Shells have various decorative uses in craftwork—you can glue them on to things, embed them in plastic resins, or make little animals with them. Some people just enjoy shells for their own sakes, but that's not really a craft—more an art.

If you can't find what you want on the beach, the following craft shops have varying quantities of shells for sale, singly or in packs. The main specialists are probably The Tropical Shells Company in Brighton, Eaton's Shell Shop in London and Afrasian Imports in Royston. Specialist suppliers tend also to sell related objects—bits of coral, mother-of-pearl and sharks' teeth.

ABERDEEN

The Craft Centre (see page 9)

ALDEBURGH

The Beachcomber (see page 36)

ALTRINCHAM

The Handicraft Shop (see page 9)

ANDOVER

Arts and Crafts Centre (see page 10)

BEESTON

The Handicraft Shop (see page 11)

BISHOPS STORTFORD

Galaxy (see page 12)

BOLTON

Bolton Handicrafts (see page 12)

BRIGHTON

Geobright and The Glass Animal Man (see page 38)

Handicrafts (see page 12)

BRIGHTON

The Tropical Shells Company Limited 22 Preston Road, Brighton, Sussex BN1 4QF   Brighton 63178

Open: Monday to Friday 09.00 to 17.30; mail order; catalogue

Wholesale and retail suppliers of sea-shells for craftwork and for amateur and advanced collectors. Minimum order they will send would cost £2.00, but if you call in you can buy a single shell. Good range of shells and also coral, sea urchins, etc. Make up Standard and Quantity packs for craftwork.

BRISTOL

Craftwise (see page 38)

Ruskin's (see page 38)

CAERNARVON

Black Kettle Crafts (see page 13)

CAMBRIDGE

The Leigh Gallery (see page 13)

CHANDLERS FORD

Creative Crafts (see page 14)

CHELTENHAM

The Colourman (see page 14)

DUBLIN

Gemcraft of Ireland (see page 41)

EAST KESWICK

Westby Products (see page 16)

GODSHILL
The Island Craft Shop (see page 18)

HARROGATE
Arts and Handicrafts (see page 18)

HOVE
Handicrafts (see page 19)

HUDDERSFIELD
Arts and Crafts (see page 19)

HYTHE
Needlecraft and Hobbies (see page 20)

KEIGHLEY
Conways Arts and Crafts (see page 20)

LEEDS
Headrow Gallery (see page 21)

LETCHWORTH
The Picture Shop (see page 22)

LONDON EC1
Crafts Unlimited (see page 22)

N9
The Art and Craft Centre (see page 23)

NW3
Crafts Unlimited (see page 23)

SW19
Gemlines (see page 45)

W1
Eaton's Shell Shop
16 Manette Street, London W1
01 437 9391

Open: Monday to Friday 09.00 to 17.30;
Saturday 09.00 to 12.30; mail order; catalogue

Just round the corner from Charing Cross Road. A small, very well stocked shell shop offering a great many exotic shells and also variety packs of small shells for craftwork at 15p or 30p a packet. Also a few other fruits of the sea—corals, seahorses, starfish and 'loose shark teeth'. They have large stocks of serious collectors' items and will do their best to fulfil requests for minerals, crystals, cut stones and fossils. Helpful and informative whether you call in person or order by mail. Even the mail order stock list tells you things like 'Chank Shells—sacred in the East' and 'Worm Shells—strange twisted species'. They also sell beads and cane and are one of the best sources of natural raffia in London. They will make bead curtains to order and have quite a few ready-made items— mostly suspended from the ceiling, raffia table mats, baskets and lampshades, mattings and bamboo and cane roller blinds.

W8
Crafts Unlimited (see page 24)

MALVERN
Fearnside and Company (see page 25)

NEWTON STEWART
Country Crafts (see page 27)

PRESCOT
The Art Shop (see page 29)

PRESTWICK
Stones and Settings (see page 48)

READING
Inspirations (see page 48)

REDBOURN
Atelier (see page 29)

ROYSTON
Afrasian Imports
2 Kneesworth Street, Royston, Herts
  Royston 43211

Mail order only; catalogue

It is perhaps a pity that one cannot visit a firm with such a tremendous range of exotic seashells with names like Daybreak Cowry, Spider Conch, Music Cone, Spiky Drupe and Half-Hearted Cockle. Almost worth having for the names alone—but the shells themselves are even more beautiful and extraordinary. The large ones are sold singly but you can also buy packets of mixed shells, and the smaller craft shells (like Baby Button Tops and Chinese Gold Ring Cowries) come by the pound. They also supply mother-of pearl, coral, broken abalone pieces and, should you need them, sharks' teeth, dried flying fish, beetles, grasshoppers, butterflies, moths and snails.

SHEFFIELD
H R Whitehead (see page 36)

SOUTHAMPTON
Hampshire Hobbies (see page 31)

SOUTH SEA
Solent Lapidary (see page 50)

SKIPTON
Craven Art Centre Limited (see page 31)

STURMINSTER NEWTON
Clarkes Handicraft Supplies (see page 31)

SWANSEA
Arts and Crafts (see page 32)

THORNBURY
Arts and Crafts (see page 32)

TWICKENHAM
Bits and Bobs (see page 54)

WAKEFIELD
Glenjoy Craft and Lapidary Supplies (see page 51)

WELLING
Crafts Unlimited (see page 33)

WELLINGTON
New Age Handicraft Centre (see page 33)

WOKING
Arts and Crafts Shop (see page 34)

WOOLER
Glendale Crafts (see page 80)

23 Paper

General stortages permitting, it is not hard to find origami paper, craft paper, tissue paper, etc. Every well stocked craft shop has, or can obtain, a reasonable supply (see Chapter 1) and the same applies to art shops and large stationers. The papers which are hard to find are the special ones—handmade, marbled vellum or whatever. And since most paper merchants like to deal in overwhelmingly large quantities it isn't easy to find someone who will sell a few sheets of something suitable for the endpapers of a hand bound book. Here are a few people who will help.

ANDOVER

Reckner and Company
21 Ferndale Road, Andover, Hampshire
  SP10 3HQ Andover 2636

Mail order only

Suppliers of hand-made papers, coloured papers, art paper, cartridge paper and boards. Generally sell the handmade paper by the quire and the cheaper papers by the ream. Telephone your enquiry through, or send a letter. You can make an appointment to call if you wish. Can supply endpapers and boards for bookbinding. Will send samples but prefer not to now that paper is scarce.

BRENTFORD

H Band and Company Limited (see page 120) Vellum and parchment

COMPTON CHAMBERLAYNE

Compton Russell
Compton Chamberlayne, Near Salisbury, Wiltshire Fovant 630

Mail order only; catalogue

Producers of hand marbled papers—especially suitable for endpapers in bookbinding. Prices on application and quantities by arrangement.

GRANTCHESTER

Douglas Cockerell and Son
Riversdale, Grantchester, Cambridgeshire
  Grantchester 2124

Open: By appointment only; mail order; catalogue

Produce cartridge, kraft and handmade marbled papers, suitable for endpapers. The pattern books are free and they will deal in small quantities (by which they mean as little as one sheet). But place your order by post or telephone—*don't* call in person. They haven't the time or facilities to cope with visitors.

LANCING

Rogate Printers (see page 121)

LEICESTER

Dryad (see page 22)

LONDON SE1

R K Burt and Company Limited
37 Union Street, London SE1
  01 407 6474

Open: Monday to Friday 10.00 to 12.30 and 14.00 to 16.30; Saturday closed; mail order; catalogue

Not a retail shop, so you must write or ring in for an appointment. They deal in print-making papers suitable for silk-screening (as well as drawing and water colour papers) and might be able to supply you with endpapers for bookbinding as well—depending on what you want. Minimum order supplied is normally 25 sheets.

WC1
Frank Grunfeld Limited
32 Bedford Square, London WC1
01 636 5295

Open: Monday to Friday 09.15 to 13.00
and 14.00 to 17.15; mail order

Paper merchants who are used to ordering large quantities of materials for printers and publishers. But you can call in at the office where they are happy to sell to casual customers. If your order is small then they will only sell from the stock they have around the place and will only get in special stocks if you need massive amounts. Go to them for rather expensive endpapers and boards for bookbindings.

WC1
Kettles
127 High Holborn, London WC1
01 405 9764

Open: Monday to Friday 09.00 to 16.45; mail order

Specialist retailers of all kinds of paper—pasting papers, art papers, tissue papers, flock papers, hand marbled papers, wrapping papers; and also related products like cardboard boxes and tubes. If they don't have what you want they can probably get it. Deal with customers all over the country, and will send out samples free.

SW6
Falkiner Fine Papers
302 Lillie Road, London SW6 7PU
01 381 3366

Open: Tuesday to Thursday 10.30 to 16.30; mail order; catalogue

Fine papers for artists and craftsmen, supplied in single sheets if you wish. The opening hours are brief but you can call at other times if you make an appointment first. Gabrielle Falkiner will also attempt to locate hard-to-find papers for customers.

W1
Paperchase
216 Tottenham Court Road, London W1
01 637 1121

Open: Monday to Friday 10.00 to 18.00; mail order; catalogue

A treasurehouse of paper and paper craft kits, books and stationery. They have brass rubbing materials and a very good selection of papers to rub them on to; origami and flower-making paper; tissue paper, etc. Also hessian, veneers and metallic PVC by the yard. They stipulate £2.00 minimum on mail order sales. No minimum if you go in person.

MAIDSTONE

Green's Fine Papers Division
Springfield Mill, Maidstone, Kent
Maidstone 61681

Mail order only; catalogue

Manufacturers of handmade and mould-made drawing, watercolour and printing papers—natural and tinted. If you have trouble locating their papers they will try to give you the address of your nearest supplier—or you can order direct so long as your order comes to not less than £10 before VAT. Orders over £20 are sent free of carriage charges. Samples and full details on request.

Acknowledgments

I would like to thank everyone who offered help, information and encouragement—and especially Fred Aldous Limited, Mr Santer of Artstraws, Mr Robinson of Joseph Bell and Son Stained Glass, Graham Spite of Bindercraft, Mrs Dempster of the British Plastics Federation, Mary Howard of the Buckinghamshire Gild of Weavers, Mrs Bull of the Buckinghamshire Pottery and Sculpture Society, Louise Littleton of the Cheshire Guild of Handloom Weavers, Mrs Burt of the Cotswold Craft Centre, Mrs Johnson of the Cowley Recreational Institute, Hans Theilade of Craft O'Hans in Nannerch, Anne French of the Crafts Advisory Committee, Chris Palmer of the Craftsmen Potters' Association, Lt-Col P Honnor of the Devon Guild of Craftsmen, Helen Lee of the Devon Guild of Weavers, John Rome of the Dorset County Crafts Association, The Embroiderers' Guilds of London and South Wales, Enamelaire Limited, Mrs D L Gill, Mr Hayes of the GLC Supplies Depot, H O Williams of the Guild of Herefordshire Craftsmen, Raie Barnett and Mike Halsey of the Handweavers Studio and Gallery, Mr Edwards of Harris Looms, Mrs Jackson of the Herefordshire Art and Craft Society, Miss Johns of the Holloway Adult Education Institute, Prudence Holton, Mr Offer of Hydebourne Limited, Mr McGregor of ICI, Mr Jennings of the Kent Small Industries Committee, Miss Brenton of the Lace Society of Wales, Mrs McQuitty of the Local Enterprise Development Unit, Belfast, Elizabeth Gale and George Dixon of the London College of Furniture, Mrs Walker of the Marquetry Society, Joan Hudson of the Marylebone Institute, Isabel McGraghan of the Monmouthshire Guild of Weavers, The National Federation of Women's Institutes, The National Jewellers' Association, Mr Wall of Reeves Limited, Nellie Richardson, Mrs Bird of the Sheffield Lace Makers, Sally Smith of the Small Industries Council for Rural Areas of Scotland, Elizabeth Fearon of the Society of Designer Craftsmen, Alun Williams of the Society for Education Through Art, Mrs Smith of the Somerset Guild of Craftsmen, Brian Marshall of the World Crafts Council, Colonel Barton of the York and District Guild of Weavers, and everyone included in the book, who so willingly gave me all the information I asked for.

J A

Index